A Private Choice

A Private Choice

Abortion in America
in the Seventies

John T. Noonan, Jr.

THE FREE PRESS
A Division of Macmillan Publishing Co., Inc.
NEW YORK

Collier Macmillan Publishers
LONDON

The Free Press
A Division of Macmillan Publishing Co., Inc.
866 Third Avenue, New York, N.Y. 10022

Collier Macmillan Canada, Ltd.

Library of Congress Catalog Card Number: 78–67752

Printed in the United States of America

printing number

2 3 4 5 6 7 8 9 10

Library of Congress Cataloging in Publication Data

Noonan, John Thomas
  A private choice, abortion in America in the seventies.

  Includes bibliographical references and index.
  1. Abortion--Law and legislation--United States.
2. Abortion--United States. I. Title.
KF9315.N66   344'.73'041   78–67752
ISBN 0-02-923160-4

Contents

Acknowledgments

I am indebted for comments, criticism or discussion of various portions of this book to Jesse Choper, Paul Mishkin, and Robert Mnookin, my colleagues at Boalt Hall; Ian W. Monie and P. S. Timiras, my colleagues in other parts of the University of California; James Burtchaell of the University of Notre Dame; André Hellegers, director of the Joseph and Rose Kennedy Institute; Henry P. Monaghan of Boston University; my father, John T. Noonan; and my wife, Mary Lee.

I am also indebted for very capable typing to Louise McCahan.

John T. Noonan, Jr.

Inquiry 1
On the Nature of the Present Conflict and Its Resolution

Once or twice in a century an issue arises so divisive in its nature, so far-reaching in its consequences, and so deep in its foundations that it calls every person to take a stand. Abortion, it once appeared, was an unlikely candidate to be such an issue. The nature of the act of abortion, for those who contemplated it steadily, and the unpleasantness of the procedures for anyone involved in them induced most persons to turn their attention elsewhere. Politically, the subject was untouchable before the 1960s. No one in a public forum sought to challenge the accepted limits. Later, when challengers did come forward, few politicians wanted to take sides: The issue cut across party lines, the parties had no pat partisan formulas for containing it, and each side was good at remembering its enemies. The politicians wished that the subject had never come up. Then they wished it would go away. In this respect abortion became what slavery had been: a plague for the parties and the party professionals.

Abortion has not gone away. Today it divides the country. Neutrality for a legislator is impossible. Each side believes with deep conviction that it is right. But both sides cannot be right, and conflict in theory means conflict in practice. Legalized as a private act, abortion has become a public issue. It has become the kind of public issue that compels almost everyone to take a stand.

Each act of abortion is, by declaration of the Supreme Court of the United States, a private decision. Yet each act of abortion bears on the structure of marriage and the family, the role and duties of parents, the limitations of the paternal part in procreation, and the virtues that characterize a mother. Each act of abortion bears on the

1

orientation and responsibilities of the obstetrician, the nurse, the hospital administrator, and the hospital trustee. The acceptance of abortion affects the professor and student of medicine and the professor and student of law. In the United States, abortion on a large scale requires the participation of the federal and state governments.

Overarching the whole system of private choice is the command of the judiciary, whose will has brought abortion to public acceptability and whose power has intervened constantly to sustain the liberty of abortion against public repudiation. The duties of the judges vis-à-vis an elected legislature, the respect of federal judges for the states in a federal system, the constitutional authority of judges to appropriate money from the federal Treasury—all of these questions of judicial conduct have become entwined with the abortion controversy.

The "issue" of abortion is not a single dispute over a hairline distinction. It is many-faceted. It has turned into a multiplicity of issues. Response to one aspect or another of the controversy has affected the consciences of college students in San Diego, jurymen in Boston, physicians in Philadelphia, and Treasury officials in Washington. As abortion has acted on their consciences, their responses have shaped their sense of their social obligations. What is by decree of the Supreme Court the most private of choices has become in recent American experience the center of the most public of conflicts.

In *Democracy in America,* Tocqueville describes the key role in American government of "the party" of lawyers. By that phrase he does not mean to indicate that the lawyers were organized like the Democrats or Whigs or that they acted by prearranged concert. He means that by education, interest, and values the lawyers shared certain goals and, without the necessity of consultation as to specific plans, worked together to achieve those goals.

To adapt Tocqueville's concept of party to the present, there is in the United States today a group of persons, connected by no organization or formal tie, whose common education, interest, and values are such that having worked together to create the liberty of abortion in America, they now work to maintain it. Their dynamism expands the conflict and makes its consensual resolution chimerical.

Part of the public controversy is intractable. It depends on assumptions and judgments about what human beings are and about what human beings should do for one another. These convictions and conclusions are not easily reached by argument. They rest on particular perspectives that are bound to the whole personality and can shift only with a reorientation of the person. But much of the controversy lies in a less personal domain and can be resolved by looking at evidence, the kind of evidence which is normally decisive in any battle over social policy, evidence of what a policy means for the society. In this case the evidence is how acceptance of abortion as a private choice affects American society.

Tocqueville long ago observed that we are a nation of lawyers and that every national issue is turned into a judicial question.[1] Abortion as a public matter has been primarily a matter of what judges have decided the public must do. Without the courts the whole controversy would have had a very different, and much smaller, shape. The federal judiciary has created a new constitutional liberty, fed it, fostered it, and protected it. The Supreme Court in behalf of this liberty has revolutionized the legal structure of the family. Individual federal judges have not hesitated to set aside the oldest of laws—that on murder itself—and the most basic of constitutional distributions of power—that giving Congress the power of the purse—to make the new liberty effective in America. The impact of the acts of the judges on the Constitution, on federalism, and on the legal position of the family is evidence to be assessed by every participant in the American political process as each participant decides whether the judge-made liberty of abortion should be fortified, expanded, or expunged.

Other evidence is of a more palpable kind: One should be able to touch it with one's finger or see it with one's eye. It includes what happens in dilation and curettage, in suction vacuuming, and in saline or prostaglandin injection. It includes the nature of the object of these operations. This evidence is physical, and it is far more than physical, since the response of a human being to phenomena is more than a physical reaction. Such facts can be read in the light of human experience and have a strength and significance beyond their gross physical dimensions. One can look at them and intuit how the issue should be decided.

Walter Jackson Bate, in his memorable life of that master moralist, Samuel Johnson, observes that the secret of Johnson's power was his unblinking perception of reality, his refusal to put up with fashionable sham. Johnson had the ability, Bate writes, to attend to "that rarest of all things for confused and frightened human nature —the obvious." [2] The evidence to be examined is of that rare kind.

Yet the obvious is hard to see for a physical reason: The living unborn child is not normally accessible to perception, although ultrasound, television, and fetology have been lifting this physical barrier. The evidence is also hard to see because the legends embroidered by partisans and conveyed by the press have shielded Americans from what has happened in their courts and in their hospitals. The evidence is hardest to see because we are reluctant to see it.

Inquiry is the mode I have chosen here to present what must be seen. By inquiry I do not mean the asking of abstract questions in the air. As I use the term, inquiry presupposes a point of view. Since Socrates, it has pointed in a direction. It excludes no evidence. It proceeds inductively. It points to a resolution which can be achieved only by looking at the evidence.

There are those who hold that abortion, like war, is a social necessity. Very few say that it is good in the abstract, in the best of all possible worlds. Many claim that it is necessary now in the United States of the 1970s, a land of sexual freedom, imperfect contraception, and limited resources. Inquiry has always been the preferred mode of Western culture for challenging those who accept a social practice not because it is good but because they can see no alternative.[3]

It is to those who have reconciled themselves to the hard reality of a society regulating reproduction by abortion that my inquiries are addressed. Is the reality compatible with our Constitution, our family structure, our notion of governmental power, and our sense of the human person? Is the reality beyond reshaping? Can we rationally defend the reality by continuing to categorize abortion as a private choice?

Inquiry 2

On the Creation of the Constitutional Liberty of Abortion

The makers of the Constitution of the United States do not appear to have contemplated the subject of abortion. There is no mention of it by name or by circumlocution in the original articles or in the Bill of Rights or in any of the later amendments. If a Martian were told to examine the document carefully for a clue to the framers' intention regarding abortion, he would have to admit himself baffled. The Constitution, within its four corners, says nothing.

A Martian with a sense of history might say, "Tell me what the laws and practices and beliefs were when the Constitution was made. From them I shall infer what was intended by the framers." He would find

1. that in 1789, when the original articles were adopted, Blackstone was the bible of American lawyers, and Blackstone taught that a "person" was one "like us" who had been "formed by God" in the womb [1]
2. that abortion, although not widely practiced because of medical difficulties in doing it safely, was a crime at common law if the pregnancy had reached the stage where movements by the child were perceptible; and if the child in the womb was injured by an abortifacient, was born alive, and died from his injury, the crime was murder [2]
3. that the articles gave the new government no power to disturb the administration of the common law by the states

4. that in 1790, when the first ten amendments or Bill of Rights was adopted, the common law and the beliefs expressed by Blackstone were unchanged

5. that the Fifth Amendment declared the life, liberty, and property of no person should be taken by the national government except by due process of law

6. that the Ninth Amendment declared that all powers not expressly conferred upon the national government belonged to the People, thereby leaving to the People the protection of life, liberty, and property through the legislatures and courts of each state

7. that "the most important burst of anti-abortion legislation in the nation's history" occurred between 1860 and 1880,[3] and that the Fourteenth Amendment, adopted in 1868, belongs to that era of American politics

8. that in 1868, when the Fourteenth Amendment was adopted, the common law made abortion a crime after quickening, and a number of states, including such leading Northern states as Connecticut and Pennsylvania, made abortion a crime from conception [4]

9. that in the 1860s the federal territories of Arizona, Colorado, Idaho, Montana, and Nevada had all made it a crime to abort "a woman then big with child," [5] and such territorial legislation was subject to the approval of the same congressmen who adopted the Fourteenth Amendment

10. that the Fourteenth Amendment imposed upon each state the obligation already imposed upon the national government not to take life, liberty, or property without due process of law

So informed, our Martian might reason: What the framers knew to be a crime at common law in the states when they made the Constitution, they did not intend to legalize; indeed the protection afforded the unborn at common law accorded with their view of the protection to be afforded persons. When the framers reserved to the People all powers not expressly conferred upon the nation, they did not intend to disable the People from legislating to protect life; indeed, in the distribution of governmental power intended by the founders, the states were to protect life by the ordinary laws against murder, manslaughter, and abortion.

By the time the Fourteenth Amendment was enacted, our Martian would observe, every state employed the sanction of the criminal law to regulate abortion. Surely the authors of the amendment must have approved or at least accepted this practice; for nothing in their language, or in any of the debates surrounding the adoption of the amendment, suggested that the amendment aimed at the abolition of the abortion laws of the federal territories and all the states.[6] Indeed, our Martian might suspect, the states, now under constitutional obligation not to take life without due process, might have a constitutional obligation to have laws regulating abortion.[7]

Certainly, he would conclude, the obligation not to limit liberty without due process of law could not affect an abortion law. In a hundred ways, he could observe, the laws of the states impair your liberty. You cannot walk at will on your neighbor's grass, you cannot keep your children at will from school, you cannot sleep with your father's wife, you cannot practice surgery without a license or perform it on a minor without the parent's consent, you cannot refuse to support the child you have conceived. In these and many other ways, liberty of private action is curtailed. It is curtailed by "due process of law," and such curtailment has never been supposed to be unconstitutional. The laws restricting abortion do not appear to differ in kind from the laws restricting trespass and incest or the laws requiring the support and education of one's children or the laws regulating surgery. There is nothing in the text of the Fourteenth Amendment to suggest that there is a liberty which no process of law may touch, restrict, or regulate. So, the Martian would conclude from the clues of history, the articles and amendments of the American Constitution do not forbid the governmental regulation of abortion.

The Martian, however, if he came to earth in the bicentennial year of the American Republic, would be wrong. For the Constitution of the United States means not only what its words say or its framers intended. It is a document, like the scriptures of a religion, whose words are sacred, but whose meaning changes as it is reinterpreted in the light of changing circumstances. Its interpreters control its meaning.

The process of interpretation is often beneficent. The framers could never have thought of television when they guaranteed the freedom of speech, but interpretation now makes that freedom include freedom to communicate electronically.[8] The framers did nothing to provide counsel to a defendant too poor to afford a lawyer even when they adopted the Sixth Amendment guaranteeing the right to counsel. Interpretation has made that guarantee include the right of a poor man, in some circumstances, to have his lawyer furnished by the government.[9] The Constitution has expanded beyond its letter and beyond the practice of the day it was made. When such expansion is true to the most fundamental purposes of the framers, it may be called a true development of their thought.

Every citizen is, to a degree, an interpreter of the Constitution; the President and the Congress have to be, and the courts are in a special way. By its own decisions, accepted by nearly everyone, the final interpreter is the Supreme Court of the United States. What the Supreme Court determines to be the law is the law of the land. What the Supreme Court says the Constitution means is what the Constitution means.

Such a conclusion, of course, is not as absolute as it appears. The Supreme Court can be wrong. What the Supreme Court says the Constitution means can do violence to every criterion of history and logic. Instead of developing the purposes of the framers, the Court can subvert them. The Supreme Court can find in the term "liberty" in the Fourteenth Amendment the liberty of a factory owner to work his employees more than ten hours a day, and the Court can be outrageously wrong in so finding. But the law of the land, the meaning of the Constitution as a legal document, will be what the Court says the meaning is, until it admits its error or is corrected by a constitutional amendment.

A decision of the Supreme Court, then, is the last word on the meaning of the Constitution—for the time being. The interpretation offered by the Court can last only as long as the Court is convinced that the interpretation is correct. The Court's conviction of its own correctness does not depend solely on its own precedents; otherwise there would be no change and no reversals of direction by the Court. Like it or not, the Court is engaged in an exchange with its critics, in which its critics always have the power to persuade the Court that it was wrong, or the power to persuade the President to appoint successor justices who believe the Court was wrong, or the power to persuade the country to adopt an amendment to the Constitution correcting the error of the Court.

At one time the Court thought that "liberty" in the Constitution prevented regulation by the state of the terms of employment, because any regulation interfered with the self-evident liberty of each man to set his own terms for his own work.[10] It was contrary to the Constitution for a state to say a man could not dispose of his own body by agreeing to work ten hours a day. Twelve years later the Court said that the Constitution permitted such regulation of liberty.[11] The change occurred not because the words of the Constitution changed but because the critics persuaded the Court that it was wrong.

In the matter of abortion the words of the Constitution did not change, but on January 22, 1973, its meaning did. On that date Justice Harry Blackmun found in the Ninth Amendment's reservation of power to the People or in the Fourteenth Amendment's reference to liberty—he was not entirely sure in which [12]—a liberty to consent to an abortion. On that date the Constitution came to mean that abortion was an American freedom.

Inquiry 3
On the Full Dimensions of the Liberty

The liberty proclaimed by Mr. Justice Blackmun was no narrow license or grudging concession. It was, rather, a radical or basic right located in every childbearing woman. It was a liberty of every carrier of a child to decide whether or not, for any reason or none at all, she chose to carry the child to term or consent to the child's destruction.[1]

As the liberty was located in the pregnant woman, it could make no difference to its exercise whether she was married or single, of mature or tender years, a resident of the state or a transient.[2] Whatever her age and whatever her status, she should be able to decide in privacy, without the interference of public authority, what should be done with the child within her body. The liberty of the pregnant woman, or gravida, was the liberty of an author over his manuscript, of a farmer over his crop, of a girl over her doll. It was hers to say whether the child was disposed of or grew to infancy.

No liberty is absolute, for every act of liberty must ultimately touch the liberty of some other person or group; and the liberty here granted to the gravida was restricted in time. For the first three months of pregnancy, however, the liberty was as perfect as a human liberty can be. For those first three months, all governmental authority was forbidden to intervene in the decision to abort. For those first three months, no power on earth save the gravida's own will was to decide whether or not she kept her child. A liberty that was absolute except in its duration was accorded her.[3]

In the second stage of pregnancy, at the end of the third month,

Mr. Justice Blackmun interpreted the Constitution to say a governmental interest in abortion might be recognized. That interest, however, was the government's interest in the health of the gravida, its citizen. Recognizing that abortion after the third month had increased hazards for the gravida, the Constitution permitted the government to require late abortions to be performed within hospitals or other facilities licensed to perform abortions.[4]

This mandate of the Constitution was scarcely a restriction on the absolute will of the pregnant woman. It did not permit her to have an abortion during an office visit to the doctor, if the state chose to prescribe that she must enter an accredited facility for a late abortion. But what physician would have performed a late abortion in his office? The gravida was guarded from shoddy surgery, but the unborn could be given no protection whatsoever. The passage of time had the effect of limiting the location of the abortion. An abortion in the second phase of pregnancy must be in what the state accepted as a hospital or abortion clinic. The liberty to abort remained in its essentials absolute.

In both the first phase of pregnancy and the second the Constitution gave no recognition of any kind to the unborn. The Constitution did not appear to perceive the unborn's existence, except as that existence had to be conceded to make the performance of an operation destroying the unborn comprehensible. Wearing the glasses of the Constitution, Mr. Justice Blackmun spoke only of "a theory of life" when he spoke of the states' contention that rights of the child should be recognized.[5] The child became less than a being; on the way to becoming a ghost it became a ghost—a theory whose tenuous and debatable character suggested that no living reality was present at all. To express the matter mathematically, the child became a zero when weighed against the liberty of the carrier.

In the third and final phase of pregnancy, reached at viability (reckoned by Justice Blackmun to occur ordinarily at seven months) the zero graduated from existence as a theory to "potential life." [6] When this third stage was reached, the Constitution acknowledged a kind of being in which the state may take an interest. When the third stage was reached, the state might restrict abortions beyond a restriction as to place. When this stage was reached, the Constitution permitted the state to protect the potential life against the unrestricted liberty of the carrier of the child.[7]

The Constitution, however, added—in fine print, as it were, as though it were a medical insurance policy—a cunning clause. The Constitution said that even in the final stage of pregnancy the gravida had the liberty to kill the child if her health required it.[8]

That proviso carried a further proviso. In the true fashion of insurance policies, it was necessary to consult the "definitions" to understand what all the exculpatory clauses implied. To understand what the Constitution meant when it said the health of the gravida overrode the life of the child, you had to know how the Constitution defined health. The Constitution as of 1973 defined health in the terms of the World Health Organization. It was a state of "well-being."

Whether the health of the gravida required an abortion was a medical judgment, Judge Blackmun wrote, to be made "in the light of all factors—physical, emotional, psychological, and the woman's age—relevant to [her] well-being." [9] The absolute freedom of the childbearing woman was curtailed by the necessity of a physician's finding that she needed an abortion. But it would be a rare case where a doctor willing to perform an abortion would not be convinced that his patient's emotional well-being required the abortion she asked for.

The Constitution, in short, withdrew with one hand the protection it appeared to extend with the other. The state in the last two months of pregnancy was permitted to protect the child, but subject to a proviso which undercut the protection. Could a physician ever be convicted for an abortion if concern for the childbearer's well-being were a constitutional defense? Did a doctor ever perform an asked-for abortion without preservation of the childbearer's well-being in mind? The restriction on the liberty appeared to be illusory. For the nine months of life within the womb the child was at the gravida's disposal—with two restrictions: She must find a licensed clinic after month three; and after her child was viable, she must find an abortionist who believed she needed an abortion. When the full dimensions of the liberty were realized, the liberty was little short of unlimited.

Inquiry 4
On the Jurisprudence of the Liberty

By jurisprudence is commonly meant those larger principles and assumptions that undergird a legal system and are the postulates of reasoning on any specific problem within it. Where the Constitution is concerned, jurisprudence and constitutional law overlap, for the fundamental concepts of the latter have the breadth of jurisprudential notions. It is worth, however, isolating the most basic views of legal power and responsibility in the American system from those which are constitutional law for the time being because they have been adopted by the Supreme Court.

Those most basic views constitute a paradigm or model of what the government is and of those it serves. In the American paradigm, the government is men and women acting according to laws they have made to serve the community and its members. The government is not an absolute sovereign with a will above the law. The government is not a mythic state, whose fiat creates rights and duties. Human beings exist before the government exists and are the reason why the government exists.

These observations are so obvious that they might not need to be made were it not for the existence of a competing viewpoint, whose most prominent modern exponent was the Austrian jurisprudent Hans Kelsen. In Kelsen's view, the legal order is the source of all legal rights, and a "person" is merely the personification of such legal rights.[1] In his words, "The physical (natural) person is, thus, no natural reality but a construction of juristic thinking."[2] If the legal order does not recognize any rights in a human being, such a human being is not a person. As Kelsen put it, "That a slave is legally no person, or has no legal personality, means that there are no legal norms qualifying any behaviour of this individual as a duty or as a right." [3] To have no rights is to be a nonperson, and the legal order is to determine if you have rights and are or are not a person.

Kelsen did not go so far as to say that whether you were a human being or not depended on the legal order. But he went almost that far by stating, "There is no kind of human behaviour that, because of its nature, could not be made into a legal duty corresponding to a legal right." [4] If there is no kind of human behaviour which cannot be made into a legal duty, it can be made law to disregard the humanity of certain classes of human beings. This doctrine, strangely prophetic of what the Nazi regime was to do, was framed by a fierce opponent of Nazism who thought that he put the law beyond politics by postulating a self-contained legal order.

In the United States Kelsen had been anticipated in only one important area: the law of slavery. Implicitly, not explicitly, it was assumed by the founders of the American Republic that the law could ignore the biological character of blacks as human beings and treat them as things. [5] That blacks were persons like whites was rarely put directly to the Supreme Court, so that the jurisprudence underlying this monstrous division was not articulated. Two famous cases, however, illustrated the practice.

In *The Antelope*, 281 Africans, rescued from an illegal slave ship, were claimed as property by representatives of Spanish and Portuguese slave-traders. The United States argued for their freedom, and Francis Scott Key on their behalf told the Court he represented "persons" who could not be treated as property under the American law against the slave trade. [6] But Chief Justice Marshall upheld the ability of the law to turn free men into slaves. [7] In *Dred Scott* v. *Sanford*, Chief Justice Taney treated the issue as one not of "personhood" but "citizenship" and held that the descendant of black slaves could never be a citizen of the United States. [8] In Taney's decision, as in Marshall's, there was an implicit Kelsenian jurisprudence: the law, not nature, determined who would count in the American constitutional scheme. In general, however, slavery aside, such a viewpoint was aberrant.

Before abortion became an issue, the Supreme Court had been strongly committed to the position that certain rights relating to marriage, procreation and education were prior to the state. In *Meyer* v. *Nebraska* in 1922 the issue had been posed whether the state could prohibit the teaching of languages other than English in elementary private schools. The Court ruled such a prohibition invalid as interfering with rights of teachers, students, and parents which did not depend upon the state for their existence.[9] Writing for the Court, Justice McReynolds recalled Plato's ideal republic where children were to be taken from their parents for upbringing. He observed, "It hardly will be affirmed that any legislature could impose such restrictions upon the people of a state without doing violence to both letter and spirit of the Constitution." [10] Three years later, in *Pierce* v. *Society of Sisters,* the Court held unconstitutional an Oregon law requiring children be sent to the public schools.[11] "The child," Justice McReynolds summed up, "is not the mere creature of the State." [12] The child's parents had the right, within broad limits, to determine the child's education, and that right was not a mere concession or creation of the state.

In the 1940s, in clear response to the association of compulsory sterilization with the Nazi regime in Germany, the Court in *Skinner* v. *Oklahoma* invalidated on equal protection grounds an Oklahoma law requiring the sterilization of habitual criminals.[13] Justice Douglas for the Court observed, "There is no redemption for the individual whom the law touches." [14] Justice Jackson, concurring, observed, "There are limits to which a legislatively represented majority may conduct biological experiments at the expense of the dignity and personality and natural powers of a minority." [15] The individual's procreative powers were not held by license of the state. The "natural powers" of persons were a check on fiats by the state.

In *Griswold* v. *Connecticut* in 1965 the Court held a law banning the use of contraceptives unconstitutional because it "invaded the sacred precincts of the marital bedroom." [16] For the Court, Justice Douglas wrote, "We deal with a right of privacy older than the Bill of Rights—older than our political parties, older than our school system." [17] Two years later, in *Loving* v. *Virginia,* the Court held invalid a statute prohibiting the marriage of persons of different races. Chief Justice Warren for the Court declared, "Under our Constitution, the freedom to marry, or not to marry, a person of another race resides with the individual and cannot be infringed by the State." [18] In both cases the power of the state was measured by the nature of marriage and the rights of persons anterior to the state and not dependent on it.

Meyer, Pierce, Skinner, Griswold, and *Loving* are the most famous cases of the Court treating the marital and family rights of persons as superior to the state. There are, of course, a host of cases where the rights of individuals to speak, to publish, to worship, and to defend themselves against the state have been vindicated. None of them are easily comprehensible if the state always had a fundamental power to decide who a person is. The ground of all these cases is that persons have certain rights and liberties. How easily the ground could have been removed by definition if that fundamental power to abolish personhood belonged to the state to exercise! How readily each case could have been won by a state claiming the capacity to determine for itself who was a person!

When the New York legislature in 1970 permitted abortion on demand for the first six months of pregnancy, Robert Byrn obtained appointment as guardian ad litem of unborn children who might be aborted under the statute, and he won a court order restraining the New York municipal hospitals from performing abortions except to save the life of the mother. The court appointing him treated the New York law as an unconstitutional infringement of the right to life of the unborn.[19] On appeal, the highest court of the state saw the question as turning on whether or not the unborn were persons; it held that they were not.

Speaking for the majority, Judge Charles Breitel granted that the unborn in the womb were "human" and "unquestionably alive." [20] But, he continued, "It is not true that the legal order corresponds to the natural order." Who was a legal person was "for the law, including, of course, the Constitution, to say." Kelsen was invoked by name to justify the conclusion that it was "a policy determination whether legal personality should attach and not a question of biological or 'natural correspondence'." [21]

In dissent, Judge Adrian Burke rejected the view that the state had the option to determine who was a person. He invoked the Declaration of Independence, "the basic instrument which gave birth to our democracy." The Declaration proclaimed that all men were "created equal" and were "endowed by their Creator with certain inalienable rights." These inalienable liberties preceded the state and arose from a source superior to the state, and the state could not deny them by classifying "a group of living human beings as fit subjects for annihilation." [22] Calling on the Declaration of Independence, Burke sought to give concreteness to what was a much larger idea, the "higher law" above the Constitution.[23]

In the clash between Breitel and Burke, two different jurisprudences were in conflict. It was that of Breitel and Kelsen which Justice Blackmun followed, up to a point, in *The Abortion Cases*

(*Roe* v. *Wade* and *Doe* v. *Bolton*). But while Breitel had left the making and unmaking of persons to the legislature with a reservation as to what the Constitution might say, Justice Blackmun, speaking as the Constitution, described the unborn as less than "persons in the whole sense"—a reduction which in fact treated them as less than human.[24] The biological evidence that they were human he ignored. Less candid than Breitel, he did not concede their humanity, nor did he cite Kelsen. He merely acted as a Kelsenite might feel free to act. The law created persons, and any human conduct might be given valid legal form.

The paradox of Justice Blackmun's opinion was this: To invalidate the state abortion statutes it was necessary for him not only to ignore the unborn child but to recognize a liberty anterior to the state in the carrier of the child. The invocation of liberty which was the very heart of his opinion was the invocation of a standard superior to enacted law. His radical use of "higher law" was only disguised by his claim that something in the Constitution supplied the standard by which the state laws on abortion were invalid. The ultimate basis of his decision was nothing in the Constitution but rather his reading of the natural law liberties of an individual.

The Abortion Cases themselves thus left the two jurisprudences in conflict. The negation of the unborn was inexplicable if the legal order had to bear some correspondence to the real order. The exaltation of individual liberty over a state statute was unintelligible unless the individual had rights not dependent on the state.

Only a sequel to *The Abortion Cases* showed how completely the courts were willing to accept the separation of the legal and natural orders to carry out the cases' basic thrust. In reaction to *Roe* v. *Wade,* Rhode Island enacted a law declaring that within its borders the unborn were persons. The constitutionality of the statute was promptly challenged in the federal court by lawyers for the Planned Parenthood Federation and the American Civil Liberties Union. In response, the State of Rhode Island offered witnesses to testify to the human character of the unborn.[25]

Sitting by himself and applying a rule that permitted him to declare unconstitutional by himself only "frivolous" legislative acts, Federal Judge Pettine refused to hear the state's witnesses. He invalidated the statute as "frivolous." "To me," he wrote, "the United States Supreme Court made it unmistakably clear that the question of when life begins needed no resolution by the judiciary as it was not a question of fact. . . . I find it irrelevant to all the issues presented for adjudication." [26] Once the Supreme Court had denied personhood to the unborn, there appeared to be no evidence on earth that would be permitted into the judicial system to persuade it that it had been wrong.[27] Personhood was a question not of fact but of fiat, and only the Court's fiat counted.

It sometimes makes debating points in the perennial quarrel between "positivists" and "natural law lawyers" that one or the other view of the law has led to, or justified, the worst consequences. One version of the natural law was once used to defend laissez-faire capitalism. On the other hand, the Nazi system of justice appears as a purely positivist monstrosity. It is clear that any jurisprudence may be misused, and that the worst consequences are not all to be laid at the foot of a legal philosophy.

Nonetheless, there is a difference between the two approaches in capacity for self-correction. From the eighteenth century on, from Blackstone onward, the legal system of slavery was attacked in the name of humanity and natural liberties; natural law was used to correct the mistaken claim that slavery was natural.[28] But if a pure positivist view of the law prevails, there appears to be no outside criterion to which to appeal if some human beings are excluded from the system. A revolution may overturn the system, but there is no vehicle for rational criticism of what the will of the judges has determined the Constitution to be.

This consequence is of special importance to our constitutional system. We have set up an elaborate protection of constitutional rights, especially for those who in Justice Harlan F. Stone's phrase constitute "discrete and insular minorities." [29] Such minorities can enjoy the liberties of the Bill of Rights secure in the knowledge that the Supreme Court will defend them against any infringements by the majority.

But all rights in our constitutional jurisprudence are premised on humanity. Your rights flow from your human character. None of them have security if it rests with a group of nine men, or a majority of them, to define you out of the human race. No discrete and insular minority is safe if all its liberties can be removed by defining it as subhuman. If the legal order is a universe which can be developed without reference to the natural order, only the will of the makers of the legal order controls the recognition of legal existence. In the jurisprudence of Hans Kelsen, now officially that of the Supreme Court for the purposes of law on abortion, any human conduct can be made legally valid, and any human being can be expunged from the legal order and left without protection.

Such is the jurisprudential significance of *The Abortion Cases.* Their full legal significance, however, can be measured only in the more particular terms used by the scholars of constitutional law. The judgment from this perspective is no more reassuring.

Inquiry 5
On the Constitutional Foundation of the Liberty

If the full-dimensioned liberty is to be found neither in the Constitution nor in a jurisprudence of the natural rights of the person underlying the Constitution, is there a basis somewhere in American legal theory for what the Supreme Court did? Was the creation of the liberty an exercise of a discretion constitutionally entrusted to the Court? Or was its creation an act of usurpation, a fiat of "raw judicial power," as one dissenting justice suggested that it was? On these questions the persons in the best position to answer are the scholars whose profession is to study the Constitution and the Court.

Three principal elaborations and justifications of *The Abortion Cases* have been offered. Philip B. Heymann, professor of law at Harvard Law School, and Douglas E. Barzelay, a recent Harvard graduate, explain the decisions as continuing a long line of cases protecting "fundamental rights" from state interference—specifically, such private rights as the right to marry, the right to procreate, and the right to educate one's children.[1] They invoke the great cases that have built a bulwark around the family, including the cases protecting the rights of parents, *Meyer* [2] and *Pierce*.[3] They cite the assertion of the right to procreate in *Skinner*.[4] They point to the protection of rights centered in marriage in *Griswold*[5] and *Loving*.[6] They add one further case, decided in 1972, *Eisenstadt* v. *Baird,* which held that the state unconstitutionally violated the privacy of the individual by forbidding the distribution of contraceptives to the unmarried.[7] Taken together, Heymann and Barzelay say, the cases "delineate a sphere of interests—which the Court now groups and denominates 'privacy'." That privacy is implicit in the "liberty" protected by the

Fourteenth Amendment. At the core of this "sphere," subject only to limited social restrictions, is the right of the individual to make "the fundamental decisions that shape family life: whom to marry; whether and when to have children; and with what values to rear those children." The cases that created this protected zone are justified because "our political system is superimposed on and presupposes a social system of family units, not just of isolated individuals. . . . [T]he family unit does not simply co-exist with our constitutional system; it is an integral part of it." [8]

Heymann and Barzelay are far more articulate than the Court. They make an impressive case for the rationality of *Roe* v. *Wade*. Constructing a consistent rationale for each decided case in the line they cite, they make the line speak for *Roe* v. *Wade*. In doing so they turn *Roe* v. *Wade* itself into a vindication of the family. What they do not notice or care to acknowledge is that *Roe* v. *Wade* was profoundly hostile to the family. The family unit which they say is "an integral part" of our constitutional system was rejected by *The Abortion Cases* and destroyed by their logical sequelae.[9]

The only case these scholars invoke which bears on the Court's true rationale is *Eisenstadt* v. *Baird*. That case followed by seven years *Griswold* v. *Connecticut*'s upholding of the right of the married to use contraceptives. *Griswold* v. *Connecticut* was based on the immunity of "the sacred precincts of the marital bedroom." [10] Invoking *Griswold, Eisenstadt* turned the liberty on its head. What had been founded on marriage was now said to be the liberty of the unmarried. For the Court, Justice William Brennan, Jr., wrote, italicizing the key word, "If the right of privacy means anything, it is the right of an *individual,* married or single, to be free from unwarranted governmental intrusion into matters so fundamentally affecting a person as the decision whether to bear or beget a child." [11] In those words a liberty that had been based on the special position of the married was made universal in a way that repudiated the legally privileged status of marriage.

Eisenstadt—decided after *Roe* v. *Wade* had been argued to the Court, so that its revolutionary rationale was probably invented with *Roe* v. *Wade* in view—was in fact *Roe* v. *Wade's* only true precedent. Each was premised on precisely the society that Heymann and Barzelay claim does not exist in America—a society of isolated individuals. Each rejected what Heymann and Barzelay say is integral to our constitutional system—the family unit. Each was a massive departure from the long line of cases that Heymann and Barzelay correctly portray as a vindication of the family. The attempt to show that *The Abortion Cases* were rooted in precedent ends in what is in effect a counter-proof. Except for a single case decided by the same judges at almost the same time, *The Abortion Cases* floated without mooring in the Constitution or in any decided case; indeed they denied the premises of the line of cases that put the person and the family beyond the power of the state.

Heymann and Brazelay came to the defense of *Roe* v. *Wade* in the spring of 1973. By the fall a new theory had matured. It was fashioned by another professor at Harvard Law School, Laurence H. Tribe. His thesis was that *Roe* v. *Wade* was an instance of the constitutional prohibition against establishment of religion. The Constitution, he noted, forbade the establishment of religion. Laws regulating abortion, he claimed, were an establishment of religion. Therefore, he concluded, they were unconstitutional.

To be sure, no one before Tribe had ever considered laws on killing to bear this kind of religious stamp. Tribe, however, argued that "whenever the views of organized religious groups have come to play a persuasive role in an entire subject's legislative consideration for reasons intrinsic to the subject matter as then understood," then the legislature cannot act without favoring a particular religious doctrine and thereby "establishing" a religion. A controversy, he contended, "may be so structured in a particular social and historical context that no attempt to resolve it in a public forum can avoid explicit confrontation with the religious differences that divide the disputants." Abortion was such a controversy and, as he put it, "triggered" the constitutional barrier to legislation.[12]

Tribe's explanation, like Heymann and Barzeley's, suffered from the disadvantage of not having been formulated by the Court. But as a rationalization of *The Abortion Cases* it was more plausible, as it was contradicted by nothing that the Court had said. It had the additional merit of describing the abortion battle as an advocate of abortion might view it: the sheer imposition of religious views on a dissident minority. But there were also serious problems with Tribe's account.

First, as stated by him, it scarcely applied to statutes that, when they were adopted, were not the subject of religious controversy. The abortion statutes in question were of that character. It was not at all evident what "organized religious groups" had led the Texas legislature to adopt its abortion statute in 1911 or even what "organized religious groups" had prevailed when Georgia had adopted the American Law Institute model in 1970. What Tribe had to mean in order to sustain the Court was that if, after a legislature had passed a law, a minority contended that the law was "intrinsically religious," then the Court should invalidate the law. This position seemed to suggest that any group that could point to "intrinsic" religious postulates behind legislation should be able to obtain the invalidation of the legislation. The law on marriage, for example, rested on religious belief. By Tribe's criteria, it was open to any group—polygamists, say, or mere believers in free cohabitation—to attack the intrinsic religious character of the law and procure its invalidation.

Even more serious was the way Tribe was forced to use his theory one-sidedly. His basic contention was that abortion was a subject of a religious nature because it involved "a decision as to what characteristics should be regarded as defining a human being," and that that decision "depended on a statement of religious faith upon which people will invariably differ." [13] If his contention were accepted, *any* decision as to who is human would be a religious decision. Why was his decision, then, to be preferred to someone else's? Why was it unconstitutional for the legislature, making what he called a religious decision, to treat the unborn as human, and constitutional for the legislature, making the same kind of decision, to treat the unborn as nonhuman? Tribe did not address these fundamental questions. However, "on reflection," as he put it five years later, Tribe rejected his own argument.[14]

A third and by far the most candid effort to defend *The Abortion Cases* was made by Michael J. Perry. Perry, an assistant professor of law at Ohio State, boldly made the claim that the phrase "due process of law" in the Fourteenth Amendment meant more than "process." It had a "substantive" content, and the states were bound to observe that substance. Not only were the states bound not to violate that substance; they were under a positive duty to enact only laws which "involved" it.[15] Perry identified this decisive "substance" with "the public welfare." And what defined the public welfare? To that crucial question, Perry answered forthrightly, "The scope of the 'public welfare' is a function of social conventions." Or, as he put it alternatively, "The basic determinants of the public welfare are the conventional attitudes of the sociopolitical culture." [16] The Court was assigned the task of making the states conform to the conventions of the day.

For the Supreme Court to determine public welfare in this way, Perry argued, the Court had to exercise "an ethical function." [17] In fulfilling this function, the Court propounded "general, fundamental ethical principles for the moral education and guidance of the political process." [18] Perry did not disguise or regret the teaching role he gave the Court. The Court was in a better position than any legislature to say what public morals should be, for it was "insulated from the bartering and pressures of a legislature process" and could "look beyond the demands of self-interested minority lobbies in an effort to discern the attitudes characteristic of the moral culture at large." [19] In an era of shifting sexual morality, the Court could act as "a jury." As "a matter of political reality" the Court was a jury that "generally will reflect and mediate the temper of the dominant political and moral culture." Acting as a juryman, "each Justice must ask whether particularized claims about that culture resonate with him or her." [20] In the vernacular, the "vibes" felt by the Justices were to guide their exposition of the Constitution.

Perry's defense of *Roe* v. *Wade* was bold, clear, consistent—consistent with the decision and internally coherent. Despite his own doubt as to "whether individual Justices are even aware of what they are doing," it sounded very much like what Justice Blackmun and his colleagues had been doing. His defense had the ring of realism and the innocence of the child who noted the emperor's absence of clothes. If there was any rebuttal to it on its own terms, the rebuttal could come only from the political process, showing that "the jury" had misread "the sociopolitical culture." But this kind of rebuttal depended principally on the political process; it escaped the confines of scholarly debate where Perry's candor enthroned the flat assertions that substantive due process had been employed by the Court and that substantive due process, reflecting the ethics of the nation as interpreted by the Justices, was a good thing.

Perry's defense, nonetheless, had a deficiency. It ran against the meaning of "liberty" that for seventy years had been accepted as valid by the best minds which had struggled to understand the Constitution. It gave a latitude to judicial lawmaking which generations of scholars had perceived as subversive of the limits of the American Constitution and destructive of American democracy and the distribution of organic powers by the Constitution.

For almost a century the nature of the liberty litigated in *The Abortion Cases* had been explored in another context by the Supreme Court and by scholars evaluating the Court's work. The context was the social legislation of the industrial states and the challenge to that legislation in the name of the constitutional liberty that the Fourteenth Amendment said could be taken only by due process of law. In that context, a theory of constitutional meaning and the limits of the judicial role had been worked out with a comprehensiveness and universality of principle that could not be confined to the cases decided but seemed to stand as general criteria which the Court could defy only at enormous cost. The criteria were summed up in Justice Holmes's dissent in the landmark case of *Lochner* v. *New York*.[21]

The New York legislature had passed a statute making it a crime for a baker to employ workers for more than sixty hours a week or ten hours a day in a biscuit, bread, or cake bakery. No general limitation on hours of work existed at the time or could have passed the legislature, and any "labor law" was regarded with suspicion by the courts. A sixty-hour work week was bold innovation. But the highest court of New York sustained the regulation on the ground that the law was intended to guard the health of the public by protecting it from the products of overworked men, exhausted by fatigue and thus likely to be careless in their baking, and on the additional ground that it was intended to protect the health of the workers themselves, subject as they were to the inhalation of particles affecting their lungs.[22] The decision was challenged in the Supreme Court by Joseph Lochner, a baker convicted in the Oneida County Court of a misdemeanor for permitting an employee to work more than sixty hours.

The Supreme Court held for Lochner. "The right to purchase or to sell labor," the Court declared, "is part of the liberty" protected by the Fourteenth Amendment. The state could not regulate Lochner's right to buy labor on his own terms. To be sure, the liberty was not absolute. The state in extreme cases could abridge the liberty in order to protect health; it could, for example, limit employment in underground mines to eight hours a day. But the state had no business protecting the health of bakers, even if "very likely, physicians would not recommend the exercise of that or of any other trade as a remedy for ill health." Statutes "of the nature of that under review are mere meddlesome interferences with the rights of the individual, and they are not saved from condemnation by the claim that they are passed . . . upon the subject of the health of the individual whose rights are interfered with." Work in any department "carried with it the seeds of unhealthiness." That did not make state intervention lawful.[23]

Interpreting the moral conventions of their day and reading them into the meaning of "liberty," the Justices found that the

Constitution had created a virtually complete barrier to laws regulating the conditions of labor. Viewing the law not as a health measure but "as a labor law, pure and simple," the Court said that the constitutional answer might be given "in a few words." The "liberty of person" and the liberty of contract of the baker and his workers could not be interfered with. The Fourteenth Amendment was an absolute barrier to state regulation of the hours of work.[24]

Four Justices disagreed, and Justice Holmes wrote the dissent, which became classic. He repudiated the role of Platonic guardian. He would not read his view of a controverted matter into the meaning of liberty in the Constitution. He wrote:

> This case is decided upon an economic theory which a large part of the country does not entertain. If it were a question whether I agreed with the theory, I should desire to study it further and longer before making up my mind. But I do not conceive that to be my duty, because I strongly believe that my agreement or disagreement has nothing to do with the right of a majority to embody their opinions in law. . . . The Fourteenth Amendment does not enact Mr. Herbert Spencer's Social Statics.

Holmes then set out what was to be the touchstone for constitutional interpretation where an issue was one of political controversy and the legislature of a state had resolved it. The Court was not to see itself as possessed of resources or rationality superior to the political process:

> I think that the word liberty in the Fourteenth Amendment is perverted when it is held to prevent the natural outcome of a dominant opinion, unless it can be said that a rational and fair man necessarily would admit that the statute proposed would infringe fundamental principles as they have been understood by the traditions of our people and our law.[25]

Every law restricts a liberty. Unless a "rational and fair man" would "necessarily" admit that a state statute infringed "fundamental principles," the Court perverted the Constitution when it invoked "liberty" to invalidate a law. If a law took sides on an issue on which rational and fair men disagreed as to the fundamental principles at stake, the Court was not to take sides too. The Court was not to substitute its theory for the legislature's. As Holmes put it again near the end of his life, the Court's "own discretion" was not the criterion. The Fourteenth Amendment, he wrote, had not given the Justices "*carte blanche* to embody our economic or moral beliefs in its prohibitions."[26] The measure for constitutionality was provided not by the preferences of the Justices or by abstract theorizing about society, but by fundamental principles as they had been comprehended by Americans and set out in American tradition and law.

The criterion of Holmes became the watchword of great judges and scholars of the Court. It undergirded the dissent of Justice Brandeis in *Adams* v. *Tanner* a decade after *Lochner,* when the Supreme Court read "liberty" to mean that the state of Washington, attempting to regulate private employment agencies, had violated such agencies' liberty to do business as they chose.[27] And Holmes joined Brandeis's dissent in 1924 when, again on behalf of bakers, the Supreme Court held their liberty to be violated by a statute prescribing specific weights for loaves of bread. The Court, said Brandeis, engages in "an exercise of the powers of a super-legislature —not the performance of the constitutional function of judicial review."[28] Such a redistribution of organic powers originally distributed in a different way by the Constitution was seen as a gross deformation of the Constitution.

Laissez-faire economics masquerading as the voice of the Constitution were what Holmes and Brandeis fought, and they fought men too unself-conscious and too unself-critical to realize that what they put forth as the pure voice of the Constitution were only the clichés of one side of a debated question. Self-conscious and self-critical themselves, they could not but see the folly of their brothers deluding themselves that they were more reasonable than the legislators and that Justices in the shelter of their chambers had the special wisdom needed to be super-legislators. Why would anyone suppose that nine men picked by politicians to be designated "Justice" acquire by virtue of their office an insight superior to all other mortals in the country?

The evil Holmes and Brandeis protested was succinctly summarized by Felix Frankfurter, while he was still a scholar off the bench. Celebrating "Mr. Justice Brandeis and the Constitution," Frankfurter wrote:

> The veto power of the Supreme Court over the social-economic legislation of the States, when exercised by a narrow conception of the due process and equal protection of the law clauses, presents undue centralization in its most destructive and least responsible form. The most destructive, because it stops experiment at its source, preventing an increase of social knowledge by the only scientific method available; namely, the tests of trial and error.

The least responsible, because it so often turns on the fortuitous circumstances which determine a majority decision, and shelters the fallible judgment of individual Justices, in matters of fact and opinion not peculiarly within the special competence of judges, behind the impersonal authority of the Constitution.[29]

Destructive, irresponsible centralization and fallible judgment put forward as Constitutional mandate—these were the evils of "due process" when the Justices acted as though they were specially inspired in giving a substantive content to "liberty" which no legislature had the ability to perceive.

The criticisms of Holmes, Brandeis, and Frankfurter carried the day in the world of legal education. In time the Supreme Court came to make their criteria its own. In 1963, upholding a state statute regulating debt collectors, Justice Black stated for a unanimous Court, "There was a time when the Due Process Clause was used by this Court to strike down laws which were thought unreasonable, that is, unwise or incompatible with some particular economic or social philosophy." That doctrine "has long since been discarded. . . . We refuse to sit as 'a super-legislature to weigh the wisdom of legislation'." [30] The dissents of Holmes and Brandeis were now the accepted rule of the Court. It was not for the Justices to decide what social philosophy a legislature must follow to enact constitutional legislation.

Three years before *The Abortion Cases,* Justice Stewart (later to be part of the *Roe* and *Doe* majority) declared that once "the Court thought the Fourteenth Amendment gave it power to strike down state laws 'because they may be unwise, improvident, or out of harmony with a particular school of thought' . . . That era long ago passed into history." [31] To quote from Justice Stewart may only demonstrate that the memory of judges is short, that judges like other men are fallible, and that when a judge wants very much to achieve a result he may use the discredited techniques of his predecessors. Yet unless ideas mean nothing, unless great constitutional principles are produced ad hoc as flummery to rationalize the desires of the moment, everything that Holmes, Brandeis, and Frankfurter held to be true was disregarded by *The Abortion Cases.* No matter could have been said to fall less "within the special competence of the judges." No decisions ever sheltered more behind "the impersonal authority of the Constitution." No opinions were so clearly the work of fallible individuals acting as a super-legislature drafting rules for the nation.

The incompatibility of *The Abortion Cases* with the criteria of Holmes and Brandeis was quickly remarked by modern scholars who were, in many cases, not unsympathetic to abortion on moral grounds but who would not abandon their most cherished view of constitutional government in order to accommodate or rationalize a personal preference. For example, Archibald Cox, the former Solicitor General, the hero of the Watergate prosecution and the present Williston Professor of Law at Harvard Law School, wrote, "The failure to confront the issue in principled terms leaves the opinion to read like a set of hospital rules and regulations. . . . Neither historian, nor layman, nor lawyer will be persuaded that all the prescriptions of Justice Blackmun are part of the Constitution." [32] Cox could not discover the principle that led Blackmun to act as a superlegislator for the nation.

Alexander Bickel, Sterling Professor of Law at Yale and *The New York Times*'s counsel in the *Pentagon Papers Case,* described Justice Blackmun's opinion in *The Abortion Cases* as a "model statute" of the kind usually drafted by the Commissioners of Uniform State Laws. How did the model statute become the mandate of the Constitution? A great constitutional lawyer, Bickel was puzzled: "One is left to ask why. The Court never said. It refused the discipline to which its function is properly subject." [33] The Court, in Bickel's view, was "not excused in transgressing all limits, in refusing its own prior discipline." The Court, he reminded the Justices, was in the end subject to "the discipline of the political process," and that discipline was "subsequent." [34] The answers the Court was attempting to give today were "derived, not from Spencer's Social Statics, but from fashionable notions of progress." It may take time, Bickel observed magisterially, "before the realization comes that this will not do." [35]

Richard Epstein, professor of law at Chicago, evaluated *The Abortion Cases* in the journal professionally devoted to commentary on the Court's work, *The Supreme Court Review.* He began by observing that Janet Roe, the pseudonymous plaintiff in *Roe v. Wade* had presented a case which was moot—that is, by the time the Court came to decide her liberty of obtaining an abortion, she was no longer pregnant. Applying the usual rules, the Court would have dismissed her action; in its eagerness to resolve the issues it leaped over its own procedural standards and pressed on to decide her case.[36] There was a second, telltale stain: The plaintiff had claimed that the Texas statute was adopted when abortions were surgically unsafe and was intended to protect the mother's health. This rationale was a piece of fancy appealing to Justice Blackmun; [37] but even as fancy it had no relevance, because the Texas law at bar had been re-enacted in 1911 when surgical abortions were safe.[38] Justice Blackmun did not notice how late the law had been legislated, and he swallowed the plaintiff's theory whole.

Epstein moved to a frontal attack upon *The Abortion Cases.* "In the case of the Supreme Court," he noted, "only principled grounds for decision stand between it and the charge of arbitrary decision based upon its naked political preferences." [39] Epstein could not find in the Constitution the "principled grounds" of Justice Blackmun. He had produced "comprehensive legislation," which he had "enacted in the name of the Due Process Clause of the Constitution." How had the Justice determined that the unborn child was not a person within the meaning of the Constitution? He had not said. He had claimed that there was substantial disagreement as to when life began, and that the Court need not resolve the disagreement, but he had in fact resolved the disagreement—to the detriment of the unborn.[40] He had decided that life did not begin before birth. Even in doing this, he was inconsistent. He had spoken of "potential life" in the third trimester. "But is there not," Epstein asked, "potential life in the unborn child from the moment of conception?" [41] How would Justice Blackmun describe the child from conception to viability? His principles and his standards were "invisible." [42]

Harry Wellington, professor, and later dean, of the Yale Law School, observed, "The Court would have put it better had it been candid enough to quote *Lochner:* 'Statutes of the nature of that under review are mere meddlesome interferences with the rights of the individual, and they are not saved from condemnation by the claim that they are passed . . . upon the subject of the health of the individual whose rights are interfered with'." [43] By *Lochner,* Wellington meant the majority opinion in *Lochner,* and he found the parallel to it exact in *Doe* v. *Bolton,* where Justice Blackmun had held invalid the requirement of Georgia law that *two* physicians concur in the need for an abortion. Such a cautious restraint on physicians, "most" of whom, Justice Blackmun thought, were "good men," had been found to run afoul of the Constitution. The Court, Wellington remarked, "treats the private physician with the reverence that one expects only from advertising agencies employed by the American Medical Association." [44] Even if only the health of the pregnant woman were to be considered, Wellington continued, Justice Blackmun had not explained why the state could not regulate early abortion with an eye to her health, unless liberty meant "instantaneous gratification." Even the First Amendment, he added, "grants no such right." [45]

But more than the carrier's health was at issue. To justify the taking of fetal life, the Court had invoked precedents on the privacy of the marital bed. The Court's use of privacy, Wellington declared, was "Pickwickian." [46] Abortions were performed not in marital beds but in hospitals. As far as Wellington could determine, "conventional morality" in America justified some kinds of abortion, but not all. Conventional morality was "the outer limit of the Court's legitimate authority." The Court had no "mandate" to create new morality "when elaborating the concept of liberty in the Fourteenth Amendment." [47] The Court had acted as though it had such a mandate and imposed the ethical preferences of the Justices on the people.

John Hart Ely, a professor of law at Yale and then at Harvard Law School, made a close comparison between *Lochner* and *The Abortion Cases* and concluded that they, like it, answered questions the Constitution had not made the Court's business. The decision was "a bad decision." It was bad for one basic reason: It did not explain how its elaborate regulations were constitutional law.[48] Like the other constitutional law scholars, Ely could find no principle or standard which had guided Justice Blackmun in his extraordinary interpretation of the Constitution.

Ely did observe that the result was congruent with the judicial philosophy of Richard Nixon (who had appointed Justice Blackmun and two of the other judges making up the majority in *The Abortion Cases.*) Nixon had enunciated a result-oriented view of the Court's function. "That this sort of invitation, to get in there and Lochner for the right goals, can contribute to opinions like *Roe* is obvious. In terms of process it is just what the President ordered." [49] Political pragmatism, not constitutional principle, appeared to be the *raison d'être* of *The Abortion Cases.*

Critics did exist who condemned *The Abortion Cases* by asserting that the Court could not add to the written Constitution.[50] Critics did exist who were as outraged by what the Court had done to the unborn as by what it had done to the Constitution. Bickel, Cox, Ely, Epstein, and Wellington, however, were five critics who were neither fundamentalists in constitutional theory nor champions of the cause of the unborn. They accepted constitutional development by judicial interpretation as necessary, ranging in their views on this point from the pure Frankfurtian position of Bickel to Wellington's acceptance of "conventional morality" as a guide. They showed no special commitment to the anti-abortion side. In their cool professional judgment, *The Abortion Cases* were indefensible because they had a basis neither in the Constitution nor in a principled interpretation of the Constitution.

There is a tendency for any layman to rate one expert in a field as good as another. But to the experienced in any field, experts are not fungible. In the field of constitutional law, persons of experience would probably conclude that Barzelay, Heymann, Perry, and Tribe were outweighed by Bickel, Cox, Ely, Epstein, and Wellington. The balance of expert opinion viewed the liberty as a disaster. As the critics successfully evoked Holmes, Brandeis, and Frankfurter, the weight of their judgment was overwhelming.[51]

The judgment was remarkably harsh: without principle, a failure; a refusal of the Court's own discipline, a transgression of all limits, something that will not do; naked political preference, comprehensive legislation, invisible standards; a replay of *Lochner,* an advertising agent's view of doctors, Pickwickian, beyond the outer limit of legitimate authority; none of its business, a bad decision, an out-Lochnering of *Lochner* in the result-oriented style of a result-oriented Nixon.

Scholarly authority judged the liberty to lack constitutional basis. Its establishment, as Justice White had said, was an act of raw judicial power.[52] If the liberty did not have a foundation in the Constitution or in constitutional principle, its basis had to lie in politics.

Inquiry 6
On the Political Constituencies
of the Liberty

A liberty so comprehensive, so central, and so uncircumscribed as that conferred by *The Abortion Cases* could not have been created out of the air. Seven men, even though endowed with life tenure and the power to make their ideas the Constitution's, would not have embarked on such a legislative program without a political constituency or constituencies seeking the change. Mr. Dooley's words of seventy years ago are still the most dispassionate comment on a large part of the conduct of our highest tribunal: "No matter whether th' constitution follows th' flag or not, th' supreme coort follows th' iliction returns" [1]—if not literally the election returns, the demands of the politically potent. Who were its constituents here?

Prior to *The Abortion Cases,* between mid-1967 and the end of 1972, most state legislatures had considered changing their abortion laws, and nineteen states had changed them.[2] All nineteen states permitted abortions to preserve the health of the gravida, six to destroy an unborn child conceived in rape, five to destroy an unborn child conceived in incest, and four to destroy an unborn child who would probably be born with a substantial deformity; four required no grounds whatsoever. All, however, set set limits in terms of age of the child, ranging from four lunar months in Washington to six months in New York.[3] Most states acted by their legislatures. One of the states (Massachusetts) changed its law by judicial fiat, one (Washington) by popular referendum. New York attempted to reverse its change, but the legislative repeal was vetoed by Governor Rockefeller.[4]

The other thirty-one states did not change their laws despite being lobbied to do so. In two states, Michigan and North Dakota, the rejection of change was by referendum less than three months before *The Abortion Cases* were decided. In those states, abortion on demand up to five months was defeated by heavy majorities—61 percent in Michigan, 77 percent in North Dakota.[5] In other states, proposals for change were killed in committee or by legislative action.

In no state, whether it approved or rejected change, was abortion made legal for the nine months. Except in four states, abortion on demand was not authorized. In the typical states adopting change, specific grounds were set out which abortions had to meet to be legal. No state adopted anything as expansive as the broad charter of the abortion liberty decreed by the Supreme Court on January 22, 1973. If the action of legislatures elected by the men and women of the country in the late 1960s and early 1970s was any index of popular desire, if the referenda in three states were a fair reflection of the people's will, there was a wide disparity between what the people wanted on January 22, 1973, and the liberty they were given.

No one aware of these struggles for the public mind between 1967 and 1973 could have said that the abortion laws in force were the result of apathetic acquiescence in the values of an earlier age. No one aware of the changes made and the changes rejected could have termed the laws archaic. They were either freshly minted, carrying the seal of approval of the American Law Institute on their alterations,[6] or freshly affirmed, carrying either the seal of newly elected legislatures composed of men and women or the stamp of the people voting as a body directly upon the issue.

The votes confirmed what public opinion polls had indicated: Eighty-four percent of married women under the age of forty-five were reported in a National Fertility Survey of 1970 as opposed to permitting abortion to be legal after the third month of pregnancy.[7] Sixty-seven percent of all American men and women were reported in a Gallup poll of 1972 to oppose elective abortion.[8]

In January 1973, when Justice Blackmun wrote his opinion in *Roe* v. *Wade,* a Gallup poll showed that more than eighty-five percent of all Americans believed that human life began *before* birth. By the time an unborn child was viable, and so merely "potential life" to Justice Blackmun, more than seventy-five percent believed actual human life existed; less than fourteen percent thought that human life began at birth. As for the views of American women alone, exactly half believed that human life began at conception.[9] The legislation in force in a majority of states faithfully reflected the conviction that human life should be protected.

The abortion liberty was conferred by the Supreme Court with a spaciousness, a latitude that no legislature had attempted and no majority had sought. Who were its sponsors?

Abortion had not been in the American consciousness at all before the 1960s, when small elites began to press for changes in the law.[10] Only a few persons, even in the early 1960s, were dedicated in principle to the liberty of abortion. Glanville Williams, a teacher of criminal law in England and president of the British Abortion Law Reform Association, was the leader of the "Fundamentalists" in the association, who insisted on the joint liberty of the carrier and her physician, but even they did not champion the liberty beyond the thirteenth week of pregnancy, and as late as 1963 Williams's extreme views represented a minority in this group dedicated to revising the abortion laws of England.[11]

As it happened, Glanville Williams was to have a major part to play in America by being invited to participate in the drafting of the penal code of the American Law Institute (ALI). The institute, a group of judges, lawyers, and law professors, had the custom of publishing "Model Codes" for adoption by state legislatures. In 1962 its official draft of the code adopted the majority views of the British Abortion Law Reform Association, and its commentary adopted Glanville Williams's account of why anyone opposed early abortion.[12] The ALI, a small, prestigious, mostly male body, became the first prominent champion of change in the abortion laws.

The legal elite was then joined by doctors who argued that the existing law made hypocrites of them—claiming, in effect, that they violated the existing law but should not suffer for their violations.[13] It is difficult to recall in the late 1970s how the banner of abortion was borne in those early years by doctors. But the freedom the doctors sought, like the freedom the lawyers sought, was severely limited. No major American group sought abortion on demand. Alan Guttmacher, the president of Planned Parenthood, argued for change in the abortion law only to protect the integrity of doctors. Robert E. Hall, President of the Association for the Study of Abortion, a strongly pro-abortion group, argued as late as 1967 that his objective was to have current abortion law conform to current medical practice. A work on "the population dilemma," published in 1968 with a grant from John D. Rockefeller III's Population Council, observed that "most Americans" were opposed to abortion on demand.[14]

One powerful organization, however, had already decided that the time had come for abortion without legal limitations. In 1968 the American Civil Liberties Union (ACLU) decided to work for "total repeal" of all laws prohibiting abortion prior to the viability of the fetus.[15] The ACLU provided what was indispensable to the establishment of the liberty and its expansion—a cadre of specialists spread throughout the land, centrally directed from New York, expert in constitutional litigation. Symbolically, the ACLU assigned its best constitutional lawyer, Norman Dorsen, to the appeal of *Roe* v. *Wade* in the Supreme Court, as the cause of the liberty rode to victory.[16]

Since its foundation in the 1920s the ACLU had shown no concern about the abortion laws that were standard in every state; it had given no indication that it believed a fundamental right was daily violated everywhere. Why did it change its mind in 1968? In part, the burgeoning women's liberation movement was responsible. Already organized and articulate in New York by then, the movement put forward a view of women that included liberty of abortion as necessary to the liberty of women. The movement had had little influence as yet on the legislatures. But it had access to the press, and leaders of the ACLU responded to its demands.

The other organization mighty in influence that entered the battle was the Planned Parenthood Federation (PPF) of America. The ACLU had earlier worked hand in glove with the PPF to establish the liberty of contraception, and PPF's entry into the abortion field was a second important reason for ACLU's new posture. Divergent in fundamental aims but interlocked in key ways, especially in the person of a lawyer, Harriet Pilpel, the ACLU and the PPF reinforced each other.

Like the ACLU, the PPF had taken many years to see liberty of abortion as a desirable objective. In its early and growing years under Margaret Higgins Sanger, the birth control movement had opposed abortions as "barbaric" and as being, along with infanticide, "the killing of babies." [17] Contraception was set out as the rational and humane alternative. An increase in contraceptive practice was supposed to mean a decrease in abortions. To say birth control meant abortion was regarded by the movement itself as a vicious slander by the opposition. Alan Guttmacher, president of Planned Parenthood in the United States, had written in 1961 about the beginning of life: "Fertilization, then, has taken place; a baby has been conceived." [18] This observation coincided with his earlier account, *Having a Baby* (1947), where he referred to the being who was produced by fertilization as "the new baby which is created at this exact moment." In a still earlier version of the same work (1937) he had quoted, with apparent approval, an English physician on the abortion statutes: "To extinguish the first spark of life is a crime of the same nature, both against our Maker and society, as to destroy an infant, a child, or a man." [19]

The Third International Conference on Planned Parenthood, held in Bombay in 1952, heard the President of the Japan Birth Control League, Kan Majima, discuss the decriminalization of abortion in Japan, note that abortion was to be looked on only as an emergency measure, and declare that abortion "could be done away with when more logical and humanitarian concepts are widely accepted." At the same congress, Hans Harnsen, President of the West German Committee on Planned Parenthood, spoke on "The Medical Evil of Abortion" and denounced its acceptance as a means of birth control.[20] Even as late as the Eighth International Conference of Planned Parenthood, held in Santiago, Chile, in 1967, the *rapporteur* of the discussion of induced abortion concluded, "In summing up, it was stressed that abortion is today a widely used method of controlling family size, but it cannot be recommended as a method of family planning because of its effects on the life and health of the women who undergo it and their future children." [21]

In 1968 everything changed. Alan Guttmacher declared, "My feeling is that the fetus, particularly during its early intrauterine life, is merely a group of specialized cells that do not differ materially from other cells." [22] Dr. Guttmacher and the organization he headed were now avowed friends of abortion. The National Medical Advisory Council of Planned Parenthood–World Population (the international embodiment of the birth control movement) recommended "the abolition of existing statutes and criminal laws regarding abortion when performed by properly qualified physicians with reasonable medical safeguards." [23] Put more succinctly, Planned Parenthood had come to favor abortion on demand.

Had a revolution in biology occurred that necessitated the new appraisal of the biological evidence by Guttmacher? Nothing of the sort. The 1969 edition of his 1961 book still said "a baby has been conceived" at fertilization.[24] What brought about the *volte-face* of the birth controllers? Three things—one of a background character, the other two specific and immediate—had happened. The ideological and intellectual turmoil of the 1960s had led to a rethinking of traditional views of sexual morality; the revolutionary spirit of the times called for changes. In this milieu of shaken values, the old-line birth controllers found themselves assailed by Zero Population advocates who contended that the population crisis required far more drastic solutions than their genteel and gingerly approach had encouraged. At the same time the safety of the oral contraceptive, the famed "pill," which had seemed to be the magic solution of the early 1960s, was questioned. It no longer appeared that a sure, safe, economical way of controlling population by contraception existed. At this desperate pass, under heavy pressure to do more at a time when their principal weapon had been challenged, the birth controllers threw over their devotion to the baby in the womb.[25]

The views of the libertarians of the ACLU were now matched by those of the population professionals, and both converged to meet the new consciousness of medical professionals who saw themselves as an elite with special responsibilities to discharge that the law should not dictate. *The New England Journal of Medicine* published an article by Dr. Robert M. Sade contending that medical care was not anyone's "right"; it was the doctor's responsibility to ration it. His basic analogy was with the baker's control over the food so often used to symbolize life. As the Supreme Court had once taught that the baker had the right to work his men as long as he could bargain for, and again had taught that the baker could measure his loaves as he thought just, so Sade now taught, "In a just society with a moral government it is clear that the only right to the bread belongs to the baker." [26]

An editorial in *California Medicine* expressed an even stronger view of the doctor's autonomy:

> The reverence for each and every human life has also been a keystone of Western medicine and is the ethic which has caused physicians to try to preserve, protect, repair, prolong and enhance every human life which comes under their surveillance. This traditional ethic is still clearly dominant, but there is much to suggest that it is being eroded at the core and may eventually be abandoned. . . . Abortion is being accepted by society as moral, right and even necessary. . . . It is not too early for our profession to examine this new ethic, recognize it for what it is and will mean for human society, and prepare to apply it in a rational develop-

ment for the fulfillment and betterment of manhood in what is almost certain to be a biologically oriented world society.[27]

This editorial was so respectful of the ethic of life that was being abandoned and so candid in recognizing that what was being put in its place was an ethic of "killing" that it might have been written by a Swiftian moralist. But it concluded resolutely that the doctor should take his part in the new society and learn from his part in performing abortions, for his part there might "well be a prototype of what is to come." [28] The baker who owned the bread and the doctor who controlled access to health were to make their own determination as to who should live or die.

To the ACLU, Planned Parenthood, the feminist organizations, and the physicians was added the voice of economizers in government. Abortion was a cheap way to reduce the rising costs of welfare. In the view of some black persons, these welfare bureaucrats also saw it as a way to reduce the black population.[29]

The motivations of the several groups favoring abortion were distinct, and the appeal of their arguments was to different sections of the country. None of the groups were themselves poor. Each was an elite. But some claimed to speak for the poor, while others spoke for their own or some other economic interest.

In ideology and self-identity the most disinterested were the upper-middle-class lawyers who composed the leadership of the ACLU. Nourishing a vision of themselves as champions of the downtrodden, they were conscious of a motivation which was at once libertarian and humanitarian. They accepted the rhetoric of the women's movement; they saw themselves as freedom fighters for women. They viewed abortion as a human good, available to the rich and inexplicably withheld from the poor. They fought under banners proclaiming "Women's Rights" and "No Discrimination Against the Poor."

The least disinterested were a portion of the doctors. At the crassest level, freedom of abortion meant freedom to increase their incomes. After abortion became legal in New York, abortion clinics sprang up and became substantial sources of income for the doctors they employed.[30] The clinics were even to find that their clientele could be increased by out-of-state advertising.[31] The majority of doctors, not so moved by mercenary motives, had both self-interest and their patients' well-being to assert. They wanted to be free to practice their profession as they chose without interference from the community. Abortion was a medical procedure. Therefore its use should be decided by doctors. Ethical standards imposed by law were an infringement of independence. Self-interest in independence merged, usually unconsciously, in a concern for patients—that is, for the women who wanted abortions. The physician in favor of abortion saw himself as unnecessarily confined in responding to women who depended on him. He wanted to be able to help them as he saw best.

The motivations of the welfare administrators were mixed. They needed to keep their budgets down to politically acceptable levels. They wanted to help the poor who were visible to them. They did not want to eliminate their clientele. Neither did they want it to get out of hand. They were subject to electorates increasingly aroused by the rising costs of welfare. To the extent that their clientele was black, they were subject to the covert racism which the black population suspected.[32]

The substitution of abortion for childbirth presented savings, which could be calculated in several ways. At the end of the first year of the new liberty, the Department of Health, Education, and Welfare (HEW) reported to Congress that it had funded "at least" 220,000 abortions. Desiring to motivate Congress to continue appropriations for abortion, it added, "For each pregnancy among Medicaid eligible women that is brought to term, it is estimated that the first year costs to Federal, State and local governments for maternity and pediatric care and public assistance is [sic] approximately $2,700." [33] Subtracting the cost of the abortions—$200 apiece—each Congressman could calculate that the net savings *in the first year alone* were "at least" $500 million.

The estimates of HEW bordered on the conservative. The National Abortion Rights Action League (NARAL), arguing to Congress for the federal funding of abortions, was less inhibited. According to NARAL, delivery of a child, "plus welfare 1 year," cost $4,600.[34] The savings in the first year on this basis went over $1 billion.

These estimates were just the beginning. Suppose one added welfare support of mother and child for five years. Suppose one increased the number of abortions paid for by the government. Suppose one looked at the savings in criminal conduct eliminated because potential criminals had been eliminated. Suppose one estimated the benefits of the abortion liberty over a period of ten years.

It was scarcely an exaggeration to say that, brought home to the poor with government financing, it would save the government and the taxpayer more than $50 billion a decade.[35] Not to have been moved by such mammoth material inducements would have required a vision of humanity difficult to sustain in a welfare bureaucracy.

The motivations of the leaders of Planned Parenthood were the most complex. The leaders consisted of donors and professionals. The donors were, necessarily, rich. They had been convinced that a socially acceptable way of using their wealth as to reduce the number of the poor. At the level of conscious motivation they were altruists, anxious only to spread a blessing. Often they were the descendants of religious believers; their own religious beliefs were attenuated, but they could bring to a cause like "Population Control" the righteous convictions that had animated their forefathers and gain an analogous sense of bringing light to the heathen and doing good to humanity.

The population professionals were in the front line of what was often seen as a war. Their enemy was population growth. It was a powerful enemy and growing more powerful. It was not being contained by present methods. Like most generals in the field, the professionals yearned for more potent weapons. If the war was to be won, escalation was essential. As the donors listened to the professionals, they came to feel that objections to the methods used were irrelevant if the methods were effective; or rather as the method of abortion came increasingly to appear necessary, a new moral judgment was made in its behalf.

In American political terms the ACLU and the women's movement were on the Democratic Left; the doctors were on the Republican Right; the population professionals were often mildly Democratic; the donors tended to be Eastern Republicans. Cutting across the political spectrum, the proponents of abortion were a tacit and effective coalition.[36]

The abortion liberty itself was proclaimed during the regime of Richard Nixon at a time when he had appointed four of the nine justices of the Court, when the Chief Justice was his appointee, and when the Court was already "the Burger Court" to its friends and "the Nixon Court" to its foes. Three of the four men appointed by Richard Nixon voted for the liberty, and it was proclaimed by Harry Blackmun, in whose "wisdom, uprightness, and learning" Richard Nixon had declared he reposed special trust.[37] Even when all allowance is made for the independence of the judicial from the executive branch, it has seemed paradoxical that so great a liberty should issue from a Court so largely shaped by such an illiberal hand.

The paradox appears greater when Richard Nixon's own rhetoric against abortion is recalled. In his most spectacular intervention on the subject he attacked the liberalization of the New York abortion law in a letter to Cardinal Cooke.[38] He seemed embarrassed by the report of his own appointees to the Commission on Population Growth and the American Future, which endorsed abortion.[39] He was fictionally portrayed by Philip Roth, with some basis in his rhetoric, as making his last stand in office as a defender of the fetus.[40]

But Philip Roth showed less than his usual acumen as a novelist and as a prophet in taking Richard Nixon's rhetoric at face value; and today no one would. The shape and thrust and meaning of any Administration are to be measured not by presidential platitudes but by presidential actions and appointments. Richard Nixon's celebrated letter on the New York law was a gesture in the air, because he had no authority of any kind over the legislature of New York. It was like his famous comment on the desirability of a California court's convicting Charles Manson of murder—a gratuitous assertion in an area beyond his responsibilities, intended to please the people with no cost to the President and no commitment of his power.[41]

It is hard to guess what the President as a man thought on the matter. He viewed abortion as a sign of a decadent, permissive morality; but he also opposed government interference with private decisions. William Safire has suggested that personally he was influenced by his daughter Julie's conviction that abortion was an evil.[42] But the President was also the chief of a party with factions to conciliate and the head of an administration whose officers were chosen with attention to values other than the value of embryonic life. His domestic chief of staff, John Ehrlichman, was sympathetic to the abortion liberty.[43] When *The Abortion Cases* drew a storm of criticism, the mantle of the presidency was drawn about Justice Blackmun with an invitation to the first National Prayer Breakfast with the President and Billy Graham.[44]

Rhetoric and gesture aside, the Nixon Administration was the midwife of the liberty of abortion in America. In the Administration's first year, a White House Conference on "hunger" significantly linked the feeding of the poor to the reduction of the number of the poor, and President Nixon chose the occasion to propose a "Commission on Population Growth and the American Future." [45]

The Commission was to become a principal vehicle for making abortion acceptable as federal policy. The appointment of its chairman and most of its members was to be the work of the President.

About the same time as the Conference on Hunger, President Nixon designated Louis Hellman to be Deputy Assistant Secretary for Population Affairs of the Department of Health, Education, and Welfare. Hellman's qualifications were several: He was Professor of Obstetrics and Gynecology at the State University of New York. He was director of a family planning clinic whose clients were entirely "from ghetto population." [46] He had served for four years as the chairman of the Food and Drug Administration's Advisory Committee on Obstetrics and Gynecology judging the pill and in that capacity, balancing the social good against the risk to individuals, had interpreted the law to permit the pill's distribution despite doubts raised as to its safety for some women.[47] He had come to work for the Administration because "the threat of population growth" was "real to each and every individual in this country." [48] He was sponsored by Alan Guttmacher, Frederick Jaffe, and Joseph Beasley of Planned Parenthood, and by Nelson Rockefeller, and he was a director of the Association for the Study of Abortion.[49]

In 1970, the year of his appointment, Louis Hellman, using his new federal title, was co-chairman of a planning and strategy conference on abortion in America, held in New York City. The conference brought together medical and legal leaders sympathetic to the abortion liberty.[50] The other chairman was Allan C. Barnes, vice president for medical affairs of the Rockefeller Foundation. Featured speakers were Norman Dorsen and Harriet Pilpel of ACLU and Dr. Robert Hall, the president of the Association for the Study of Abortions. The funding of the conference came in part from the federal government through the Agency for International Development, whose Population Affairs section was headed by a zealous advocate of population control, Reimert T. Ravenholt. In the six subsequent years, under Presidents Nixon and Ford, Hellman and Ravenholt worked to staff their agencies and to make federal policy serve the abortion liberty.

The first limited move was made with tactical adeptness. In the summer of 1970, while abortion was still an issue of debate in almost every state, the Department of Defense declared a new policy on abortions to be provided for American military personnel and their dependents. The new policy was to be followed in the United States "without regard to local law." [51] It was to permit abortions in military medical facilities on the grounds of "mental health." In a period when no state had appropriated money for elective abortions, the Defense Department overrode all state law to provide federal facilities and federal medical staff to perform abortions that were, in all but name, elective. The decision to override local law had been opposed by the Surgeons General of the Army, Navy, and Air Force. It was imposed by the Defense Department because the department was so instructed by the Department of Health, Education, and Welfare.[52]

In the face of criticism the Administration eventually drew back on this initiative. But it also made a more substantial move. In the spring of 1970 the Congress had responded to the President and created the Commission on Population and the American Future.[53] President Nixon had the appointment of twenty out of twenty-four members. Of these presidential appointees sixteen turned out to favor abortion on demand. At a time when two-thirds of the voters and all of the state legislatures opposed abortion on demand, it required foresight and planning to compose a commission with such views.

The Commission's staff were professionals in population control. Its chief consultants were also professionals in population control, many of them coming from the leading private foundation in the field, the Population Council. At the head of the Commission, as an appropriate symbol of its orientation, the Administration placed the philanthropist whose name, throughout the world, was a symbol of population control, John D. Rockefeller III.[54]

John Rockefeller had already made clear his views on abortion. This occurred on November 17, 1968, two weeks after Richard Nixon's election, when Rockefeller keynoted a conference at Hot Springs, Virginia. The conference was under the auspices of the Association for the Study of Abortion, that imperfectly disguised committee for the promotion of the abortion liberty. It was organized by Alan Guttmacher, Louis Hellman, and Planned Parenthood's chief lawyer, Harriet Pilpel.[55] Announced as a meeting to "discuss" abortion, the conference had the kind of ratio of proponents to opponents not uncharacteristic of pro-choice symposia— twenty of the pro-choice side to one of the other. In his keynote address Rockefeller assured his audience that the "long-run answer" to the "evil" of restrictive abortion laws was not to amend them but "to eliminate abortion laws altogether." [56] The most important donor to the cause of population control emerged as a public advocate of removing regulation of abortion from the law. The course he set in 1968 did not prevent his appointment by the President in 1970.

In the spring of 1972 the Rockefeller-headed Commission reported. Among its many recommendations was specific advice on abortion and the law. It declared, "The majority of the Commission believes that women should be free to determine their own fertility, that the matter of abortion should be left to the conscience of the individual." In this terse and clear language, abolition of the abortion laws was called for. The statutes of fifty states were to be replaced by "the conscience of the individual." Abortion according to the "conscience of the individual,"—difficult in practice to distinguish from abortion on demand—was articulated as a major component of population policy.[57]

The Rockefeller report was not the act of the President, and if he did nothing to endorse it, he would pay no political price for it. He did not endorse it. Its recommendation on abortion, beyond the power of a President to implement, was to be implemented within the year by the Nixon Court. The report itself was the act of an Administration which, knowing the issues in contention, had packed the commission with professionals in the population field and set at its head the greatest of donors to the cause of population control, whose views as to the measures necessary were a matter of public record two years before his appointment.

The Administration's third significant appointment, that of Harry Blackmun, was also made in the spring of 1970, when the Commission on Population was appointed. Apart from his availability as a Republican circuit judge and his friendship with the Chief Justice, Harry Blackmun's outstanding qualification was his identification with the medical establishment. At the height of his professional career, before his appointment to the bench, he had been "resident general counsel" of the Mayo Clinic.[58] For nine years in Rochester, Minnesota, he had bathed in the mystique of the medical profession at one of its most hallowed shrines. To suppose that he was put on the Court to write *The Abortion Cases* is to attribute a foresight to the Administration and a predictability in judges that border on fantasy. But the Administration chose a man congenial to the Administration. Choosing him, the Administration put on the Court a champion of the autonomy of the physician. Measured not by the subjective and shifting intentions of a very political President but objectively in terms of the commitments and values of those appointed, Blackmun's nomination, like Hellman's and Rockefeller's, was a significant step in providing a governmental welcome to abortion.

By different and convergent paths a powerful de facto alliance on abortion had come into being. Its effective leaders were male—Alan Guttmacher, Louis Hellman, John D. Rockefeller III. Harriet Pilpel was the only prominent exception. All were very far from being poor, although only Rockefeller was extremely rich. None was a black or an Indian or a Chicano or a Puerto Rican. None was from those more silent ethnic minorities, the Poles, the Slovaks, and the Italians. Despite their personal qualifications, they presented themselves as the spokespersons of women, the ethnic minorities, the poor.

Each of the groups they claimed to represent had symbolic significance, and beyond the symbolic values they held up, they themselves represented important and powerful sections of the population. Each of them came from constituencies connected with the opinion makers, the media, the courts and the federal bureaucracy. Each of their own groups carried weight with a member or members of the majority of the Court. It was to the political weight of these groups that seven members of the Court responded by creation of the liberty of abortion. Once launched, the liberty was to be cloaked with protective legends appealing to the wider constituencies the elite spokespersons said they spoke for.

Inquiry 7
On the Legends of the Liberty

No doctrine with the massive momentum of the liberty of abortion, no revolution as radical as that accomplished by *The Abortion Cases,* could have survived without the aid of legends—popular myths used to convey the necessity of the liberty, rationalize its existence, and explain why opposition to such an obvious human benefit existed. The principal legends were five.

The first was that abortion laws were invented by men when men alone made the laws and when women and their offspring were regarded as male property not to be disposed of without male consent; that some men today still wanted women to be "compulsorily pregnant"; and that feminine emancipation would come only when women exercised their right to control their own bodies.[1]

The legend had elements of truth: Prior to the Nineteenth Amendment women did not, of course, possess the vote, and legislators, judges, and prosecutors were men. A married man at common law possessed extensive rights over his wife. Pregnancy has always been a serious interference with a woman's physiology: Her hormonal balance is affected; her digestion and other vital functions may be upset; her size, shape, and weight are changed. No man is subject to such biological alterations except by illness, which he has every right to combat. Men have oppressed women when against their will they have forced them to endure such changes in their bodies and the psychological and social effects accompanying them.

But the legend also distorted the right it celebrated. The right to control one's body was shorthand for a larger principle, which, put as a popular slogan, suffered in its phrasing. It suggested that there was a person and then there was a person's body, a dualism scarcely respectable in any contemporary philosophy. What the slogan meant was that every human being should be respected by every other human being; a corollary was that no one should affect another's body without consent. It was each person's decision to say whether he or she would be hot or cold, fat or lean, tired or rested.

The principle was not absolute, but it was a good guide in most matters: We should be able most of the time to control the conditions affecting our bodies. The difficulty was that the application of the principle in the case of pregnancy could not be made without affecting the body of someone else. In the general understanding of the right of self-control, it is assumed that the right is exercised without harm to another—you starve or you feast, you delight in snow or in sun without injury to anyone else. But control over one's body in pregnancy could not be exercised without injury to the body of another being. That other being had eyes and ears, hands and feet, skin and genitals that were not the mother's; blood, heart, and circulation that were not hers; lungs, breath, and respiration that belonged to another; mouth, stomach, and digestion that were not hers.[2] The intuitive basis for the principle of self-determination was that each human being was to be respected. The principle was not consistently applied if it were invoked on behalf of mothers and denied to their unborn children. The legend oversimplified the issue of abortion by ignoring the existence of the unborn child.

The legend contained other elements of error and distortion. A general objection to laws that were first made when only men were legislators would render all common law and the Constitution itself infirm. The abortion laws were not obsolete survivals of a patriarchal age, but, as Inquiry 6 has shown, laws reconsidered and retained or newly enacted between 1965 and 1972. The revolution effected by the Supreme Court was not desired by the great majority of American women, and its fundamental postulate that no human being existed in the womb before birth was repudiated by most of them.[3] The legend's focus on the male legislators of the past was a distortion.

The distortion was of the kind that was almost the reverse of reality. When strong and comprehensive anti-abortion statutes were being enacted in nineteenth-century America, the militant feminists had been outspoken in their scorn and condemnation of abortion.[4] Their journal, *Revolution,* urged anti-abortion measures upon the New York legislature in 1869. If the practice was resorted to at all, their leader Elizabeth Cady Stanton said, it was because of "the degradation of women" by men.[5] Abortion, the physicians attacking the practice agreed, was often imposed on women by men anxious to avoid their responsibility for children they had fathered.[6]

These themes of the era in which abortion statutes became stringent were heard a century later when abortion statutes were being relaxed. In the words of Grace Olivarez, dissenting from the Rockefeller Commission's report, the liberty of abortion was "anti–women's liberation," because it subverted the equality of men and women. Equality, she observed, meant "an equal sharing of responsibilities *by* and *as* men and women." Legalized abortion freed men "from worrying about whether they should bear some responsibility for the consequences of the sexual experience." Liberty of abortion simply excused men "from their responsibility for participation in the creation of life." Abortion on demand confirmed "the existing irresponsible attitude some men have toward their relationship to women and their offspring." [7]

Who wanted the liberty of abortion most in 1970? Only a minority of any section of the population favored it, but the stablest and strongest supporters of the liberty were white upper-class males.[8] The federal judges, the donors and professionals of the population movement, and the leading lawyers of the ACLU came from this class. Why was this minority the best friend of the liberty? Judith Blake, head of the Demography Department at Berkeley, offered a hypothesis after studying the public opinion polls from 1960 to 1970 which established this category as the core of its supporters:

> [U]pper-class men have much to gain and very little to lose by an easing of legal restrictions against abortion. For some time, these men seem to have been satisfied with relatively small families extending over a limited period of their lives. Thus the increased availability of abortions is not likely to damage whatever interest they have with respect to the family. Furthermore, their sexual freedom has been curtailed, both within marriage and outside it, by restrictions on contraception and pregnancy termination, since as a class they are especially vulnerable to being held financially and socially responsible for accidental pregnancies. For this reason, they are likely to favor a lessening of those restrictions. And when one takes into account the fact that birth-control reforms—whether advanced contraceptive methods like the pill and the coil, or abortion itself—cost men virtually nothing, their positive attitude toward legalizing abortion becomes even more plausible. After all, it is women who must undergo abortions, not men.[9]

The motivations attributed to upper-class males by Blake, Olivarez, and Stanton apply to only a minority of this class and do not show a uniform and universal male trait. But that the primary group wanting legalized abortion is found among upper-class white males appears indisputable from Blake's demographic analysis, and it is confirmed by observation of those who effectuated the abortion liberty. The motives of all these men cannot be reduced to those Blake hypothesizes; but her speculations suggest why a minority of this class so staunchly welcomed the liberty; and the existence of this male attitude and the fact that the primary supporters of the liberty are male destroy the legend that equates abortion law with male oppression.

The strongest confirmation of what Elizabeth Cady Stanton said in the nineteenth century and Grace Olivarez and Judith Blake say today has been afforded by American literature, that witness to how experience is perceived by the most gifted of our race. In Eugene O'Neill's *Abortion* (1914), the protagonist, Jack Townsend, is a rich young college student who has had an affair with a "townie" while engaged to a girl of his own class. The "townie" has become pregnant; he has arranged for an abortion; it is fatal to her as well as to the child. The play is unswervingly focused on abortion as the upper-class male's escape from the consequences of sexual adventure. Townsend's father, who pays for the abortion, regrets its necessity but treats it as an expense of his son's education. The girl who is killed is portrayed as passively complying with Jack's decision.[10]

In Ernest Hemingway's "Hills Like White Elephants" (1926), the scene is a railroad station in Spain, but it could as easily be set in Illinois. A man and a woman sit on a bar waiting for the train, which will take the woman to an abortionist:

> "It's really an awfully simple operation, Jig," the man said. "It's not really an operation at all."
> The girl looked at the ground the table legs rested on.
> "I know you wouldn't mind it, Jig. It's not really anything. It's just to let the air in."
> The girl did not say anything. . . .
> "You've got to realize," he said, "that I don't want you to do it if you don't want to. I'm perfectly willing to go through with it if it means anything to you."
> "Doesn't it mean anything to you? We could get along."
> "Of course it does. But I don't want anybody but you. I don't want anyone else. And I know it's perfectly simple."
> "Yes, you know it's perfectly simple." [11]

In Joan Didion's *Run, River* (1963), Lily Knight obtains an abortion after she has told her husband, "I'm pregnant and I don't think by you," and he has said, "Any Mexican would know better. Any

West End whore." [12] Lily's resentment at what she does is focused on him and on the man by whom she is pregnant, who has counseled the abortion, and who after it is over says "I would have cut off my right arm if I could have gone down there for you." She thinks, "He knew what he could cut off." [13] Trapped by weak and egocentric males, Lily's "choice" is a response to the expectations of both of them.

The legend attributed to women was what was wanted most by a core of upper-class males. The legend did not explain why the majority of American women did not desire the liberty fashioned by the Supreme Court. The legend did not explain why, if the women of America were able to vote upon it today (they cannot directly, for the Court has read it into the Constitution), that liberty would be rejected. The legend's function was to make the male the enemy, to assimilate sexual intercourse to rape, to rationalize the creation of the liberty.

The second legend was precisely the opposite of the first, but none the worse for that in the eyes of those fostering the liberty. It was that the original abortion laws, made by men though they were, were designed to protect women. Their object was to prevent the exposure of women to unsanitary surgery at a time when surgery was dangerous. They were health measures for the benefit of the mother, not the child. This understanding of the old laws was put forward by Governor Rockefeller's commission on the abortion laws of New York State; was reiterated by Governor's Rockefeller's friend on the New York Court of Appeals, Charles Breitel; was repeated by John Rockefeller's Commission on Population and the American Future; and was recited by Justice Blackmun in *Roe* v. *Wade*.[14]

The truth in the legend was that, since time immemorial, hazard to a mother's health had been a stock theme. As an objection to abortion it was at least as old as St. Jerome in fourth-century Rome.[15] Mention of it appealed to the self-interest of those not moved by higher considerations, much as the danger of venereal disease was sometimes emphasized by those attacking prostitution. But neither in the case of prostitution nor in the case of abortion was the health hazard the primary reason for the objection to practices condemned on their own account.

To begin with, there was not a whit of evidence in the nineteenth century that abortion carried out in a hospital was any more dangerous than childbirth. The surgery required to deliver a baby was just as unsanitary as the surgery required to perform an abortion.[16] The relative safety of early abortions was commonly accepted in the early nineteenth century.[17] The ease with which abortions were performed was a common theme of reformers objecting to abortion in the 1820s. Abortion appeared to legislators at that time as "minor surgery." [18] A celebrated advocate of abortion in the 1840s could boast that abortion was "attended with no danger, especially in the earlier stages of pregnancy." [19] In the 1860s, as the anti-abortion campaign increased, a prominent opponent of abortion saw no special physical risks to the mother in the practice.[20] As the laws everywhere became stringent in the 1880s, New York's leading professor of obstetrics, T. Gaillard Thomas, in a special series of lectures on abortion at the College of Physicians and Surgeons in New York, pronounced abortion to be a reasonably safe procedure.[21] Indeed the harshest laws against abortion were enacted as antiseptic practices became prevalent in hospitals, so that if the legislators' intent was primarily to guard the health of the gravida, they were passing the antithesis of sensible legislation, forcing the women bent on abortion to resort to abortion in unsanitary nonhospital conditions.[22] By the standards of modern courts, the nineteenth-century American legislators who had comprehensively banned abortion acted irrationally if they intended to prevent maternal deaths. But that comfortable sense of superiority to our ancestors depended on attributing to them a primary purpose they did not have.

The health of the mother was in fact not the prime objective of the vigorous anti-abortion drive led by the American Medical Association in the nineteenth century. As a modern historian puts it, educated physicians "objected strongly to snuffing out life in the making." [23] What he describes as "the physicians' crusade against abortion" began with the work of Dr. Horatio R. Storer of Boston. His report to the AMA in 1859 on behalf of its Committee on Criminal Abortion objected to the unscientific distinction between the status of the unborn before and after quickening and noted how the distinction permitted abortion in early pregnancy. Storer called for new legislation to stop "such unwarrantable destruction of human life."[24] Throughout the next twenty years, as American abortion statutes tightened, it was the physicians who led the defense of human life in the womb.[25]

The two Rockefeller commissions (Nelson's and John's) and the judges who accepted the "law-office history" version of the motivation for the nineteenth-century statutes appeared to be ignorant of the real history and, as they purveyed the legend, indifferent to it. The function of the story they told was to reassure persons solicitous for their predecessors' wisdom and to persuade persons who hesitated to abandon the abortion laws if they served a purpose. These doubters were boldly assured that the purpose was obsolete, that modern surgery no longer endangered the gravida, that the woman-protecting laws of the past might safely be jettisoned. That the "law-office history" was not the actual history was not the legend-carrier's concern.

The third legend was that the abortion laws were the product of religious dogma, supported only for sectarian religious reasons. The first statement of the legend was composed by Glanville Williams, Professor of Law at Cambridge University and President of the Abortion Reform League of Britain. He speculated that abortion was opposed by Christians because of their view of the necessity of infant baptism. Abortion, by killing unborn in the womb, prevented baptism. Therefore to save the fetus's soul, the Christian Church had opposed the practice.[26] William's hypothesis was incorporated in the draft of the Model Penal Code circulated by the American Law Institute as *the* explanation of the opposition to abortion.[27]

Williams failed to show that the reasoning he described had animated the Christian opposition to abortion. In fact, some Christians had taken precisely the opposite stand: They had argued that the fetus should be aborted in order to be baptized before dying. But neither this reasoning nor that so thoughtfully put forward by Glanville Williams was accepted by the Christian mainstream.[28] His hypothesis was without foundation.

The legend was patched up and restated in this form: It is because of religious dogma on the soul that Christians, especially Catholics, believe that abortion is wrong. It is because of a theological view that each fetus is ensouled at conception that persons adhering to this theology object to destroying the unborn.[29]

What the legend left out of its account was that the general Christian opposition to homicide could, if one so desired, be put in precisely similar terms. One could characterize as "theological" every Christian claim that human beings should be respected, for every such claim derived from a view of human beings as created by God and destined for God, as "ensouled" in traditional parlance. It was that creation and destiny which forbade their treatment as things.

To say that the Christian position rested on a theory of ensoulment and to proceed therefore to disqualify it in the realm of secular law was to imply that Christians had no right to be heard on killing in general. The Christian opposition to genocide, to urban air raids, to the war in Vietnam was no more and no less theological than the

Christian opposition to abortion. The legend, focusing on the esoteric term "ensoulment," encouraged defenders of the abortion liberty to believe that the Christian objection was founded on an idiosyncratic theology when it depended on the general principle of respecting other human beings, supplemented by the biological observation that unborn children were part of the human species.

The most popular and pervasive form of the legend abandoned the effort to compose a theology for religious opponents of abortion and simply spread it abroad that opposition to abortion was a peculiar tenet of the Catholic Church. In this form the legend was able to assure supporters of the liberty that their opponents were moved by irrational religious motives; to use the Catholic Church as a scapegoat for any setbacks suffered; and to play upon and inflame the still substantial anti-Catholicism present in America.

There was an understandable element of self-deception in this form of the legend. Even since the "birth control" movement had taken shape in the United States under the leadership of Margaret Higgins Sanger, its most vocal and persistent opponent had been the Catholic Church.[30] Despite the opposition of the Church, the movement had succeeded. Contraception had become widely accepted in the United States. American public policy supported contraception. The federal government paid for "family planning programs." Within the Catholic Church itself a strong strain of opinion argued for the moral acceptability of contraception.

When the abortion battle opened, it was entirely natural for the old birth controllers to see it as a replay of the battle over contraception. Their nemesis, the Catholic Church, appeared again to them as the principal foe. The scenario was clear. They would attack the Roman menace. Secular, Protestant, and Jewish opinion would rally to them. The Church's own ranks would divide. After a struggle, abortion would be triumphantly established as national policy. It was tempting to believe that what had happened before would happen again, so tempting that the warriors of birth control ignored all the signs that the issue was different, the opposition deeper, and their scenario a fantasy. The legend was nonetheless framed and circulated that, but for the Catholics, abortion would be accepted as an American good.

In the quietest but most persistent manifestation of the legend, the media habitually identified a person who publicly opposed abortion by his religion, if he happened to be a Catholic. It was not the general practice of the media to point out the religion of public officials when they took public stands on moral issues. Senator Mansfield did not become "the Roman Catholic Senator Mansfield" when out of conscience he opposed the war in Vietnam. Hugh Carey did not become "the Catholic Governor of New York" when he objected on moral grounds to the mistreatment of the elderly. But just as a racist press once identified every thief if possible as black, so the press identified every public opponent if possible as Catholic. The implication of this kind of identification was evident: "Only a Catholic would see the matter this way; there must be some quirk of Catholic dogma that makes Catholics take this extraordinary position." Done a thousand times by the media, the identification was a highly effective technique of perpetuating the legend.

The legend, steadily fostered by the press, permitted a law professor at Harvard Law School to say, in treating of "religious entanglement," that Justice Blackmun had recognized "the highly charged and distinctly sectarian controversy that the abortion issue had predictably come to stir" and to add in documentation of this statement the following remarkable footnote: "As Governor Rockefeller of New York observed in vetoing a repeal of his state's liberalized abortion law: 'The extremes of personal vilification and political coercion brought to bear on members of the legislature raises serious doubts that the votes to repeal the reform . . . represented the will of a majority of the people of New York State'." [31]

It was not clear that Governor Rockefeller's claim that his opponents had used "personal vilification" and "political coercion" was proof of "distinctly sectarian controversy" or "religious entanglement," unless one was meant to read such charges against a background assuring one that the opponents of abortion were unscrupulous religious bigots. It was not evident that extreme vilifiers and coercers were proof of a religious presence unless one already possessed strong stereotypes of who one's religious opponents were and what they were like.

At another level, the legend permitted the defendants' counsel on appeal in the *Edelin* case to put the attempted enforcement of the state's manslaughter statute into a context of a "bitter clash of religious, moral, and political beliefs" and to refer darkly to the use of criminal accusations as "an instrument of ideological or religious warfare." [32] The code message transmitted to the court, in case it had not been reading the press, was not difficult to decipher in the context of Massachusetts history: The Catholic Church in Massachusetts has put an innocent doctor on trial.

In pre–World War I English politics, it was recognized that one way for the Conservative Party to win votes was for it to "play the Orange Card"—that is, to appeal to anti-Catholic feeling on the issue of home rule for Ireland. At times the Conservative Party played the Orange Card to its advantage. Yet what a bitter harvest it sowed for all of England, what festering hatreds it left in Ulster for such prejudice to have been politically cultivated! Some friends of the abortion liberty played their "Orange Card" with no apparent care for the harvest it was sowing.

Friends of the liberty created an ad hoc lobby, the Religious Coalition for Abortion Rights, composed of groups ranging from the American Ethical Union to the Women's Division of the American Jewish Congress to the Board of Church and Society of the United Methodist Church. The stated rationale of the coalition was that "in a pluralistic society the state should not embody in law one particular religious or moral viewpoint on which widely different views are held by substantial sections of the religious community." The statements of the Coalition were perceived by some Protestants as an effort to turn abortion into a "Catholic issue." Baptists for Life and American Citizens Concerned for Life, two Protestant groups, explicitly warned the Religious Coalition for Abortion Rights that Americans "will not tolerate the creation of another Northern Ireland in which religious differences are polarized and then manipulated for political gain." [33]

When, in 1976 and 1977, the pro-choice cause began to lose in Congress and the courts, the temptation increased to appeal to this powerful bias. In January 1978 the National Abortion Rights Action League circulated potential contributors with a flyer entitled "Who Finances the Anti-Abortion Movement?" [34] There followed an enumeration of contributions from Catholic dioceses to the National Committee for a Human Life Amendment. It was noted that there were "a number of other anti-abortion groups" which had "also raised large sums"; but the message of the flyer was that the Catholic Church was financing the campaign for an Amendment. If a comparable flyer had been run by opponents of the civil rights legislation of the 1960s and had listed *only* the Jewish groups favoring such legislation, ignoring all the other Americans opposed to discrimination, the anti-Semitism of the message would have been apparent. The flyer would have been saying, "The Jews are for this; therefore, oppose it." No less blatantly, NARAL asked for contributions on the implicit ground that if the Catholic Church was the principal sponsor of something, right-thinking people must be against it. The appeal was to a latent anti-Catholicism.

This theme became explicit later in 1978 when several abortion clinics were victims of violence by anonymous arsonists setting them on fire. With great deliberation, certain defenders of the abortion liberty declared the firebombings were "part of a national campaign of violent opposition to abortion encouraged by the Roman Catholic Church" and that the Catholic Church was "responsible for the escalating violent opposition." Regional affiliates of Planned Parenthood circulated a cartoon showing a mitred bishop gloating over the success of the attacks.[35] Proof was not offered in support of these sensational charges. The murky depths of religious hatred were stirred. These friends of the abortion liberty invited the American public to hold the Catholic Church guilty of vicious atrocities.

At a more civil level, the legend was decked out by lawyers as a First Amendment claim. When it appeared probable that the Hyde Amendment, restricting the federal funding of abortion, would be held constitutional by a federal court (see Inquiry 12), Planned Parenthood attacked the Hyde Amendment as "enactment into law of one religious belief respecting abortion." [36] Apparently Planned Parenthood wanted unwillingness to aid abortion to be understood as a religious rule of the same order as, say, unwillingness to eat pork or unwillingness to eat meat on Fridays. But the foundation of Planned Parenthood's position was that there was no secular criterion by which human life could be determined to exist. If that foundation were sound, then *any* position on the beginning of human life was "religious." Planned Parenthood could not evade its own characterization of the issue. Its position was as "religious" as anyone else's; and there was no more reason for a court to prefer its religion and require funding than to accept the determination of the legislature. Failing to distinguish its position as uniquely secular, Planned Parenthood's claim functioned only to inject the venom of prejudice into the judicial process. That it was indeed the strategy of some defenders of the abortion liberty to focus attention on the Catholic Church as *the* opponent was openly confessed by the director of the Religious Coalition for Abortion Rights.[37]

The strategy was deployed in 1978 in lawsuits in California, Illinois, New Jersey, New York, and West Virginia in an effort to have declared unconstitutional laws that failed to fund nontherapeutic abortions. Although the Supreme Court had already held it to be within the power of a state to decide not to fund such abortions (see

Inquiry 11), it was the contention of these suits that a religious point of view was established whenever a legislature voted not to use public money to finance the private choice of an abortion.[38]

Information as to the characteristics of the life to be taken by abortion would appear to be essential in order for a childbearing woman to rationally exercise her choice to bear or destroy her off-spring. An Akron City Ordinance, followed in substance by several state statutes, provided that in any abortion the woman be informed by her physician "that the unborn child is a human life from the moment of conception" and be told "in detail the anatomical and physiological characteristics of the particular unborn child at the gestational point of development at which time the abortion is to be performed, including, but not limited to, appearance, mobility, tactile sensitivity, including pain, perception or response, brain and heart function, the presence of internal organs and the presence of external members." [39] Although the basic ideology of the ACLU is a commitment to the free flow of ideas, lawyers for the American Civil Liberties Union of Ohio Foundation informed the mayor of Akron that he might be personally liable in damages if he enforced the statute, and, joined by lawyers for the Reproductive Freedom Project of the parent ACLU in New York, they attacked the Akron Ordinance in toto. "Chapter 1870," they told the federal court, "constitutes enactment into law of religious belief concerning abortions and the nature of the fetus." [40] In this legal assault the facts of biology (see Inquiry 17) were treated as though they had a religious coloration.

At the highest level of ecumenical dialogue, the legend permitted two hundred ethicians, mostly Protestant clergymen, to denounce "the bishops of the Roman Catholic Church" for attempting "to enact religiously based anti-abortion commitments into law." [41] Many of the same ethicians had been vigorous in expressing their own religiously based commitments against the war in Vietnam—but that, of course, was noncontroversial!

As brought to bear on American abortion statutes, the legend was a travesty. The statutes of the nineteenth century had been enacted as the result of a "physicians' crusade" led by the American Medical Association at a time when Catholics did not play a major role in American social legislation. The leaders of the crusade had even been able to appeal to anti-Catholic nativist sentiment in urging the enactment of abortion statutes to stop the self-destruction of the white Protestant American stock.[42] The recent American statutes of the kind declared unconstitutional in *Doe* v. *Bolton* had been designed by the American Law Institute and criticized by Catholics for permitting too many exceptions to the defense of the unborn child.

There was an element of truth in the legend: The Catholic Church was opposed to abortion. But there were elements of distortion when this truth was isolated from its context. First, it implied that the Catholic Church was the sole religious opponent of the liberty of abortion conferred by the Court. Second, it suggested that in some way Catholics had a grudge against the race or that it was some special ecclesiastical doctrine that made them the obstinate and only defenders of the fetus. That the anti-abortionists acted on biological knowledge common to all Americans coupled with a respect for human life basic to the Western ethic could be forgotten. Smoldering sentiments of antipapalism, whether they were fundamentalist Protestant or rationalist, could be depended on to do the work of argument.

From the time the Christian Church had emerged in the Mediterranean world in the first century A.D., opposition to abortion had been one of its moral tenets and one of its most distinctive behavioral injunctions. The use and the user of abortifacients were denounced in the New Testament itself. A first-century catechism, *The Teaching of the Twelve Apostles,* placed those who are "killers of the child, who abort the mold of God," between murders and adulterers, all embarked on "the Way of Darkness." The early Christian *Epistle of Barnabas* declared, "You shall not slay the child by abortions." The Greek Church and the Latin Church in the course of time developed specific sanctions against the sin.[43]

The Reformation marked no break in the moral opposition to abortion. The Church of England and the Lutheran Church were steadfast in their opposition.[44] Calvin wrote with particular feeling against the practice: "If it seems more disgraceful that a man be killed in his own home than in his field—since for every man his home is his sanctuary—how much more abominable is it to be considered to kill a fetus in the womb who has not yet been brought into the light." Benjamin Wadsworth, a Puritan divine of outstanding orthodoxy and later president of Harvard College, declared in his sermons entitled *The Well-Ordered Family:* "If any purposely indeavor [*sic*] to destroy the Fruit of their Womb (whether they actually do it or not) they're guilty of Murder in God's account." He repeated the same doctrine when he expounded the Sixth Commandment in Boston in 1719; after speaking of those who violated "Thou shalt not kill" by using poisons, Wadsworth continued: ". . . and so do those who purposely indeavor to destroy the Life of the Child in the Womb, whether the Woman her self or another does it." [45]

In the twentieth century the Protestant opposition to abortion was equally manifest. The Lambeth Conference of 1930, announcing Anglican doctrine, declared, "The Council records its abhorrence of the sinful practice of abortion." [46] The popular Anglican writer Dean W. R. Inge rejected abortion "as involving the destruction of a life which has already begun." [47] The Encyclical Letter of Anglican Bishops, issued in connection with the 1958 Lambeth Conference, recommended contraception as a means of population control in overpopulated countries and simultaneously declared, "Abortion and infanticide are to be condemned." [48] In the mid-1960s it was evident that some Anglicans were in favor of a much more permissive stance, and their views, focused primarily on legislation, were circulated as a church committee's report.[49] But as another Anglican writer noted, these persons spoke only for themselves; the Church of England stood committed to its historic opposition to abortion.[50]

On the Continent of Europe, the heirs of the Reformers were articulate in opposition. Helmut Thielicke, the Lutheran theologian, pronounced abortion permissible only where a life had to be sacrificed to the save the mother's life. Apart from such a rare case, he wrote, "The genesis of human life is a sacrosanct domain which dare not be invaded by human hands or 'rationalized,' that is, subjected to utilitarian considerations." [51] Life in the womb was not to be sacrificed for any of the reasons pragmatic argument could suggest.

Karl Barth, the giant of Calvinist neo-orthodoxy, declared, "Our first contention must be that no pretext can alter the fact that the whole circle of those concerned [in an abortion] is in the strict sense engaged in the killing [*Tötung*] of human life. For the unborn child is from the very first a child." When life had to be sacrificed for life, a "rare, genuine exception existed." But abortion had become a plague. It was "the great modern sin." As practiced among "so-called civilized peoples," it was "secret and open mass murder." Repeating his denunciation, Barth concluded, "Deliberate abortion is irrefutably seen to be sin, murder, and transgression." [52]

A minister whose own martyr's death at the hands of the Nazis gave his witness particular authenticity spoke against abortion as he wrote under the shadow of death in the 1940s. Dietrich Bonhoeffer said:

Destruction of the embryo in the mother's womb is a violation of the right to live which God has bestowed upon this nascent life. To raise the question whether we are here concerned with a human being or not is merely to confuse the issue. The simple fact is that God certainly intended to create a human being and that this nascent human being has been deliberately deprived of life. And that is nothing but murder.[53]

The womb as a sacred sanctuary—Calvin and Thielcke; abortion, murder (*Mord*)—Barth and Bonhoeffer; the widespread practice of abortion, mass murder—Barth; the right to life inviolable—Bonhoeffer. Such was the teaching of leading Protestant thinkers on abortion.

In the United States by the 1970s some Protestant churches took a permissive stand as to what the law on abortion should be. For example, in the 1960s the Unitarian–Universalist assembly went on record in favor of permitting abortion to be legal if there was any "compelling reason" for wanting it. Similar stands were taken by the Eighth General Synod of the United Church of Christ in 1971 and by the General Conference of the United Methodist Church in 1972.[54] Such permissiveness as to what the law should be was not permissiveness as to the act of abortion itself. The major Protestant churches continued to maintain the traditional Christian condemnation of the act.

The 1972 General Conference of the United Methodist Church, for example, while calling for the removal of "abortion from the criminal code," affirmed its "belief in the sanctity of unborn human life" and declared, "In continuity with past Christian tradition, we recognize tragic conflicts of life with life that may justify abortion." The Methodist position now disagreed with the traditional Anglo-American way of restraining abortion by the criminal law; it still justified abortion in terms of the conflict of life with life. A change of this kind on the means of implementing the moral condemnation of abortion was easily misread by the pro-abortion party as a change in the Protestant position on abortion. Such a change obscured the fact that a large body of Protestant opinion was against the legalization of abortion. Such a change fed the religious legend that made the Catholic Church the only opponent of abortion. But the main moral position of Christians that abortion was the taking of human life was not altered. Although some Protestant churches, such as the Presbyterian Church in the United States, developed a casuistry permitting abortion under some circumstances and although a spectrum of Protestant views existed on the use of the law to restrict abortion, no Protestant church endorsed abortion as a human good or taught that what was once regarded by all Christians as sin was now desirable. As this fundamental premise remained, the judgment about the use of law to regulate abortion was a prudential or tactical conclusion. It was left open, for example, to leading Methodist theologians such as Paul Ramsey, Harrington Spear Paine Professor of Religion at Princeton University, to argue that only legal protection of the unborn would fulfill the Methodists' commitment to the sanctity of unborn life, and to urge restoration to the states of the power to protect life taken from them by *The Abortion Cases*.[55]

In the political sphere, the leaders of the movement to restrict abortion by law were often Protestants. The president of the largest anti-abortion group, the National Right to Life Committee, was Mildred Jefferson, a Methodist. The president of Americans United for Life was George Huntson Williams, Hollis Professor of Divinity at Harvard Divinity School and an ordained Unitarian minister. The president of American Citizens Concerned for Life was Marjory Mecklenburg, a Methodist. In the Congress, early sponsors of a Human Life Amendment included Senator Mark Hatfield, a Baptist, and Senator Harold Hughes, an ordained Methodist minister.

The opposition to abortion as an evil form of taking human life was not confined to the traditional Christian Churches. The Mormon Church considered it "one of the most revolting and sinful practices in this day." [56] Spencer Kimball, a Mormon president, expounded the Mormons' position with a lawyer's clarity: "Rare special cases" might exist where it would be justified. In general, "We place it high on the list of sins against which we strongly warn the people." [57]

In classic Jewish law, abortion was permitted only to save the life of the mother.[58] Life in this case was sacrificed for life. In the same way, in rabbinical responsa, it was permitted to break the Sabbath only to save a human life, and this exception was understood to include the life of an unborn child.[59] The Chief Rabbi of Israel, following the tradition, described abortion in 1963 as "an appurtenance of murder." [60]

In the 1960s and 1970s some broad rabbinical readings of "life" to include health were made, and the head of the Rabbinical Court in Jerusalem went beyond the traditional exception to permit abortion in cases of rape, incest, or a handicapped child.[61] Yet the main line of Orthodoxy held: "Jewish law permits abortion only when a potentially lethal deterioration in the mother's health might ensue if pregnancy is allowed to proceed to term. . . . Abortion 'on demand' purely for the convenience of the mother or even of society is strictly prohibited and morally repugnant." [62] Although liberal and reformed Jews were not bound by the Orthodox position, and many held more permissive positions, it was evident that the religious opposition to abortion extended well beyond the boundaries of Catholic Christianity.

Old and modern religious condemnation of abortion does not prove that every Christian or Protestant or Mormon or Jew opposes abortion or favors laws restricting its practice. They do demonstrate that the view of abortion as an evil taking of nascent human life is not confined to the official Catholic hierarchy, and that the legend is grossly in error when it portrays opposition to abortion as the peculiar tenet of Catholics. But, although it is not true, the legend has been wonderfully effective.

The story that abortion laws were invented by men to oppress women; the story that abortion laws were invented by men to spare women; and the story that abortion laws were invented by Christians or by Catholics to harass the human race were genetic legends. They furnished explanations for the existence of abortion laws and for their defenders' attachment to them. But the most powerful constructions have been those setting out the moral position of the pro-liberty cause and the consequences of its opponents' position. The fourth legend said that abortion was a profoundly personal decision; it was to be made freely by the sole person affected; it was a private choice. "Choice" became the watchword. Personal autonomy became the banner. The opposition were "moral absolutists" who had substituted an iron rule for rational decision-making by the individual affected.[63]

The legend tapped the deepest wellspring of Western consciousness—respect for the conscience of the individual. Its moral dimension was reinforced by its political dimension, its appeal to libertarian ideology. In an age where the power of the state was ubiquitous, the legend said that there was one corner immune from the state's interference. In privacy, in liberty of conscience, the pregnant woman was free to bear or jettison her burden. This legend was indeed the form in which Justice Blackmun presented his decisions in *The Abortion Cases*.[64]

No society in history had ever regarded the reproductive process as without social consequences: It did not matter to the legend. No act of reproduction was possible without a partner, no medical abortion was possible without a physician: It did not matter. The act of

abortion imposed the childbearer's choice upon the unborn child beyond argument and beyond recall: The existence of another human
being was eliminated by the legend.

After the victory of private choice in the Supreme Court the
liberty was immediately seen to have social implications: It could not
be effectively exercised without vast governmental aid. The consciences of opponents could not be left free if the exercise was to be
effected. Students in colleges were told to pay for the abortions of
their fellow students, whatever their conscientious opposition to abortion, or be expelled. Hospitals founded by persons who abhorred
abortion were assaulted by lawsuits to make them provide facilities
for abortion or be held in contempt of court. Doctors who failed to
counsel abortions about which they had moral scruples were threatened with money judgments in tort. Students who wanted to become
doctors were interrogated on their beliefs on abortion before being
admitted to medical schools. Towns that wished to exclude abortion
clinics were instructed by judges that they must allow them. Parents
who objected to their daughters' abortions were told by judges that
their parental rights were second to the liberty. Civic hospitals that
refused to perform abortions were, from 1973 to 1976, ordered to do
so. The consciences of whole states opposed to abortion were overridden by judges or governors determined to fund and facilitate the
practice. The personal decision of the pregnant woman for abortion
had social consequences for college students, medical students, hospitals, doctors, parents, towns, cities, and states. The dedicated defenders of choice were dedicated to making everyone else agree with
the choice of abortion. The defenders of conscience—the ACLU
foremost of all—recognized only their own consciences as right. The
liberty, so peculiarly private in legend, was ubiquitously social in
reality.[65] "Choice" remained the code word.

The fifth and most politically potent legend was that the liberty
was necessary to prevent discrimination against the poor. The rich,
it said, could always get abortions, either from complaisant doctors
at home or from physicians acting lawfully in some foreign country.
The poor were condemned to self-induced abortion by coat hanger
or the butchery of a back street abortionist. Eight thousand poor
women a year, the legend said in 1967, die because of the discrimination of the law. The liberty will end the evil.[66]

After the liberty was granted, the legend was rephrased. Now, it
said, abortions are denied to the poor not because of the law, but because of economics. The doctors who formerly would oblige only the

rich in breaking the law will still practice their profession only for money. Legalizing abortion will not have the hoped-for effect unless abortion is also paid for by the community. The person who opposes payment is an enemy of the poor, an advocate of the coat hanger. The poor, the legend once said, will pay exorbitant fees to unskilled abortionists for illegal abortions in septic conditions; the poor, the legend now said, will not be able to pay reasonable fees to skilled obstetricians for legal abortions in antiseptic surroundings.[67]

The legend embodied one principle, one truth, one lie, one implication, and two assumptions. The principle was that the law should be equal for all. Equality before the law is a foundation stone of democracy. To assert that the abortion laws were unequal laws was to invoke in condemnation of them the massive weight of democratic ideology.

The truth was that the rich can do things the poor cannot. When that truth was coupled with the principle of equality the combination was a powerful criticism of *any* law. In a society based on money as an incentive, discrimination based on money is bred into the society and into its legal processes. When this fact was related to abortion, it was made to appear that abortion law in particular was open to avoidance or evasion by the rich when every law was open to such a charge. If the legend was to have bite, it was necessary to suggest why this fact called for abolition of this law alone, why the unevenness in the law's impact was peculiarly odious here. It was at this point that the lie was serviceable. The lie was that 8,000 women per year died from illegal abortions. The true figure was between 250 and 500.[68] The true figure had to be increased over 1,000 percent to shock and make its point.

The impact of the lie was further enlarged by an implication. Presenting only the figure on maternal deaths carried the implication that pregnant women were the only human beings affected by abortion. Again and again, the legend was stated in such a way that so many "lives" would be saved by eliminating restrictions on abortion. It was never conceded that a second set of lives, those of unborn children, had to be taken into account in any fair quantification of the human life saved or lost by eliminating the law. By the conservative calculations of a demographer friendly to abortion, the liberty increased the number of abortions per year by 250,000 in 1975. Projecting this figure throughout 1977 and allowing for the increase that had already occurred in 1973 and 1974, it could be inferred that by 1978 the liberty had, at a minimum, cost more than one million lives.

The number of human beings actually aborted in the United States in the four years 1973–1976 was more than 3.5 million. If the abortion rate prior to *The Abortion Cases* was substantially lower than the pro-abortion party guessed, the new liberty had cost the lives of more than 3 million human beings.[69]

The underlying assumption of the legend was that abortion was a human good—indeed, a specially prized human good. To deny it to anyone who wanted it was to inflict a deprivation. That the opponents of abortion considered abortion a human evil, indeed a specially pernicious human evil, was overlooked in the presentation of the legend. Because they did not accept the legend's assumption, they were wicked in wanting to keep this great blessing from the poor. Although they would not concede the assumption, they were still supposed to share it. Their objection to providing the poor with means to have abortions was portrayed as the cruelest of hypocrisies. But how devoted to the poor were the purveyors of the legend?

The Court that granted the liberty of abortion voted to uphold as constitutional the refusal of many states to provide welfare assistance for more than a fourth child. The fifth and subsequent children of a poor family had no constitutional right to eat. So strong was the enchantment of the legend that Justice Blackmun could see no inconsistency in treating the denial of assistance for an abortion as far worse than the denial of assistance for food.[70] Rejecting the legend, Edward C. Smith, one of the few black members of the Carter White House staff, wrote that "poor women" was "a popularly understood euphemism for *poor minority* women—blacks, Hispanics, Indians, etc.—in other words those women more prone to have large families (four or more children)." It was these families to whom the Court said the states could deny the right to eat. "These poor minority women with their government Medicaid cards," Smith sharply observed, "represent a very lucrative supplemental income market for middle- and upper-income (and mostly white) male physicians." [71]

The Court that granted the liberty voted to deny assistance to unborn children under the Social Security Act. So seductive was the power of the legend that this real injury to the poor, consequent on the liberty, was forgotten. The evil of malnourishment of poor unborn children was made to seem nothing compared to the good of eliminating them altogether.[72]

Attacking this kind of reasoning, Jesse Jackson, perhaps the best known spokesman for the black poor, sent an "Open Letter to Congress." He urged that governmental funds spent on abortion be cut off and the money be "expended to meet human needs." Instead of a "federal policy of killing," he proposed a federal policy of caring for the "most precious resource we have—our children." Like Edward Smith, he doubted that those who wanted to reduce the ethnic minorities had their welfare primarily at heart.[73]

If the assumption underlying the legend was true, it was not cause for suspicion that a rich and powerful country should offer to help a poor and weak country by saying, "We'll help you if you'll first abort your children." In the world of the legend it was not strange that a rich man should tell a poor man, "I'd love to help you. Let me show you how to kill your unborn children."

Dissenting from the Rockefeller Commission, Grace Olivarez, herself a Chicano, had a different view of the liberty's meaning for the poor. She wrote:

> To talk about the "wanted" and the "unwanted" child smacks too much of bigotry and prejudice. Many of us have experienced the sting of being "unwanted" by certain segments of our society. . . . One usually wants objects and if they turn out to be unsatisfactory, they are returnable. . . . Human beings are not returnable items. . . . Those with power in our society cannot be allowed to "want" and "unwant" people at will. . . .
>
> The poor cry out for justice and equality, and we respond with legalized abortion.[74]

In this view the offer of abortion was an evasion of responsibility, and the legend was a lie.

There was a second assumption as basic to the legend as that abortion was a human good: It was that the poor to be held in view were the women unable to pay for abortions. But there was another way to view the poor. It was taken by Jérome Lejeune, the discoverer of the genetic basis of Down's Syndrome, which produces the condition popularly known as mongolism. Addressing the American Society of Human Genetics after receiving its award for his work, Dr. Lejeune expressed his horror at the use to which his discovery might be put: amniocentesis to detect the defective gene, followed by abortion of those found to have it. The children who suffered from this handicap would never be among the elite of the world, but they could lead lives harmless to others and even pleasing to themselves and to those who came to love them. On what basis would one extripate them from the human race? Perhaps, Lejeune suggested with mordant irony, a National Academy of Death should be established, which would establish the criteria and select those who should die. Lejeune, for his part, did not know how to judge them. These were "the poorest of the poor." [75] He could only be "their advocate." [76]

The legend looked past such cries as Olivarez's, such defiances as Lejeune's. Like each of the other four legends it was firmly based on the belief that there was no good reason to challenge the liberty. Hence those opposing it must be male chauvinists or uninstructed traditionalists or religious bigots or hypocritical enemies of the poor.

The champions of the liberty were high-minded idealists—the libertarians of ACLU and NOW, the donors and professionals of Planned Parenthood, the doctors and welfare administrators who sought not to promote their own interests but the good of their patients, their clients, their society. Convinced of their own morality, believing their own legends, the political constituents of the abortion liberty were able to focus exclusively on the act of will by which a pregnant woman chose to continue her pregnancy or not. This moment of interior choice was the foundation of the legend that abortion was a uniquely private act. The massive social repercussions of the resolution of that issue could be forgotten. The poorest of the poor were silent, so their voices could not disturb the tale. Wrapped in legends, the liberty expanded with a logic and an internal dynamism of its own; and its legends were purveyed by the press.

Inquiry 8
On the Propagation of the Liberty by the Press

That the press is the fourth branch of the American government, although unrecognized as such by the Constitution, is a truth which today stands in no need of demonstration, if "press" is read exclusively enough to mean the *New York Times*, the *Washington Post*, *Time*, and *Newsweek* and inclusively enough to include the three television networks. Legally, the truth received indirect acknowledgment in the *Sullivan* case, where the Supreme Court, to the immediate benefit of the *New York Times*, virtually repealed the law of libel as to criticisms by the press of public officials' official conduct,[1] and in *The Pentagon Papers Case,* where the Supreme Court found that the *New York Times* had greater constitutional rights in not disclosing its sources than the executive branch had in keeping its papers secret.[2] Practically, the removal of Richard Nixon as President, a governmental act of magnitude, could not have been accomplished had not the press taken the matter in hand.

In both this special governmental sense of "press" and in the larger sense of all newspapers, magazines, and radio and television stations, the press was for the abortion liberty. Virtually every major newspaper in the country was on its side, as were the radio stations, the news commentators, the disc jockeys, the pollsters, the syndicated columnists, the editorial writers, the reporters, the news services, the journals of information, and the journals of opinion. With the notable exception of three or four syndicated writers—Nick Timmesch, William Buckley, George Will, and Michael Novak—every major molder of public opinion in the press was pro-abortion or indifferent to the issue. With the single exception of the *National*

Review, no journal of secular opinion was open to articles hostile to the liberty. With the exception of the anti-abortion movement's own creation, James McFadden's *Human Life Review,* no scholarly magazine was receptive to criticism of the liberty.

There was a massive barrier through which any news or opinion contrary to the liberty had to travel. There was not a single large urban newspaper regularly carrying the anti-abortion viewpoint the way Horace Greeley's *Tribune* had carried the anti-slavery viewpoint. There was not a single national news magazine or television network that was ever other than silent on the issue or favorable to the liberty.

If one were to enumerate all the anti-abortion testimony before Congress and the state legislatures which, as a consequence, went unreported to the public at large, one could compile an enormous dossier. If one were to tell of all the large anti-abortion rallies that, as a consequence, went unnoticed by television cameras or newspaper photographers, one could make a list as large. If one were to catalogue the number of anti-abortion articles rejected, the number of anti-abortion books unreviewed, the number of anti-abortion stories untold, the number of anti-abortion opinions unrecorded by the press, one could compose what would itself be a book. Buoyed by the currents of the time and creating those currents, self-confident and safe from challenge, the American press swept aside almost all signs that abortion as a liberty was unwelcome to the majority of Americans.

In a major way, the press muffled the issue. The *New York Times* had a reporter, Warren Weaver, Jr., specializing in reporting the Supreme Court. On January 23, 1973, under the headline "High Court Rules Abortion Legal," a front page story by Mr. Weaver began,

> The Supreme Court overruled today all state laws that prohibit or restrict a woman's right to obtain an abortion during her first three months of pregnancy. The vote was 7–2.
>
> In an historic resolution of a fiercely controversial issue, the Court drafted a new set of national guidelines that will result in broadly liberalized anti-abortion laws in 46 states, but will not abolish restrictions altogether.[3]

Weaver then gave a summary of the Court's principal conclusions and, in a burst of realism, referred to the Court's pronouncements not as the teaching of the Constitution but as a draft of "guidelines."

Every word he wrote was matchable in something the Court had said. Every word was true. But his story was not fair. Focus and emphasis, not literal factuality, determine the meaning of a story and its fairness.

In his first sentence Weaver had emphasized that restrictions were ended for the first three months. His unavoidable implication was that there were restrictions on the last six. Of course there were, but none of the kind that anyone was interested in and none that effectively restricted abortion. Although he went on to recite portions of the Court's decision touching each stage of pregnancy, the reporter failed to notice how the Court's definition of health made abortion available on demand.

Its initial report was a prototype of how the *New York Times* would continue to play the story. It would emphasize heavily the ending of restrictions on the first three months. It would leave the impression that serious restrictions existed on the last two months. It would blur the legal situation of months four through seven.

A *New York Times* editorial endorsing the Court on January 24, 1973, took the same approach. It began, "The Supreme Court has made a major contribution to the preservation of individual liberties and of free decision-making by its invalidation of state laws inhibiting a woman's right to obtain an abortion in the first three months of pregnancy." [4] Like the news account, everything attributed to the Court had been actually said by it, but the focus was kept squarely on the first three months. Won by that moderate position, the reader was expected to accept with aplomb its further refinements.

What the further refinements were, the editorial did not make too clear. At one point it said that the Court permitted state power to be used at a later stage of pregnancy, but such power was to be "governed essentially by considerations of maternal health." Yet in almost the next breath the editorial said that in the later stage the state might "protect potential life." The editorial did not pause to ask how these statements were reconcilable, nor did it note the broad definition the Court provided for "health."

Editorial writers are traditionally inexact and rhetorical, and this editorial is of interest chiefly in revealing the close correspondence between the focus of *New York Times* reporting and editorial policy. More startling was a story run as news that purported to give the effect of *The Abortion Cases* upon state law. Accurately noting that the abortion laws of most states were invalid by the Court's criterion, the reporter reported, "In the strictest interpretation only New

York State's abortion law appears to conform in all details to the Court's ruling." [5] New York's abortion law at the time permitted abortion on demand for the first six months of pregnancy. New York's abortion law then treated as "homicide," punishable as a second degree felony, any abortion performed in the last trimester.[6] The law conformed "in all details" if "criminal homicide" and "constitutional liberty" meant the same thing. *Floyd* v. *Anders,* analyzed below in Inquiry 15, was to demonstrate dramatically the difference.

The story put out by the *New York Times* was not at first adopted by all the leading members of the press. *Time,* for example, spoke of the liberty of abortion as existing for "six months." [7] But in four years it became conventional in the press to describe the abortion liberty as confined to "the early months" or, specifically, to "the first three months." The *Washington Post* of June 24, 1977, editorially declared that "women have a clear constitutional right to terminate pregnancy by abortion, at least through the first three months." Tom Bethell's "Taking Exception" column of July 23, 1977, in the *Post* eliminated even the "at least," so that, again, three months appeared as the term of the liberty. The *Los Angeles Times* of July 2, 1977, described Justice Blackmun as "author of the Court's 1973 opinion striking down laws that interfered with abortions during the first three months of pregnancy." On October 19, 1977, reporting the new Supreme Court decisions on the funding of abortion and the controversy over funding, the *Washington Star* described "the 1973 decision that a woman has a right to choose to have an abortion in the first 13 weeks of pregnancy." The International Women's Year Conference at Houston approved a resolution specifically endorsing the Supreme Court's abortion decisions. The page-one news digest of the *Wall Street Journal* of November 27, 1977, reported the Houston Conference had approved a resolution "supporting abortion during the first three months of pregnancy." By December 5, 1977, *Time* itself had adopted the error: "The U.S. Supreme Court in 1973 gave women the right to have an abortion for any reason during the first 3 months of pregnancy" (page 20). The unavoidable impression conveyed was that the abortion liberty ended when pregnancy was one-third over.

The equation of "three months" with the "abortion liberty" affected the reporting of public opinion on abortion. On November 21 *Time* (p. 115) reported with fanfare a survey made on its behalf by Yankelovich, Skelly, and White of American opinion on sexual morality. It announced that 64 percent of those polled believed "a woman should be legally free to have an abortion if she wants one." Only a few months earlier, Judith Blake, professor of demography at UCLA, had made a careful analysis of public opinion on legal abortion which was published in the March–June issue of *Population and Development Review*. Her study of National Opinion Research Center and Gallup polls from 1965 to 1977 showed at no time more than 31 percent approving elective legal abortion and at no time more than 27 percent approving abortion after three months.[8] The discrepancy between Blake and Yankelovich was enormous. Three explanations for the discrepancy could be offered:

1. The NORC and Gallup polls were badly done, or the Yankelovich poll was badly done. Such lack of professional competence seems unlikely.

2. There was a massive shift in American public opinion between the spring and fall of 1977. Nothing at all appears as a reason for this to have occurred, and nothing else suggests that it did.

3. The pollsters and their respondents implicitly equated "legal abortion" with "therapeutic abortion before the end of the first three months." It is highly likely that this is the error that affected the Yankelovich survey and the subsequent reporting by *Time*. The press's own mistake came home to roost.

The error, which could only be inferred from the *Time* survey, was explicit in one conducted a little earlier by Louis Harris. Polling the nation on funding in July 1977, the Harris Poll introduced its question to its 1,515 respondents by stating "the U.S. Supreme Court has ruled that abortions up to three months of pregnancy are legal." On the basis of this clear misstating of *The Abortion Cases,* Louis Harris interpreted the results of the poll as showing that a majority of the public "continues to favor legalized abortions as set down in the 1973 Supreme Court decisions." [9] Harris's column and the poll were carried in his syndicated column throughout the country without correction by the newspapers printing him.

Not only did the press create and sustain and spread the error; the press was impervious to correction. Although the *Washington Post* prides itself on its own ombudsman, he never acknowledged that the *Post* had misrepresented *The Abortion Cases.* Louis Harris did not publish the correction of his mistake when it was called to his attention. *Time* declined to print a letter pointing out the gap between its poll and Blake's analysis and the probable reason for its pollsters' error. When the gaffe on the Houston Conference was brought to the attention of Frederick Taylor, executive editor of the *Wall Street Journal,* he replied, "We'll stand on what we printed." [10] When a persistent gadfly, Dexter Duggan, attempted to interest the *Columbia Journalism Review* in the constant misrepresentation, he was met by the stonewalling of the review's editors.[11] Louis Boccardi, the news editor of the Associated Press, replied, when the AP's practice of referring to only the first three months was challenged, that this summation was due to "the inevitable compression which takes place when decisions must be summarized." [12]

Because of this "inevitable compression" practiced by the *New York Times,* the *Washington Post,* the *Washington Star,* the *Los Angeles Times,* the *Wall Street Journal,* the Harris poll, *Time,* and the Associated Press, a reader dependent on the press would have had difficulty in determining what the abortion issue was.

The press, however, did have its own characterization of the issue it did choose to present. The issue was, in its eyes, religious. The opponents of abortion acted out of religious belief. There are, no doubt, occasions when the media must refer to the religious beliefs of a person. When someone presents himself as the spokesman of a church, when someone declares that his views are founded on a church's teaching, when someone speaks on an issue of doctrine in dispute within a church, his religion is a part of the story. It is also true that in-depth coverage of a man may appropriately explore his religious convictions and in-depth coverage of an issue may appropriately bring out the religious beliefs at work in forming public opinion on it.

What is entirely different from these references to religion is the use of a religious reference to stereotype and dismiss a point of view. There may have been many reasons, for example, why John Erlichman was opposed to a national health plan. It would have been an injection of religious prejudice if each time that Ehrlichman was mentioned in this connection he were identified as "the Christian Scientist, John Ehrlichman." The reporter would have reduced Ehrlichman's reasons to one, guessed that it was the predominant one, and appealed to everyone to disregard Ehrlichman's view because it was based on an idiosyncrasy of his religion. It is that kind of use of religious references that characterized the media's treatment of the abortion debate.

On January 22, 1977, the *Des Moines Sunday Register* carried this headline: "Abortion Still a Sin/Italian Bishops Warn." The headline was followed by four paragraphs on the abortion controversy in Italy, complete with quotation from "the Vatican newspaper *L'Osservatore Romano*," and then, without a break or other indication of a shift in place and focus, the column continued, "Meanwhile in Washington opponents of abortions [*sic*] marched from the Capitol to the White House Saturday to demonstrate their support for a constitutional amendment to ban abortions." The rest of the story— seven paragraphs—was devoted to a march in Washington, of between 35,000 and 100,00 Americans.

The abortion issue had been a matter of American politics for ten years. A constitutional amendment to ban abortions had been an issue in the presidential campaign of 1976. The Republican Party platform had endorsed such an amendment. But to the editors of the *Des Moines Sunday Register*, mass action in Washington in support of the amendment belonged in a story on "Abortion Still a Sin/Italian Bishops Warn."

It would have been striking enough if this inclusion of a major issue of national politics under headlines relating to religion abroad had been the aberration of a provincial newspaper. But this particular episode was brought to the attention of the National News Council, a body of journalists whose function is to judge bias in the press. The council dismissed a complaint against the *Register*, saying, "In this instance, the editor saw more merit in the story dealing with the pronouncement of the Italian bishops than in the Washington march. Many can disagree, but it remains a valid exercise of editorial judgment." [13]

The prejudice, however, had not been injected by giving headlines to the Italian bishops, but by implying a connection between the Italian bishops and the Washington march. If this combination was not an unsubtle way of suggesting that the thousands of marchers and *L'Osservatore Romano* were cut from the same cloth, how could the implication have been more offensively conveyed? The evaluation—"a valid exercise of editorial judgment"—put the stamp of the National News Council on treating an American political movement as an arm of the Vatican.

On November 28, 1977, the Associated Press put out a dispatch dealing with the report of a task force in the Department of Health, Education, and Welfare on alternatives to abortion. The task force, plainly unsympathetic to its assignment, had reported that the alternatives were madness, motherhood, or suicide. The report was not acceptable to HEW Secretary Joseph Califano. It would indeed be not acceptable to most reasonable people to put motherhood on a par with madness and suicide and to construe "alternatives to abortion" so narrowly that only the range of options after pregnancy was considered. Instead of letting the report speak for itself, the Associated Press added, "Mr. Califano, a Roman Catholic, who has said his opposition to abortion is based on religious and ethical beliefs, is virtually alone in his position among top officials in his Department."

What was the function of this religious reference? In his confirmation hearings, ten months earlier, Secretary Califano had been drawn out on the subject of his religious and ethical reasons for rejecting abortion. The specific identification of Secretary Califano as "a Roman Catholic" was intended to suggest that there was some idiosyncrasy in his religion that made him reluctant to concede that madness, motherhood, or suicide were the alternatives to abortion. The *New York Times* waited a full day after receiving this Associated Press dispatch and then ran it on November 29, 1977, complete with the identification of the Roman Catholic Secretary of HEW, on page 18.

For months in 1977 the House and Senate conferees were unable to agree on the federal funding of abortion in what Martin Tolchin, the *Times*'s correspondent covering the story, described on November 5, 1977 as "one of the longest and most intense disputes ever to divide the two chambers." This intense political battle was to be reduced to the symmetry and clarity of a cartoon. After reporting a partial compromise agreed to by the House and Senate conferees, Tolchin wrote:

> Mark Gallagher, lobbyist for the National Committee for a Human Life Amendment, which is financed by the United States Catholic Conference, an organization representing Roman Catholic bishops, attended as an observer, and privately indicated to the House conferees whether he found various Senate proposals acceptable.[14]

From a pro-abortion perspective his paragraph served several purposes. The National Committee for a Human Life Amendment, the organization connected to the bishops, had a good chance of being confused with the mass-movement Right to Life Committee, so that this grass-roots organization would be thought by the unwary to be the bishops' creature. The hierarchical character of the opposition was stressed twice over with "Roman Catholic bishops" and their national organization, "the United States Catholic Conference," both mentioned. The results were said to be dictated by the bishops' man, and the entire national issue was reduced to the nod of the influential observer. That Catholics were a clear minority of the House and that the House had voted overwhelmingly for the Hyde amendment (an abortion-restriction rider to the HEW–Labor Department appropriation bill) were facts the reader was not reminded of. That the bishops' lobbyist, Mr. Gallagher, was a young man, scarcely one-third the age of the venerable congressional veterans he was supposed to be instructing, was unstated. The story suggested that eleven senior congressmen from a variety of states spread throughout the country, each congressman backed by his own aide, and every congressman visible to an audience of pro- and anti-abortion observers, had obeyed the quiet command of the youthful spokesman for a single religious body.

Tolchin evoked the forgotten clichés of the Know-Nothing movement. He did so so quietly and so artlessly that it was difficult to believe that he did so self-consciously. He brought back from the American subconscious forgotten echoes of religious prejudice: the Pope in the White House, potbellied confessors whispering the voting instructions. His updating made the clichés plausible: the Catholic hierarchy of the United States installed at a meeting to decide national policy, passing on each proposal with an episcopal nod, and "privately" conveying their directions. The "privately" alone was a wonderful improvement on "whisper," as the hierarchy dictating to Congress was an improvement in verisimilitude on the Pope seated in the White House. The bishops gave the orders, and "the boys" did what they were told. The abortion issue was reduced to clichés of the dominant legend.

When in 1978 certain defenders of the abortion liberty sought to intensify the campaign to present the Catholic Church as *the* enemy, the media cooperated. When the firebombings of several abortion clinics occurred and the founder of the Abortion Freedom League charged that the Catholic Church was responsible, the Associated Press on February 20, 1978, did not hesitate to repeat this enormous allegation, offered without evidence or any attempt to provide evidence. The *Cleveland Plain Dealer* even ran the charge as its major page one headline on that holiday morning: "Catholics Spur Violence, Pro-Abortionist Says." Even when presented in more subdued format, as in the *Berkeley Gazette* of the same date, the story had the distinction of taking seriously and propagating the charge of malicious vandalism offered by a critic of the religious body assailed. This stirring of religious strife was passed over in silence by the usual monitors of the nation's civil freedoms.

On April 23, 1978, CBS presented a television program entitled "The Politics of Abortion," a report on the subject by Bill Moyers. The program opened with a shot of a priest selling rosaries; the camera then panned to a statue of the Virgin Mary. In this fashion, a march on January 22, 1978, mourning the fifth anniversary of *The Abortion Cases* was introduced. The number of the marchers— 70,000 to 100,000—was not stated, nor was it mentioned that the march constituted one of the largest demonstrations in Washington since the height of the national crisis over Vietnam. Without words the camera let the hawker of religious goods and the image of the Virgin declare that whoever was there was guilty of mariolatry and a probable bigot.[15]

In the hour that followed only one person opposed to abortion was identified as other than a Catholic. A priest in clerical dress was shown preaching against abortion in a pulpit. The bishops' spokesman on abortion, Monsignor James McHugh, was interviewed presenting the Catholic opposition to abortion. His voice was overplayed at one point by another voice reciting the figures on diocesan contributions to his office, the same figures that had been the staple of the NARAL circular attacking opposition to abortion as a Catholic plot. At no point in this exploration of the reasons why abortion was a political issue was it mentioned that outstanding scholars had criticized *The Abortion Cases* as deficient by the criteria of constitutional law; nor was the opposition to abortion of Orthodox Judaism, Mormonism, and the major Protestant churches referred to; nor was the fact disclosed that the great majority of American women were opposed to abortion on demand and to abortion after the third month. Bill Moyers concluded the program with a four-minute epilogue in which he drove home the theme that abortion was a "theological and religious issue." The message of the program was that Catholic theology, conveyed by priests at the beck of bishops to a fanatical laity, was the basis for the opposition to the funding of abortion and the reason for discontent with *The Abortion Cases*. The separation of Chuch and state was explicitly evoked by Moyers as the reason to reject this imposition of a religion. "The Politics of Abortion" presented the great issues facing the nation in the terms drawn by the proponents of the abortion liberty.

So secure in their own legends were the media that, when a

detailed presentation was made to CBS of the bias manifested by this film, the network replied, "The broadcast was not a 'pro-abortion presentation'. . . . It included, with equal weight, the anti-abortionists' view of themselves and their antagonists." [16] It was as though a cartoonist had shown a kind-faced Arab woman asking to enter the Sinai as her home, and a maliciously grinning figure with a machine gun stopping her, and to the complaint of bias replied, "I have given, with equal weight, the Jews' viewpoint of themselves and their antagonists." The spokesman for CBS was unwilling to accept a view of the opponents of abortion different from the stereotype created by friends of the abortion liberty.

It is more than twenty years since Peter Viereck observed that "anti-Catholicism is the anti-Semitism of the intellectuals." That is less true today, but it would be completely true if "journalists" were substituted for "intellectuals." [17] Beating on this old drum of bigotry while concealing what *The Abortion Cases* decided, the press effectually misled the American public on the issues at stake in abortion. Its service to the abortion liberty reflected the commitment of partisans to a strong dynamic movement that employed legend to live and to expand.

Inquiry 9
On the Dynamism of the Liberty

A challenged way of life, dependent on a particular view of human nature and human responsibilities, has within itself a tendency not merely to defend itself but to expand. It will expand regardless of the risks it incurs to its own existence. Its secret dynamism is moral.

Southern slavery was a way of life that began to be criticized by a handful of persons in the 1830s and continued to be criticized by slightly larger numbers of Abolitionists in the 1840s and 1850s.[1] The slaveholders might have stayed securely within the boundaries of the slaveholding states. No one could challenge them effectively there. No one, South or North, was even disposed to challenge them, save the tiny band of Abolitionists. The slaveholders could have nurtured their peculiar institution indefinitely without the application of any political power to uproot it. But they perceived that their basic concepts of humanity and human responsibility were challenged, and they responded accordingly.

They insisted upon the passage of the Fugitive Slave Act of 1850. It was an aggressive extension of the frontiers of the slave system. It brought directly and palpably into Northern communities the issue of cooperation with the slave system. It afforded Northerners the spectacle of manacled blacks being led back to bondage. The parade of Anthony Burns, a recaptured slave, through the town of Boston, at the order of a Massachusetts court, created more Massachusetts sentiment against the system that condemned him than all the harangues of William Lloyd Garrison.[2] But the dynamism of Southern slavery demanded this expansion; it did not count the costs.

The slaveholders sought to expand their system westward. The territories had to be open to slavery. The new states had to be, if feasible, slave states. The frontiers of the system were literally to be expanded. The dynamism of the system would not let it be confined to a citadel.[3]

And all this expansion had to be accomplished legally—by territorial legislatures, by state constitutional conventions, by acts of Congress. It was important that the expansion have legal foundation and legal vindication. If the democratic organs of government failed to provide this foundation and this vindication, there were always the courts. The strongest foundation, and the most authoritative vindication, would be that of the Supreme Court. In *Dred Scott* v. *Sanford,* a test case, a slaveholding majority of the Supreme Court provided all the slaveholders asked. Obligingly, the Court held up its decision for a year by ordering reargument when announcing the opinion in a presidential election year would have had an impact on the election. When it finally spoke, the Court brushed aside technical barriers to give a broad holding, read history selectively to support the slaveholders' side, and issued moral pronouncements unnecessary to decide the case before it. The slaveholders on the Court gave slavery a charter for expansion that was as broad as the West and as firm as the Constitution. The Court announced that the Constitution itself forbade any legislature from keeping slavery from the territories.[4] After the decision was given, Abraham Lincoln could ask if any legislature could keep slavery out of any Northern free state.[5] The dynamism of the slave system had propelled slavery to a pinnacle where its principles, stamped as the command of the Constitution by the Court, ruled the land.

For good measure, in that terrible and fateful decision, in words that today seem scarcely capable of having been uttered, blacks were said to have been regarded by the makers of the Constitution as "beings of an inferior order . . . and so far inferior that they had no rights which the white man was bound to respect"; and the conclusion was drawn that the Constitution, framed by persons so regarding blacks, itself relegated them forever to that status of inferiority. No descendant of Negro slaves, the Court ruled, could ever become a citizen of the United States. Nowhere henceforth could a black in the United States be protected by federal law as a person in the whole sense of the term.[6]

Such success had its risks and its cost. Abolition was not a bread-and-butter issue. Few cared for it, few would fight for it. But to turn free territories into slave territories was a matter that offended both the economic sense and the moral sensibility of free whites. There were a handful of Abolitionists. There was formed a party of Free Soilers, the Republican Party, which was destined to destroy the slave system at its roots. The opposition to slavery was, on the margin of its expansion, fought out in territories like Kansas, until the Supreme Court decision in *Dred Scott*. Then thoughtful persons throughout the country could see that the issue was national and its resolution central to the meaning of the Constitution. If federal law was disabled from treating a black as a person in the whole sense of the term anywhere, that affected every state in the Union. If black slaves were property, which Congress could not touch, what prevented such property from being brought in numbers into border states like Illinois and turning free states into slave states?[7] Indifference to the issue was no longer possible. *Dred Scott,* capping the slaveholders' drive for expansion, became a focal point of organized opposition. The dynamism of the slave system had generated a counter-dynamism that would bring it down.

Why did the slaveholders act as if driven by the Furies to their own destruction? One can, of course, give an answer in economic terms. They wanted to stop the loss of valuable property through slaves' taking refuge in Northern communities. They did not want to abandon valuable property when they moved into the territories. They wanted new markets in the West for slaves bred in the Old South. But if economic calculation had included a measure of political foresight, they would have seen that whatever they preserved and whatever they gained in these ways was little to what they would lose if they brought upon themselves the united wrath of the free states. They chose to risk that wrath despite the odds.

Why did they take such risks, why did they persist beyond prudent calculation? The answer must be that in a moral question of this kind, turning on basic concepts of humanity, you cannot be content that your critics are feeble and ineffective, you cannot be content with their practical tolerance of your activities. You want, in a sense you need, actual acceptance, open approval. If you cannot convert your critics by argument, at least by law you can make them recognize that your course is the course of the country.

Abraham Lincoln recognized this secret moral dynamism when in his famous speech at Cooper Institute in 1860 he asked what would convince the slaveholders that his party had no designs on their property or the Constitution of the Union, and he answered: "This, and this only: Cease to call slavery *wrong,* and join them in calling it *right*. And this must be done thoroughly—done in *acts* as

well as in *words*. Silence will not be tolerated—we must place our-
selves avowedly with them." [8] The slaveholders sought the moral
surrender of their critics.

Has a similar dynamism governed the expansion of the liberty of
abortion in America? Objective evidence that it has abounds. In
purely prudential terms, the champions of the liberty would have
been well advised to rest content with the legislative victories and
single Supreme Court decision they won between 1967 and 1973.
They had nineteen states scattered around the country in which
abortion might be performed for reasons other than to save the life
of the carrier. In practice, in a state like California where abortion
might be had to preserve the mental health of the gravida, complaisant psychiatrists could readily be found who would diagnose,
by telephone, a woman seeking an abortion and would find it necessary for her mental health. In all but name, abortion on demand
existed in such states.[9] In addition, the Supreme Court, passing on
the District of Columbia abortion statute, had interpreted "health"
to include "mental health." [10] The decision touched only the District, but an analogy was offered whereby every abortion statute
could have been expanded by easy degrees. If this course had been
followed, abortion on demand would have crept through the land.
But there would have been no firm foundation for the abortion
liberty, no vindication of it as a right. The pro-choice groups did
not pursue this effective strategy of gradualism.

The champions of the liberty in two test cases deliberately
framed to raise the issue sought national vindication from the Supreme Court. The Court's decision was held up for a year by ordering reargument, with the consequence that it did not have an impact
on a presidential election.[11] Then, when it finally spoke, the Court
brushed aside technical barriers to give a broad holding, read history
selectively to support the pro-abortion side, and issued moral pronouncements on "meaningful" life unnecessary to decide the case
before it. A status of permanent inferiority was stamped forever on
the unborn. Nowhere henceforth could any state protect an unborn
child as a person in the whole sense of the term. The champions of
the abortion liberty saw their principles proclaimed the law of the
land. They would have been very well advised to stick within the
boundaries of the victory. But they would not—or could not.[12]

The Supreme Court itself in *The Abortion Cases* had declared
that it was imposing no obligation upon those conscientiously opposed to abortion to perform abortions.[13] But such respect for the

consciences of others did not sit well with some friends of the liberty. Lawsuits, strategically brought in different parts of the country, sought court orders to force private hospitals, founded and operated by persons opposed to abortion, to turn over facilities for abortions.[14] Just as the slaveholders had once wanted the cooperation of their critics in returning their slaves, so these libertarians wanted their critics to cooperate in doing what their critics believed was evil. Richard Flathman, a grave philosopher, defending abortion as a woman's liberty, argued that opposition to the liberty was so ill-founded, he would force a physician against the physician's conscience to carry out the killing.[15]

Before *The Abortion Cases,* Planned Parenthood's general counsel, Harriet Pilpel, had suggested that doctors who had religious scruples about abortion might be practicing "sectarian medicine." [16] After *The Abortion Cases,* this suggestion was argued to mean that such doctors could be sued for malpractice.[17] Harriet Pilpel herself, now not only general counsel for Planned Parenthood but vice chairman of the American Civil Liberties Union, went on to attack the post-*Wade* "conscience clauses" enacted by Congress and by forty states protecting hospitals from being coerced into doing abortions against the moral beliefs of their trustees. In her view both the consciences of trustees and of the hospital corporation could be ignored. The clauses, she claimed, were "direct defiance of the United States Supreme Court." [18] Not mere tolerance, not mere silence, but active cooperation was what she desired.

A prominent ethician, Joseph Fletcher, put forward the principle that no government should resolve the moral dispute over the nature of the unborn: "The First Amendment to the Constitution forbids any such solution in a pluralist democracy." [19] If anyone thought the unborn slated for abortion were valueless, he should be free to experiment on them. From this position of pure laissez faire, Fletcher moved without conscious difficulty to the proposition that the government had an obligation to fund such experiments. The state was to give preference to no one's view of the unborn; the state was to use its taxing power to implement the view of those who thought the unborn disposable.[20] Only the absolute conviction of being right permitted such ingrained indifference to inconsistency.

When the National Commission for the Protection of Human Subjects made recommendations permitting experiments on the unborn, it was not enough for a pro-liberty law professor, Jane Friedman. One of the commission's eight consultants on ethics had expressed the belief that there is "no moral distinction between the fetus and any other human being"; four had held the fetus to be "a close analogue to a human being"; one had termed the fetus an entity that has "a legitimate claim on us for protection." All these characterizations of the unborn child, according to Friedman, stemmed from the Judeo-Christian tradition. The consultants' views and this religious tradition, she asserted, were the "underpinnings" of such regulations as the commission did propose to govern experiments on the unborn. That the actual staff was pro-liberty, that the membership of the commission itself was pro-liberty, that the regulations themselves were pro-liberty—none of this was enough for her. Because there were *any* regulations whatever premised on the humanity of the unborn, they were unconstitutional; the First Amendment had been violated; Friedman could be satisfied only by rules adopting her own view that the unborn could be experimented on as freely as any nonhuman animal.[21]

Laurence Tribe, the law professor who had defended *The Abortion Cases* themselves in the name of "no establishment of religion," took a different view of "no establishment" when it was his religion that was to be established. The state must not decide the status of the unborn if the state's decision would be for their preservation. Where the funding of abortion was concerned, the state had a duty, enforceable by the courts, to fund the killing.[22] In agreement, a celebrated judge, Thurgood Marshall, described the refusal of the majority of an electorate to fund elective abortions as one more attempt by the opponents of abortion to "impose their moral choices upon the rest of society."[23]

In some state universities, the abortion liberty led to all students being obliged to pay the costs of abortions sought by a few. When three students at the University of California, San Diego, refused to submit to such coercion of their consciences to make them support what they thought to be evil, their registration was revoked. They sued for reinstatement; the university readmitted them pending the suit's outcome; but in the motion to dismiss their complaint, the university's counsel coolly informed the court:

> Neither plaintiffs nor any other person is entitled to enrollment in the University of California. . . . Plaintiffs could have sought and obtained admission as students to institutions having health service policies which are more compatible with plaintiffs' beliefs. To whatever minimal extent University of California health services compel "participation" in activities which contradict their

beliefs, the plaintiffs have knowingly and voluntarily brought the situation upon themselves.[24]

In the jingoist argot of the 1960s, "Love it or leave it." There was no room at the University of California for the conscience opposed to paying for abortion.

In some medical school admission programs, persons suspected of disfavoring abortion were questioned closely on their views; if their answers were not satisfactory, they were denied admission to the school. At the University of California Medical School at San Diego, persons opposed to abortion were advised that for them the "competion would be intensified"—language of ominous import in a field where competition was already intense.[25] So intrusive were the practices used to promote the abortion liberty in the training of physicians that a bill to bar such discrimination was finally introduced in Congress.[26] It was not evident that a medical profession could exist which was half devoted to the care of the unborn as patients and half devoted to elective abortion as a social good.

As resistance to abortion mounted so did the temper of some of its proponents. Bella Abzug was an unlikely person to call for expanded use of the Federal Bureau of Investigation. But speaking in San Francisco in September 1978, she called for "an FBI probe of the anti-abortion minority."[27] She spoke after Congress, which acts by majority vote and is elected, had declined to fund elective abortions.

As had happened in the case of slavery, the dynamism of the liberty interlocked with the forces leading the federal judiciary to assert its will against local opposition. The truest friends of the abortion cause were the federal judges. When Sarah Weddington argued *Roe* v. *Wade* before a three-judge district court in Texas, prior to the Supreme Court hearing the case, she was uncertain of her chances. One judge was Sarah Hughes. Sarah Weddington recalls: "At one point during the hearing when my nervousness was obviously showing, Sarah winked at me as if to say, 'It's going to be all right.' Sure enough it was."[28] In case after case, there was the equivalent of that wink from the federal bench to the friends of the abortion cause. A federal jurisdictional statute, for example, permitted only a three-judge district court to declare a state statute unconstitutional. Yet so eager were certain circuit court judges to demolish a state statute refusing funds for elective abortion that they ignored this jurisdictional requirement and themselves declared the state statute unconstitutional, without even giving the state the opportunity to brief them on the merits of the case.[29] The Supreme Court itself was guilty of bending practice to help the pro-abortion cause. In the very case in which the Court unanimously rebuked the over-zealous circuit court, a majority of the Justices granted doctors the unusual right to present not their own constitutional claims but those of their patients—a procedural bonus without precedent, in the view of the four dissenters.[30] In another case, the Court could find a statute banning the cruel saline method of abortion unconstitutional only if it could be proved that prostaglandins were not available as an alternative;[31] but the Court relied on a finding about prostaglandins' unavailability which was made in another case by a judge in another state two years before the Court's decision. For a Court so attentive to medical advances this way of turning a blind eye to the spread of prostaglandins was remarkable. Justice White, dissenting, observed, "I am not yet prepared to accept the notion that normal rules of law, procedure, and constitutional adjudication suddenly become irrelevant solely because a case touches on the subject of abortion." [32] From the Supreme Court on down to the winking district judge, most judges were so prepared.

The dynamism of the liberty was to affect every level of government and to alter the distribution of governmental power in American society. At the most fundamental level, judicial interpretation of the liberty was to affect the authority of Congress to appropriate money and to color the Treasury's understanding of its obligations under the Constitution.[33] At the grass-roots level, the liberty was to override the traditional powers of a New England town meeting and to require a town's sense of appropriate community activities to be subordinated to the immune position of an abortion clinic.[34] It was to overturn a school board's control of its teachers and a school board's concern for the teaching of a casual attitude to abortion by the example of a teacher.[35] No corner of the land was to be immune from the liberty's dynamic thrust.

The liberty, which could not be confined by geographic or governmental limits, could not be confined to the womb. The practitioners of personal choice needed to be free not only to kill the unborn but to cause the death of the child already born: Only then would the exercise of the liberty not be "chilled." At a philosophical level, Michael Tooley, a Stanford philosopher, argued that there was no moral distinction between abortion and infanticide: The unsocialized infant outside the uterus was no more a person than his or her brother or sister not yet born.[36] At a legal level, adherents of the liberty undertook the defense of doctors accused of manslaughter and murder for actions alleged to have affected the newborn; they did not scruple to regard such cases as "abortion cases."[37]

The analogy with the dynamics of slavery is not absolute; no historical analogy is perfect. Yet in many ways the movement to defend slavery and the movement to defend abortion were similar.

The thrust of the analogy was sometimes misunderstood by partisans, as though saying a pro-abortionist behaved *like* a slaveholder was saying a pro-abortionist had the morals of a slaveholder. Something very different was meant by the analogy. The slaveholders, from Washington to Lee, were the epitome of social respectability in their day. They were not conscious of doing wrong but of doing right. When it is suggested that the pro-abortionists are like them, it is the respectability and the righteousness of the pro-abortionists which is attended to, and it is argued that such respectability and righteousness, when challenged, will lead to a desire to silence their critics. Today, to say one is for abortion, a friend of the abortion liberty, a champion of the abortion cause, is to pay what commonly would be taken as a compliment. It is only another age than ours which will be able to pronounce on the pro-abortionists the judgment history eventually recorded on the slaveholders—that they were blind to what they did.

The analogy held at the level of colloquial derision, where the slaveholders' taunt "nigger-lover" was matched on college campuses by the cry "fetus-lover." It held at the level of political strategy, where the slaveholders' efforts to make the Republican Party responsible for John Brown's mad act of violence at Harper's Ferry was matched by the pro-choice efforts to tag pacific critics with responsibility for the ugly violence of arson.[38] It even held when the basic defense of the slaveholders was considered: Slaves were property, protected by the Constitution, so what right had anyone else to meddle in what was the slaveowner's own business? Invoking the right of private property, the apologist of slavery defended the choice of owning slaves, free of legal restraint and moral criticism. Invoking the right to dispose of one's body, the apologist of the liberty defended the choice of taking fetal life, free of legal restraint and moral criticism.

Claiming that their concern was private choice, the pro-abortionists won the liberty they wanted and national vindication from the Supreme Court. They wanted more. The liberty, founded on almost absolute privacy, was to become absolutely social in its consequences. And those consequences were to be inseparable from the liberty itself. But why did the pro-abortionist seek these consequences?

Once the friends of the freedom had acquired the constitutional foundation and vindication of the liberty from the Supreme Court, a slower, more prudent course would have won them financial support. To make the liberty real they did not need to monitor medical school admissions, force students to violate their consciences, punish doctors with scruples about killing, try to wrest control of hospitals from their opponents, or run roughshod over the sentiments of dozens of communities and the laws of many states. They did so because of the secret moral dynamism of their position. They were committed to a particular view of human nature and human responsibilities. What would convince them that they should rest content? This, and this only: Cease to call abortion wrong, and join them in calling it right. And this must be done thoroughly—in acts as well as in words. Silence would not be tolerated; all must place themselves avowedly with them.

To achieve this, private choice was to assault the structure of the family; override the consciences of trustees, legislators, and whole political communities; alter the law of infanticide; and assert dominion over the meaning of language itself.

Inquiry 10

On the Application of the Liberty to the Family

The object of the liberty was a being located within the body of the childbearing woman. That being was the product of a joint effort of a man and a woman. Did the man have any say as to the disposition of his offspring? Announcing the liberty, Justice Blackmun observed in a footnote that he was not answering that question now.[1]

Read against the background of other decisions of the Supreme Court on the right to marry, to procreate, and to care for one's offspring, the answer to the question was "Yes, a father has a say in the disposition of his child." *Skinner* v. *Oklahoma* had held that Oklahoma could not sterilize a recidivist chicken thief—the right to procreate was so fundamental that it could not be arbitrarily taken by the state.[2] The chicken thief saved from this punishment was a man. It could reasonably be argued that if a man had a fundamental liberty to procreate, that liberty must include the protection of the child procreated throughout pregnancy. If it did not include that protection, all that a man had was a liberty to fertilize an ovum—a liberty that, if not actually meaningless, was a good deal less than full freedom to procreate.

In *Loving* v. *Virginia* a unanimous Court had invalidated laws forbidding blacks and whites to intermarry—the right to marry was so fundamental that it could not arbitrarily be denied by the state.[3] It could reasonably be argued that, if a man had a fundamental liberty to marry, that liberty must include liberty to have children. If liberty to marry did not include liberty to have children, freedom to marry meant a great deal less than full freedom to marry.

A divorced mother, the Court had held in *Armstrong* v. *Manzo*,

90

could not constitutionally arrange for the adoption of a child in her custody without giving notice to the child's father.[4] It could reasonably be argued that, if a father could not lose his rights to one of his children without a hearing, even if the child was in the mother's control, he could not lose his child within the mother's womb without at least an opportunity to object.

An unwed father, the Court had held in *Stanley* v. *Illinois,* could not have his children taken for adoption by the state without being given a special status in the adoption proceeding. Even though such a father had not married and had himself failed to adopt the children he had sired, his biological connection was a tie that the state must respect in a hearing.[5] It could reasonably be argued that, if biology conferred rights, a father had as much interest in an unborn child of eight weeks as in an infant of eight months.

These precedents on the right to procreate, to marry, and to be heard on the disposition of one's child were not ancient law. The oldest of them, *Skinner,* had been decided in 1942; the most recent, *Stanley,* in 1972. They were cases which established, if settled interpretation of the Constitution by the Court could establish, that a father had rights in relation to his children that were independent of the state; for in each of these cases state restriction of his rights had been held violative of the Constitution.

Three years after *The Abortion Cases* the question not decided by Justice Blackmun was presented to the Supreme Court by Planned Parenthood, which attacked the constitutionality of a new Missouri law passed after *The Abortion Cases* and framed in light of them. The law required the consent of a husband to any abortion performed upon his wife. It was given to Justice Blackmun to answer the question he had postponed in 1972.

The Abortion Cases had held that the state had no power to intervene in the abortion decision. Justice Blackmun now reasoned that, as the state had no power of its own, it had no power to delegate to the husband. Its grant of the right to consent was void, for it had nothing to grant. "The State cannot delegate authority to any particular person, even the spouse, to prevent abortion during the same period." [6] Authority and structure in the family, it appeared, depended upon the state.

Even Justice Brennan—Blackmun's firmest ideological ally on abortion—did not quite take Blackmun literally. A year later, in an adoption case, Brennan spoke of the family as "having an origin far older than the state," with the implication that a parent's rights did not depend on the state's delegation.[7] But where abortion was at issue, Brennan did not qualify his adherence to Blackmun's subordination of the father to the state and of the state to the childbearer. Five other Justices joined them, holding that the Constitution and, specifically, the Fourteenth Amendment gave only the carriers of unborn children the power to decide the future of those children in the womb.

The same Missouri law also provided that a girl who was not of legal age could not obtain an abortion without the consent of her parents. The legislation reflected what is the common-law rule about medical practice on children generally: Apart from emergencies in which a parent is unavailable, a physician cannot touch a child without the parent's consent.[8] The common-law rule is paternalist and maternalist, recognizing the parents' judgment as superior to the child's. At common law a child of tender years cannot have a mole removed without his parents' consent. An unauthorized touching of such a child by a surgeon is an unlawful touching, in legal language a battery, which must be redressed by damages paid to the parents.[9]

Once again there were famous Supreme Court cases of the past acknowledging that the parents' liberty to care for their children was independent of, and superior to, the power of the state. *Pierce* v. *Society of Sisters* and *Meyer* v. *Nebraska* had held that the state could not arbitrarily interfere with parents' educational arrangements for their children.[10] *Pierce* explicitly recognized "the liberty of parents and guardians to direct the upbringing and education of children under their control." [11] The upbringing of children seemed to include parental participation in a child's decision to have an abortion.

The liberty of abortion, however, overrode the liberty of the parents. Just as the autonomy of choice was not to be curtailed by the father's interest, so it was not to be curtailed by the interest of either parent in their daughter's welfare. The law requiring their consent to an abortion was declared unconstitutional.

In a companion case from Massachusetts, *Bellotti* v. *Baird*, the Court kept open a crack for parental rights. If a law gave the parents a veto on abortion, subject to a proviso that a judge could override the veto, the law might qualify as constitutional.[12] Tentative, grudging, and half-articulated, this concession took the ultimate decision from the family and conferred it on the minor and on a judge already under instructions from the highest Court that the liberty was almost absolute and belonged to the childbearer, married or not, adult or not. It was a marginal concession.

How marginal was to be demonstrated by the history of *Baird* v. *Bellotti,* a case that also cast light on the forces unsympathetic to the traditional legal treatment of the family. There were four pseudonymous plaintiffs, all named "Mary Moe," challenging the requirement of parental consent; three of them were not further identified; the fourth was a sixteen-year-old, who was aborted while her case was being decided. She was, nonetheless, permitted to remain as a plaintiff, presumably on the ground that she might need another abortion before she came of age at eighteen. The interest of the four Mary Moes, however, was clearly overshadowed by the principal plaintiffs, who managed the case: a clinic paradoxically and ungrammatically called Parents Aid; [13] its director, William Baird, a hero of the abortion movement; and Gerald Zupnich, a doctor who performed abortions for the clinic. Time, as is often the case in lawsuits, was an important factor for the litigants. If the state law was allowed to operate in normal course, the clinic and its physician would either have had to be sure that minor girls coming to the clinic had parental consent or abort them at peril of a criminal prosecution. To avoid this danger, they sought an injunction from the federal court in Boston, forbidding the commonwealth's Attorney General to prosecute them. For the court to grant the injunction it had to determine that the law was probably unconstitutional and that irreparable harm would be done the plaintiffs if the injunction were not granted. Bailey Aldrich and Frank Freedman, two members of the three-judge federal court that heard the case, made these findings. The result was that a law enacted in 1973 was still not being enforced in 1978, even though the actual constitutionality of the law had not yet been finally adjudicated.[14]

What was the "irreparable injury" the court found the plaintiffs would suffer? The fourth Mary Moe had had her abortion, and the status of the others was never determined. The clinic itself was nonprofit. Its gross receipts for the fiscal year ending 1974 were $122,000; they were $224,553 for the year ending in 1975; and they were $350,000 for the year ending 1976.[15] Those were years in which the clinic's work on behalf of minor girls was protected by the federal injunction; but by no means all of its income depended on aborting minors, and the federal judges did not treat the loss of an income source for a nonprofit organization as an irreparable injury.

Dr. Zupnich presented a different case. He was a resident of New York. He commuted to Boston and was present two days a week to perform abortions on a fee basis. It was not shown that he could not have done as well by practicing five days a week in New York.

But it was clear that he had what the court called a "substantial income" from his trips to Boston. What part of that substantial income was owed to the abortion of minors was not stated. To protect this income, Bailey Aldrich and Frank Freedman granted the injunction. At a minimum their actions gave Dr. Zupnich several years in which to practice his profession without interference from the enacted law of Massachusetts.

The Supreme Court of the United States had suggested that the state court in Massachusetts might construe the state law in a way that would make it constitutional.[16] Accepting this invitation, the Supreme Judicial Court of Massachusetts in 1977 added a new feature to the law: A minor in Massachusetts seeking an abortion against her parents' wishes was entitled to a lawyer to be paid for by "the public treasury."[17] Without any action by the legislature, the Supreme Judicial Court turned the abortion decision into family litigation and appropriated whatever money was necessary to pay for the minor's side of the lawsuit. With the aid of this public champion, the minor was entitled, the state court said, to persuade a state judge that an abortion was in her best interest, whatever her parents thought.[18] Finally, the Supreme Judicial Court added a blanket promise that whatever the Supreme Court of the United States said was necessary for the constitutionality of the state law, it would read into the state law.[19] But it professed uncertainty as to how much reading it would have to do. Unless the Constitution prohibited it—and here the state judges were unsure of what the Supreme Court justices would find the Constitution said—the parents must at least be notified of their daughter's court case seeking to override their refusal to approve an abortion.[20]

It would seem that the prostration of state law to the unfathomed will of a majority of the United States Supreme Court could not go much farther, nor could the family structure in the matter of abortion be more eroded. But this was not enough to satisfy Bailey Aldrich and Frank Freedman in the federal court in Boston. The requirement of the state court that the parents be notified when their child sought an abortion was too much of a burden on the liberty. The judges had already seen "strong reason to believe that it would be in the minor's best interests for her parents not to know of her condition."[21] The federal court now felt that any knowledge on the parents' part of a physician's operation on their daughter and grandchild would be barred by the liberty. Although commonly in a judicial proceeding it is necessary to let the adverse party know that you are suing him, when a daughter sued to get an abortion, her parents might be kept in the dark; they were eliminated as a necessary party.[22] Parents Aid and Dr. Zupnich were not to be disturbed. As this book went to press, the final decision of the case awaited action by the Supreme Court of the United States. The Court had the choice of letting the Massachusetts state court know what further judicial amendments to the legislation would be necessary to satisfy its standards or affirming the lower federal court's decision that total anonymity must protect the child seeking an abortion.

The Abortion Cases and their sequelae took from the American family much of its status in the law. *The Abortion Cases* themselves had created a liberty in which the most fundamental strand in the structure was deprived of support in the law—a mother was relieved of the duty to care for her offspring, if they were unborn, and was given the liberty to destroy them. With this strand removed, much of the remaining legal structure was dismantled by the cases that followed. The teaching of *Meyer, Pierce, Skinner, Loving,* and *Armstrong* was turned on its head. Rights that had been thought older and more fundamental than the state became delegations of power from the state. Even the right to procreate became a state-delegated power when it was exercised by a male. As the state had no power to stop abortion, it had no power to protect its delegation of procreation to a man. Parents' interest in their grandchildren was denied. Parents' interest in an operation affecting the body, emotions, and conscience of their daughter became a matter of litigation where the state must furnish the daughter with counsel. The abortion decision became a matter of litigation between minor child and the state, which the parents need never know about. The liberty of abortion became larger than any liberty located in the family structure.

Such a view of the childbearing woman was now imputed to the Constitution that she became a solo entity unrelated to husband or boy friend, father or mother, deciding for herself what to do with her child. She was conceived atomistically, cut off from family structure. The *Boston Herald* ran a picture of young girls seeking an abortion in the same months that Justice Blackmun wrote *Planned Parenthood* v. *Danforth.* The girls wore bags over their heads. Without a family identity, these carriers of children were anonymous and parentless. As they prepared to destroy their own children, they put on masks and became faceless.

Inquiry 11
On the Financing of the
Liberty: The Courts

Medicaid made it optional with the states, if they wished, to provide eyeglasses for those who could not see without them and, if they wished, to provide dentistry for those whose teeth were unhealthy. There is, one supposes, a constitutional liberty to see and to have healthy teeth; it would be unconstitutional for the state to take away your glasses or your dentures. Yet there are large unmet needs for glasses and for dental work.[1] No party argued that because the state failed to provide the poor with glasses or dentistry or dentures, its Medicaid program unconstitutionally preferred the senile elderly to those handicapped in vision or eating ability. Poor children served under Medicaid were the victims of gross inequality: They were 57 percent less likely to see a doctor in two years than children of the affluent. Black citizens on Medicaid were frequently served less well than white citizens. In particular, black males were admitted in disproportionately low numbers to nursing homes.[2] The actual bias governmentally exhibited toward poor children, poor old people, and blacks was not the focus of the litigation by libertarians and egalitarians in the 1970s. Their focus was on the funding of elective abortion.

There are few matters, it would seem, on which reasonable persons might more easily disagree than the question of whether a medically unnecessary operation should be paid for by the government. When the operation at issue was an abortion, the general question of whether the government should subsidize this kind of medical care was caught up in the larger issue of whether abortion was the taking of human life, a matter where the disagreement of

96

reasonable persons was even greater. For the courts to decide that abortion should be funded required them to hold that the Constitution itself, as interpreted by *The Abortion Cases,* did not permit dispute on either the nature of abortion or the obligation to provide this kind of medical care.

To say that the Constitution guarantees a liberty is not to say that the government must pay for its exercise. Traditional American liberties—freedom of religion, of speech, of the press—have always been thought of as giving each individual scope to do as he or she thought right, not to have the state pay for it. No one has supposed that because a rich man can afford to own a newspaper and a poor man cannot, the poor man has a constitutional right to have his purchase of a printing plant funded by the public. No one has argued that, when the government subsidizes some forms of the free press by postage subsidies to magazines, it has a duty to provide subsidies to those who want to communicate in another fashion. Where governmental funding has been implicitly required by the Supreme Court in fulfillment of a constitutional right, it has been in connection with access to the court system itself: Such access to the vindication of one's rights cannot be prevented by poverty.[3] What the Court has done in supervision of the judicial system is no precedent for the funding of all constitutional liberties. But almost every lower federal court that considered the abortion liberty in the light of *The Abortion Cases* found that the government must fund its exercise.

The new liberty carried its funding with it, so the judges reasoned. In this spirit Jon O. Newman, a federal district judge in Hartford, Connecticut, summarily invalidated a regulation of the Connecticut Welfare Department that required a doctor to certify that an abortion was necessary before Connecticut would provide Medicaid assistance for the abortion. Judge Newman ruled that "no conditions or requirements can be imposed inconsistent with the standards set forth in *Doe v. Bolton.*" A doctor's certificate was a requirement inconsistent with these standards, and the regulation imposing it was condemned by the Constitution.[4]

In the same spirit, Daniel J. Snyder, Jr., a federal district judge in Pittsburgh, held invalid a Pennsylvania regulation providing Medicaid assistance for an abortion only upon medical evidence that the life or health of the gravida was threatened or that the pregnancy resulted from rape or incest or that the infant might be born with an incapacitating deficiency. This broad regulation failed to give an indigent childbearing woman an abortion at request. The federal

Social Security Act would now be read to require the funding of such abortions. "*Roe* v. *Wade,* supra," wrote Judge Snyder, "must be considered as dispositive of the contentions in the instant case." [5] Judge Snyder differed from Judge Newman only in that he acted as part of a three-judge court, having convoked such a court to consider the "substantial constitutional question." Judge Newman did not think Connecticut's position substantial enough to bother two other judges to hear it.

When South Dakota refused to extend Medicaid for "any items or services which are not reasonable and necessary for the diagnosis or treatment of illness or injury or to improve the functioning of a malformed body member," a three-judge court declared the regulation void as it operated to bar the funding of elective, nontherapeutic abortions. In Utah a three-judge federal court overrode the Utah policy against paying for such operations. Referring to *Roe* v. *Wade* and *Doe* v. *Bolton,* the court said that "a contrary holding in the instant case would in our view fly in the face of those two cases." So it went around the country, with federal judges in Minnesota, Missouri, and New York joining their brothers in Connecticut, Pennsylvania, South Dakota, and Utah and mandating the public funding of abortion on demand.[6]

Frank M. Coffin, the Chief Judge of the First Circuit, outdid the others by extending *The Abortion Cases* to sterilization. If a city was to have a hospital providing short-term surgical services, it must provide sterilization, he ruled. Overriding the policy of Worcester City Hospital, and disregarding the consciences of the citizens of Worcester, Massachusetts, Judge Coffin compared the termination of childbearing capacity to "excisions of benign tumors which would cause subsequent neurological problems." [7] Speaking for a three-judge court, he declared that *Roe* v. *Wade* "requires that we hold the hospital's unique ban on sterilization operations violative of the Equal Protection Clause of the Fourteenth Amendment." [8]

The bluntest opinion was written by Jon O. Newman in a second round in the case involving the Connecticut regulation. As he again overrode the state's policy, he observed in a footnote, "The view that abortion and childbirth, when stripped of the sensitive moral arguments surrounding the abortion controversy, are simply two alternative medical methods of dealing with pregnancy may be gleaned from the various opinions in *Roe* and *Doe*." [9]

Jon Newman's way of eliminating the moral issue was open to easy parody: Stripped of the sensitive moral arguments surrounding them, embezzlement and the cashing of a check are simply two alternative ways of withdrawing money from a bank. Stripped of the sensitive moral arguments surrounding them, prostitution and marital intercourse are simply two alternative methods of satisfying the sexual instinct. But to parody his interpretation of *The Abortion Cases* suggests that Newman himself was without moral convictions. On the contrary, the temper of his work was that of an impassioned, high-minded man impatient with his moral inferiors, conscious of bringing the true light of the Constitution to the legislature of his state. It was a temper often displayed by federal judges as they carried out the Supreme Court's edict in communities resistant to the change.

The most unself-critical opinion, perhaps, was rendered by Federal Circuit Judge Donald Ross. The city of St. Louis had promulgated a policy of not performing abortions in the city's public hospitals except to save the gravida from physiological harm or death. The federal district court sustained the validity of the rule.[10] But on appeal a three-judge court, speaking through Judge Ross, held the city's policy to be illegal under *The Abortion Cases*. Going further, Judge Ross imposed on the mayor of St. Louis the obligation of paying the legal bill of his opponents.

Judge Ross awarded the fees under the court's power to do so when a losing party has acted in bad faith, vexatiously, wantonly, or for oppressive reasons. Mayor Poelker had won in the district court. He was to win in the Supreme Court. Judge Ross found he had been "obdurate and obstinate" and shown "a wanton disregard for the constitutional rights of the plaintiff and other indigent pregnant women in St. Louis." [11]

What had been the mayor's offense? He had made his opposition to abortion known in his campaign for mayor.[12] Judge Ross had been a mayor himself, of Lexington, Nebraska. He was also familiar with politics on a larger scale, having been vice-chairman of the Republican National Committee when Richard Nixon was the party's head and having been appointed by Richard Nixon in his judicial post.[13] The endorsement of Mayor Poelker's views by the electorate did not affect Judge Ross's view of the mayor's position. The mayor, according to the judge, had made people "conform to the mayor's personal moral beliefs." [14]

What had been his offense? Primarily, that he had banned payment for abortions and then dared to litigate the constitutionality of his action. Judge Ross pointed to nothing else except the brief filed by Poelker's counsel, which had suggested that abortion on demand

interfered with the institution of marriage.[15] For such temerity in opposing the will of the Supreme Court as gleaned by Judge Ross from
his reading of its opinions, the mayor of St. Louis was subjected to a
personal fine, in the form of his opponents' attorneys' fees, of more
than four thousand dollars.[16]

As it turned out, Mayor Poelker was to be vindicated, and Donald
Ross reversed, by Donald Ross's masters. As it turned out, all the
lower federal judges who had mandated the funding of abortion and
the providing of abortion and sterilization by cities or states were
wrong. They had misinterpreted their oracle. They were overruled
by the Supreme Court.

Writing for a majority made up of Chief Justice Burger and Justices Stewart, White, Rehnquist, and himself, Lewis Powell first held
that there was nothing in federal law itself that required the funding
of nontherapeutic abortions. Nothing in the Social Security Act
required a state to "undercut" its "unquestionably strong and legitimate interest in encouraging normal childbirth." Judge Snyder was
overruled.[17]

Writing for the same majority of six, Justice Powell next took up
the Connecticut regulation that Jon O. Newman had dispatched
singlehandedly and found that Judge Newman had "erred." Nothing
in the Constitution required the states to pay for abortions. Nothing
in *The Abortion Cases* made funding of abortion a constitutional
right. Judge Newman had "misconceived the nature and the scope"
of the liberty.[18]

In a reproof which touched not only the district judge but his
own court as well, Justice Powell declared that where such sensitive
policy choices were involved "the appropriate forum for their resolution in a democracy" was the legislature. "We should not forget,"
Justice Powell wrote, "that 'legislatures are ultimate guardians of the
liberties and welfare of the people in quite as great a degree as the
courts.' "[19]

The last part of Justice Powell's rebuke of Jon Newman was
taken from Justice Holmes.[20] The language evoked Holmes's dissent
in *Lochner*. The wisdom of the judiciary as super-legislature was once
more doubted.

Justice Powell went further. The state, he indicated, was free to
make childbirth "a more attractive alternative" than abortion. The
state had a "strong interest in protecting the potential life of the
fetus." The state's "strong and legitimate interest in encouraging
normal childbirth" was "an interest honored over the centuries."[21]

Justice Powell insisted that *The Abortion Cases* were not overturned.[22] The Constitution still debarred the state from denying access to abortions. But the underpinnings of *The Abortion Cases* had been questioned—Justice Powell denied the superiority of the Court to a legislature in this area; Justice Powell declared that the state could distinguish between childbirth and child death.

With these opinions written, the Court "per curiam"—that is, without the designation of any particular person as the author—quickly disposed of Judge Ross's opinion and fine. The city of St. Louis was under no constitutional obligation to make its municipal hospitals provide nontherapeutic abortions.[23]

The Court went on to take notice of Judge Ross's characterization of Mayor Poelker's opposition to abortion as "personal." To the contrary, the Court noted "he is an elected official responsible to the people of St. Louis. His policy of denying city funds for abortions such as that desired by Doe is subject to public debate and approval or disapproval at the polls." Judge Ross had committed "error" in awarding attorneys' fees to be paid by the mayor.[24]

These opinions produced consternation in the cadres of Planned Parenthood and the American Civil Liberties Union and distress within the Court.[25] Three dissenters accurately read the cases as a step away from the pure abortion liberty of *Roe* and *Doe*. Thurgood Marshall was the most excited.[26] The opponents of abortion, he announced, "have attempted every imaginable means to circumvent the commands of the Constitution and impose their moral choices upon the rest of society."

The phrase "circumvent the commands of the Constitution" was wonderfully alliterative. What did "commands of the Constitution" refer to? Justice Marshall meant the right to an abortion created in 1973 by seven members of the Supreme Court. Any attempt to narrow, palliate, or treat as less than absolute that right was what Justice Marshall viewed as "circumventing the commands of the Constitution." In this spirit he continued: "The present cases involve the most vicious attacks yet devised." Elective abortion had been criminal everywhere in the United States until January 22, 1973. No state or municipality had even authorized such a practice, much less paid for it. When a state or city now failed to treat as desirable what yesterday was criminal, Justice Marshall believed, it had succumbed to "the most vicious attacks yet devised."

Among the evils Justice Marshall pictured as flowing from the denial of free abortions was the birth of poor children who "will sadly attend second-rate segregated schools." His implied suggestion for this misfortune was a unique, novel, and terrible contribution to the law on school desegregation. He said, no free abortions, then segregated, second-rate schools. He implied, free abortions, then no segregated, second-rate schools. And why would there be no such schools? Because their potential pupils would be dead.

The impassioned and naive tone of Marshall's dissent continued to its very end, where he indulged in fantasy as to the forces the judge was opposing. Public officials, he declared, were under pressure by "well financed and carefully orchestrated lobbying campaigns" to restrict abortion further. His imagery was surprising to anyone familiar with the citizens struggling to restrict the liberty of abortion to its 1973 level. If they had one-twentieth of the resources of Planned Parenthood of America, or of the American Civil Liberties Union, or of the *New York Times;* if they had any campaign as "well-orchestrated" as the PPA–ACLU endeavors on behalf of the liberty, it was not known to anyone knowledgeable about the effort to eliminate *Roe* and *Doe* as the law of the land.

Justice Marshall concluded with a reference to elected leaders who "cower before public pressures." He was referring to Connecticut, where Ella Grasso had run for governor on a platform favoring a constitutional amendment eliminating *Roe* and *Doe,* and to St. Louis, where Mayor Poelker had been elected on a pledge to stop optional abortion in the municipal hospital. It was a not very usual use of language to describe as "cowering" the fulfillment of a campaign promise.

William Brennan, Jr., also dissenting, was only a modicum more restrained than Justice Marshall.[27] He cited as controlling precedent a case that addressed merely the procedural question of the plaintiff's standing to complain—a merging of procedural and substantive precedents for which he was taken to task by Justice Powell, writing for the majority. He cited as sound law Jon O. Newman's posing of the nature of abortion and added to it: "Pregnancy is unquestionably a condition requiring medical services [citing cases]. Treatment for the condition may involve medical procedures for its termination, or medical procedures to bring the pregnancy to term, resulting in a live birth." This was not very far from writing, "Life is unquestionably a condition requiring medical services. . . . Treatment for the condition may involve medical procedures for its termination or its continued support." To this adherent of *The Abortion Cases,* death had become such a bland alternative to life that the choice had become almost without legal significance.

What was most striking about this dissent was its apparently deliberate ignoring of the rationale of the majority's opinion justifying a state's preference for encouraging childbirth. Why has a state an interest in not funding abortions? Justice Brennan asked. Is it to save money? No, because if an abortion is not had, it will cause an "increased welfare bill incurred to support the mother and child." Is it the mother's health? Justice Brennan answered negatively here, too. He never mentioned the reason Justice Powell had given—"the potential life of the fetus." The life of the unborn child, which was at least potential life to Justice Powell, remained invisible to Justice Brennan.

The shortest and comparatively most restrained dissent was that of the author of *Roe* and *Doe*, Justice Blackmun.[28] In his view, the Court was letting the states accomplish indirectly what he had said they could not do directly, that is, restrict the right to an abortion. He exaggerated, of course; but his sense that the old pro-abortion majority had crumbled was clear and understandable enough. He let fly a little invective at the Court: What it had accomplished was "punitive and tragic." But his strongest words were reserved for public officials who were bowing to "the demonstrated wrath and noise of the abortion opponents." With these irate words a justice of the Supreme Court entered the political lists to taunt those who had challenged his interpretation of the Constitution. He made no acknowledgment of the possibility that public officials, like judges, occasionally act from reason and conscience.

Justice Blackmun not only imagined elected officials cowering, but took offense at their running for office on anti-abortion programs. Mayor Poelker was "one whom the record shows campaigned on the issue of closing public hospitals to nontherapeutic abortions." The majority of voters who elected him were described, strangely, as a "presumed majority." The majority was declared to have acted "punitively." "This," Justice Blackmun declared with hauteur, "is not the kind of thing for which our Constitution stands."

Instructive as the three dissents were in the ideology of abortion, impassioned though they were in personal conviction, intolerant as they were of the majority on the Court and in American society, they were of course not the law of the land. The law now was that "the appropriate forum" for the resolution of the funding question was the legislature. The battle was to continue in that forum with unusual vehemence.

Inquiry 12
On the Financing of the Liberty: The Legislature

What the voters would do, freed of the restraints set by courts but also instructed by the Supreme Court on the existence of the abortion liberty, could be determined in fact only by what the legislatures, especially Congress, did. In an intricate interplay with imperial federal judges, Congress acted. The resultant battle revealed, at the same time that it created, two legislative parties, one pro-abortion, one opposed. These parties, so firmly entrenched, so deeply divided, so unable to compromise, fought out the abortion issue in terms of funding.

Congress had not addressed the funding of abortion as national policy prior to the Family Planning Act of 1970. In that year, providing a federal program to offer contraceptive information and contraceptive services, Congress had provided that no funds appropriated under the act should be used in programs where abortion was "a method of family planning." [1]

In 1971 the Nixon Administration proposed to Congress a comprehensive revision of the Social Security Act, "the second legislative stage" in that Administration's efforts "against poverty." [2] This "monumental" bill—so monumental that Chairman Mills of the House Ways and Means Committee said it had caused more confusion "than any bill I remember having anything to do with" [3]—contained within it authorization of payment for family planning services as part of the Medical Assistance Program (Medicaid). Through such authorization the Nixon Administration sought to gain by one route what had been denied it by another in 1970. Such was the focus on the bill's "family grants," and so great the surrounding

104

confusion, that no attention was paid to the fact that abortion was not excluded from family planning. Quietly, without fuss, the congressional policy of 1970 was reversed. When the main proposal, in truncated form, passed in 1972, the "family services" provision was still intact with abortion neither included nor excluded by name.[4] Depending on the interpretation of the law, the Nixon Administration had, for the first time in the history of the nation, the authority to fund abortion as Medicaid.

At the time of the law's enactment, every state treated abortion as a crime, but a few months after its enactment *The Abortion Cases* opened up every state. The Nixon Administration decided to follow the tide, to interpret existing law to authorize federal funding of abortions, and to use Medicaid to pay for abortions sought by the indigent. Not only did it use Medicaid money, where by law the rate of reimbursement by the federal government to the states was set at maximums of 50 percent to 83 percent depending on the income of the state, but the Population Affairs section of HEW, with Louis Hellman presiding, arranged for the rate of reimbursement to be 90 percent, as though abortion were "family planning" and not Medicaid. By the end of 1973 HEW was reporting to Congress that it had funded "between 220,000 and 270,000 abortions."[5] HEW in 1975 stopped treating the states as eligible for 90 percent reimbursement, but it did not announce any recovery of money furnished at the premium rate. The basic policy of Nixon's HEW, the funding of abortion through reimbursing the states, was continued by the Ford Administration. By 1976 HEW was spending about $50 million a year to fund annually about 300,000 abortions.[6]

In 1976 Henry Hyde, a Republican congressman from northern Illinois, proposed to stop all this. To the Appropriations Act for the Department of Labor and HEW he attached a rider, to become celebrated as the Hyde Amendment, cutting off Medicaid for abortions. His rider was passed by the House, was rejected by the Senate, and went to a conference between the two branches of Congress. From June 29, 1976, to September 18, 1976, the Appropriations Bill was stalled, with each branch refusing to give way. In the House, Hyde was backed with particular effect by the Republican whip, Robert Michel; Silvio Conte, Republican from Pittsfield, Massachusetts; and Daniel Flood, a veteran Pennsylvania Democrat and chairman of the Appropriations Subcommittee on Labor–HEW.[7] The issue as it was seen by Hyde's supporters was put in a nutshell by James Oberstar, Republican from Minnesota: "Vote for life, vote for the unborn," he urged his colleagues as the issue came before the House for yet another vote on September 16, 1976. The opposition appealed to the rights of women and the needs of the poor; their most vigorous speakers were Donald Fraser and Bella Abzug, Democrats, respectively, of Minneapolis and Manhattan.[8]

In the Senate the fight against the rider was led by two Republicans, Robert Packwood of Oregon and Edward Brooke of Massachusetts. Senator Packwood enlisted on his side the United States Civil Rights Commission, whose staff director furnished him with a letter declaring, "The law virtually mandates deletion of the Hyde Amendment." With innocent self-righteousness, the staff director added that no "personal feelings about abortion" should be permitted to influence a congressman's vote.[9]

In the course of trying to establish a meaning for "abortion," Senator Packwood introduced as definitive the meaning of "abortion" as determined by the American College of Obstetricians and Gynecologists and used by all hospitals following the International Classification of Diseases. This definition limited "abortion" to an operation performed on a fetus of twenty weeks' gestation or less.[10] No one on the Senate floor that day observed that this age was four months less than age set by the Supreme Court; nor did Senator Packwood draw the evident conclusion that "abortion funding" under Medicaid should not exceed twenty weeks if the proper medical meaning of the term was to be observed.

Jesse Helms, Republican of North Carolina, chief champion of Hyde in the Senate, took up Senator Packwood's use of a "cost savings" analysis of abortion made by HEW's Louis Hellman, showing a half billion dollars of welfare costs to be saved by timely abortions. He noted that the same cost/benefit way of weighing the value of abortions was advocated by the National Association for the Repeal of Abortion Laws. In the economic calculus of this pro-abortion lobby, as in the statistics of Hellman, no place was found for the value of the lives of the unborn who were removed from existence by abortion. Helms expressed surprise that Senator Packwood would make use of such a mode of argument.[11]

Hanging over the debate in the Senate was the conviction of many Senators that the Hyde Amendment was unconstitutional. The decided cases were the federal decisions, noted in Inquiry 11, which required public funding by the states. It was not evident in 1976 that the Supreme Court would decide differently or that Congress would be treated differently from the states. Senator Helms indeed urged adoption of the amendment for the very reason that the Senate was entitled to have an opinion on the matter: "By taking affirmative action on this amendment Congress is saying that it is constitutionally permissible." [12] But Birch Bayh, Democrat of Indiana, a foe of the amendment, finally voted for it so as not to delay the whole Appropriations Act, declaring as he did so, "I am confident that any court ruling will hold this action as unconstitutional." [13] With such "insincere" pro-Hyde votes, the Senate receded and on September 19 passed the Appropriations Act with Hyde attached. The act was vetoed by President Ford. Whether or not opposition in HEW to the Hyde Amendment helped move the President is speculative—the announced reason was the excessive size of the appropriation. On September 30, 1976, the last day of the old Appropriations Act, the veto was overridden—the desire to have the Hyde Amendment played a part in drawing Republican votes to override the Republican President—and the Hyde Amendment became law.[14]

At once there was a rush to the courts by friends of the abortion liberty to win back judicially what they had lost legislatively. At the time they had in their favor the decisions requiring the states and municipalities to pay for elective abortions,[15] but there were two obstacles to be faced that the state cases had not presented. First, to obtain an injunction against the Hyde Amendment's going into effect, "irreparable injury" to a plaintiff had to be shown. Part of the case for "irreparable injury" had to be that the states would not pay for the abortions the federal government refused to fund. If the states would still pay, no individuals or hospitals could contend that the Hyde Amendment would deprive them of anything. On the ground that no showing had been made of "irreparable injury," Judge John Sirica in the federal district in Washington dismissed an attempt to enjoin the operation of the Hyde Amendment.[16]

The second obstacle was even more powerful. Article I, section 9 of the Constitution provides, "No Money shall be drawn from the Treasury but in Consequence of Appropriations made by Law." This clause was part of the organic law of the Constitution, separating the legislative branch of government from the executive and the judicial, and giving the power of the purse to Congress. By virtue of this provision the Treasury was restrained from paying out money unless it had been appropriated by a law enacted by Congress. It was to be a measure of the dynamic force of the pro-abortion cause in the courts and the executive branch that this fundamental constitutional provision was to be bent if not broken in the ensuing struggle.

Prior to the abortion funding controversy there had been little doubt as to the meaning and the force of Article I, section 9. In a classic case of 1850 brought by the widow of a post office contractor to obtain money owing from the United States, Justice Levi Woodbury had said for a unanimous Supreme Court, "However much money may be in the Treasury at any one time, not a dollar of it can be used in payment of anything not thus previously sanctioned." [17] That case, *Reeside* v. *Walker,* was reaffirmed as standard constitutional doctrine by another unanimous Supreme Court in 1937 interpreting Article I, section 9: "It means simply that no money can be paid out of the Treasury unless it has been appropriated by an act of Congress." [18] Again, in 1962, Justice Harlan, writing for the Court, had occasion to say, "Article I, section 9, clause 7 vests exclusive responsibility for appropriations in Congress, and the Court early held that no execution may issue directed to the Secretary of the Treasury unless such an appropriation has been made." [19] In other words, no court had power to order the Treasury to pay what had not been appropriated.

The doctrine was so well established that even when certain distillers paid more than $1 million into the Treasury to create a fund to be administered by the Secretary of Agriculture under the Agricultural Adjustment Act, and the act was later declared unconstitutional, the distillers could not get a judgment ordering the Treasury to pay back the money: The court allowed they had equity on their side, but they were barred "by a more important constitutional rule, that 'No Money shall be drawn from the Treasury but in Consequence of Appropriations made by Law'." [20]

In the case of *United States* v. *Lovett,* Congress prohibited payment of the salaries of Lovett and two other named individuals, suspected by Congress of being Communists, and the Supreme Court held the prohibition an unconstitutional Bill of Attainder, forbidden by Article I, section 9, clause 3; but the Court did not order the Treasury to pay the amounts owing the three (respectively $1,996, $101, and $59). [21] Instead, the Supreme Court affirmed the judgment of the Court of Claims. [22] The Court of Claims had been scrupulous not to trench on the appropriations power of Congress and had noted that the prohibition against paying the three was a part of an appropriations act passed in 1943. That act, observed the Court of Claims, had halted "the disbursing power in a special situation."[23] The act did not foreclose Congress from subsequently appropriating money to pay the three. The Court of Claims held the three were owed money, but it left to Congress the decision whether money would be appropriated to pay what was owing.[24] Affirming this judgment, the Supreme Court stopped at the limit of its constitutional power and did not cross it. *Lovett* became another case standing for the principle that the Treasury can pay only from an appropriation, and only Congress can appropriate.

On this fundamental ground, Judge Vincent Biunno, sitting as federal judge for the District of New Jersey, rejected an effort to enjoin the Hyde Amendment on October 1, 1977, the first day of the new law's operation. He interpreted the Hyde Amendment to be an integral part of the authorizing language of the Appropriations Act. He observed:

> If Secretary Mathews were to ignore the Hyde Amendment pursuant to such a judgment, the Secretary of the Treasury would remain bound to observe the Hyde Amendment and to refuse to draw any moneys out of the Treasury for payment of a federal share to a Medicaid state on account of elective abortions.[25]

It would have appeared that this interpretation of the Hyde Amendment and its effect were binding on Secretary Mathews of HEW, unless a higher court ruled to the contrary, and that the Treasury was in sufficient privity with HEW to be bound in the same way to this interpretation of the law; so that not only by force of the Constitution but by specific decision of this federal court, no money could be paid for elective abortions when no money had been appropriated for them.

On October 22, 1977, however, a different result occurred in the federal court for the Eastern District of New York in Brooklyn. Here Judge John Dooling did not make a final ruling but gave an opinion that the plaintiffs seeking to enjoin the operation of the Hyde Amendment would probably prevail on the ground that the amendment would be held unconstitutional.[26] Judge Dooling adopted the argument of Planned Parenthood that, as the morality of abortion was disputed by "Godfearing people," the government would be required to be neutral. And "neutrality" meant the government should be on Planned Parenthood's side and pay for abortions! He ordered a trial on the merits of Planned Parenthood's case. In the meantime, he issued an order requiring the Secretary of HEW not to carry out the Hyde Amendment and to announce his willingness to "provide reimbursement provided to all Medicaid-eligible women by certified Medicaid-providers." [27]

Judge Dooling's order jumped over the obstacles that had detained Judge Sirica and Judge Biunno. The first, that of showing irreparable injury to anyone in New York, was peculiarly difficult in the case. The State of New York was already under a federal injunction to fund elective abortions for indigents. That injunction had been issued by a three-judge federal court of which John Dooling was a member.[28] He could not have been unaware that no indigent could be denied abortion funding as long as that injunction held. He closed his eyes to the requirement of equity jurisdiction that irreparable injury must be shown. Even more remarkably, he made his injunction binding on the Secretary of HEW throughout the United States, although no showing had been made that the other states would fail to fund abortions if not reimbursed by the United States. He did not attempt to explain how he could enter such an injunction without a showing of irreparable injury throughout the country.

On the fundamental constitutional issue of the division of powers between the courts and Congress, Judge Dooling cited *Lovett,* but he had misread *Lovett.* He wrote:

> The language of the Act makes clear that Congress has appropriated what it judges sufficient money for carrying out Title XIX and that it has sought only to restrict the circumstances in which the funds could be used to pay providers of lawful abortional services. If that prohibition of use transgresses constitutional rights, it cannot be given effect. Payment of funds will follow, but not by an act equivalent to an appropriation.

He then cited *Lovett* as authority for setting aside "a section of an appropriations act."

In short, Judge Dooling, in direct conflict with Judge Biunno, thought the money for elective abortions had actually been appropriated but that the "use" of the money had been restrained by the Hyde Amendment. When the amendment was set aside, the appropriated money could be touched. Mistakenly, he believed that *Lovett* had similarly set aside one section of an appropriations act and reached sums already appropriated. Mistakenly, he ignored the House's own understanding of its legislative process: that a vote for an amendment to an appropriations act, forbidding use of appropriated funds for a given purpose, was a vote not to appropriate for that purpose.[29]

After Judge Dooling's order was entered, the Ford Administration could have asked the Circuit Court or the Supreme Court for a stay of its effect while the conflict with Judge Biunno's ruling was resolved by a higher court; but it did not. After the order was entered, the Ford Administration could have filed an appeal; but it did not. Instead, when Senator James Buckley, as an intervenor in the case, sought a stay of Judge Dooling's order, the motion was opposed by Robert Bork, the Solicitor General, and by William H. Taft IV, General Counsel for HEW. These lawyers, charged with the obligation of representing the United States in an adversary proceeding against Planned Parenthood, took the position of their adversaries. They could not, they assured the Supreme Court in writing, think of a single reason why Judge Dooling's order should be stayed. They even went so far as to present their own argument to the Court, making the point of Hyde's opponents in Congress that the government would save money by not enforcing Hyde, because of the "monies that would otherwise have been expended for childbirth and post-natal care if women were to carry unwanted pregnancies to term." [30] The page of the Congressional Record they cited in support of their argument for their adversaries contained Senator Helms's rebuke of Senator Packwood for relying on Louis Hellman's cost/benefit body count, in the course of which Senator Helms quoted Hellman's memorandum. The Justice Department was in the extraordinary position of using a hostile quotation of Hellman by a supporter of Hyde to undercut the law enacted by Congress and presumably binding on the executive branch.

Bork and Taft did cite the contrary decision of Judge Biunno, but they did not give Judge Biunno's reasons, nor did they point out that the Treasury was in the dilemma of having to follow one of two conflicting interpretations of law and that Judge Dooling and Judge Biunno could not both be right. As Judge Biunno's opinion was not yet in print, the foundation of his conflict with Judge Dooling was not made known to the Supreme Court. Bork and Taft did observe that the plaintiffs had shown no irreparable injury resulting to them if the Hyde Amendment were enforced—the State of New York, they observed, was under another court order to pay for abortions. Irreparable injury, the essential basis for Judge Dooling to exercise here the extraordinary powers of an equity court, was lacking. But because the federal government would not be out of pocket, these lawyers urged the Supreme Court not stay his order. As the Hyde Amendment was to last for only a year, time was of great importance.

These lawyers gave their opponents time in abundance. On the eve of the presidential election, President Ford's campaign was stressing his opposition to abortion, while the Ford Administration paid from the Treasury money not appropriated to pay for elective abortions.

Under the provisions of Title 31, Section 82 of the U. S. Code, disbursements are supposed to be made by the Treasury when a "certifying officer" of a government agency certifies that a voucher for payment is in accordance with law. When HEW, obedient to the injunction, certified that the vouchers to pay for elective abortions were lawful, the Treasury paid. No one in the Treasury asked whether the command of the Constitution was not superior to the injunction and the U. S. Code. No one in the Treasury asked if it were not bound by Judge Biunno's earlier opinion.

Only in February 1977, with the Carter Administration in office, did the government appeal Judge Dooling's comprehensive injunction to the Supreme Court; and even then the government failed to ask the Court to stay the injunction while its propriety was examined.[31] Even then, the Treasury continued to disregard Judge Biunno's ruling and to make the payments for which no appropriation appeared to exist. The result was that, for almost the whole life of the Appropriations Act, a single federal judge's quick decision was able to halt the operation of the Hyde Amendment throughout the land. In disregard of precedent, by misinterpretation of *Lovett,* and through ignorance of the House's understanding of an "appropriations" bill, a single federal judge had made his will the law of the country. Judge Dooling had effectively appropriated money to pay for elective abortions throughout the nation. The requirement of Article I, section 9—"No Money shall be drawn from the Treasury but in Consequence of Appropriations made by Law"—had been breached.

Federal reimbursement of Medicaid abortion was at least $50 million per year. It may be estimated that two-thirds of the abortions so financed were elective abortions. As of April 1978, the federal government had not sought to reclaim from the states the money it had paid them in breach of the Constitution. Like the earlier Medicaid payments at the family planning rate, payments made in aid of abortion seemed to be immune from the ordinary requirements of the legal system.

Meanwhile, appropriations time for 1977–1978 came round. Again, Henry Hyde offered his amendment. The Supreme Court had not yet decided *The Abortion Funding Cases;* Judge Dooling's injunction was still in effect. Hyde's opponents in the House attempted to embarrass him by getting the bill before the House, with no exceptions whatsoever, as a ban on all abortions including those to save a mother's life. The tactic failed to scare off Hyde's supporters. Knowing that the Appropriations Act would go to a House–Senate conference, which would iron out anomalies, they voted 201 to 155 for the bill.[32]

That was on Friday, June 17, 1977. On Monday, June 20, the Supreme Court decided *Beal, Maher* and *Poelker,* explicitly holding that there was no constitutional obligation to pay for nontherapeutic abortions.[33] On Wednesday, June 29, the Hyde Amendment was debated by the Senate, with every Senator newly conscious that the Hyde Amendment might be held to be valid law. The Senate rejected it, 65 to 33.[34] The stage was set for what was to become one of the longest and bitterest divisions in history between the two houses of Congress.

The issue now faced with a new sense of reality by the legislators was neither the question of whether the Constitution required that abortion be permitted nor the question whether abortion should be a crime. As a major issue of American politics it was a new issue: Should the government as a matter of fairness to poor women or as a matter of population or genetic engineering pay for the abortions of those unable to afford them? Congressmen could not plead that the question should be resolved by the states, nor could they take shelter behind a decision of the Supreme Court, which had left the decision squarely with them. The rhetoric that abortion should be a matter of "choice" was hardly apposite when those conscientiously opposed to abortion were being asked to tax themselves to finance it. The issue of public policy could not be effectively disguised as one of personal privacy. Nor could a congressman who personally believed that abortion was a moral evil easily excuse himself if he voted for funding: If he did so, he voted to provide the means for an action he personally said was immoral; he cooperated in the act and could scarcely, without hypocrisy or casuistry, plead that it was not his responsibility that the funds were used for abortion on a massive scale.

Some of the Republican leaders were with Hyde, most notably John Rhodes, the minority leader in the House, although Howard Baker, the minority leader in the Senate, was opposed. The Democratic leadership was slightly more anti-Hyde, with John Brademas, the majority whip in the House, and Robert Byrd, the majority leader in the Senate, both opposed. But these positions of the party leaders were no guarantee of how members of the two parties would vote, nor did the regular leaders play a strong part in the battle.

In the Senate the opposition to Hyde was led by the Republican Edward Brooke, ably seconded by the Democrat Warren Magnuson. Hyde's champions were Richard Schweiker, elected as a liberal and now a conservative after being named by Ronald Reagan as his running mate in the presidential nomination race of 1976, and Jesse Helms, the Republican from North Carolina. In the House the amendment was opposed by Republicans like William Cohen of Maine and Democrats like Elizabeth Holtzman of New York. The leaders opposing funding were the Republican Hyde himself and the Democrat Daniel Flood of Pennsylvania.

Not only were the parties split, so were the intraparty factions and the geographic regions. In general, "coast" Senators, whether East Coast or West Coast, were against Hyde. But there were notable exceptions: Hatfield of Oregon, Durkin of New Hampshire, Biden of Delaware. In general, the Middle West was pro-Hyde, but Percy and Stevenson of Illinois were anti-Hyde, as was Bayh of Indiana. Liberal Democrats tended to be anti-Hyde, but Eagleton and Proxmire were pro-Hyde. Newly elected Republicans like Danforth and Lugar were pro-Hyde, but Hayakawa was opposed.

A number of Senators must be assumed to have voted their consciences, rather than the will of their constituencies. Oregon produced Packwood and Hatfield: At opposite poles, one of them must have been exercising rare independence. Massachusetts produced Kennedy and Brooke: On the same side, they took a stance far different from legislators closer to the grass roots in the Massachusetts legislature, which was militantly opposed to abortion funding. Similarly, Ribicoff and Weicker, anti-Hyde, did not reflect Connecticut opinion. Congressman Hyde was no doubt more representative of sentiment in Illinois than the two Illinois senators who opposed his bill. Such disparities between popular opinion and senatorial conduct reflect the time lag, which tenure in the Senate assures, before the Senate fully responds to community demands.

Meanwhile action was occurring in Judge Dooling's court. On August 4, 1977, seven weeks before the Appropriations Act for 1976–1977 would expire, Judge Dooling lifted his injunction against the enforcement of the Hyde Amendment but ordered hearings before determining what his final decision would be.[35] His retreat was to have greater significance than the few remaining weeks of the 1976–

1977 act suggested. As the Congressional impasse continued, and no new Appropriations Act was passed, the 1976–1977 ban stayed in effect. Payrolls in the affected Departments were met by a "continuing resolution" maintaining the status quo.

There was tremendous pressure on the Congress to agree so as not to hold up an act containing $60 billion of appropriations, including the funding of new programs which could not be funded by a "continuing resolution." On September 27, 1977, the House conferees satisfied their Senate colleagues by letting the House vote on a Senate-backed compromise funding abortions when "medically necessary." The House defeated the compromise 252 to 164, the most massive anti-abortion vote yet registered in the Congress. The majority leader, Jim Wright, and the Chairman of the Ways and Means Committee, Al Ullman, joined in voting for Hyde. What the press was busy depicting as the idiosyncrasy of a religious minority was seen to be the settled will of the congressmen elected in the Democratic sweep of 1976.[36]

The Senate still refused to yield. Two new compromises were proposed: (1) that payment be permitted for "medical procedures necessary for the victims of rape or incest"; and (2) that abortions be funded where continued pregnancy threatened "severe and lasting physical health damage." What the first proposal meant was unclear. The House conferees understood it to refer to actions taken soon after intercourse, when there could be a reasonable doubt as to whether any human being was being destroyed.[37] The Senate conferees understood it to mean any abortion performed after rape or incest—an interpretation which raised the question why the special term "medical procedures" was employed.[38] In the words of George Mahon, the old Texas Democrat who was chairman of the House Appropriations Committee, the meaning was "a little bit fuzzy," and yet "not too bad." [39] In short, the House and Senate, unable to agree, agreed to words whose meaning would have to be determined by HEW in the administration of the act.

The other compromise, "severe and lasting physical health damage," was an attempt to meet the objection that complaisant doctors would interpret "medically necessary" or "health" in a latitudinarian fashion that would make the result equivalent to elective abortion.[40] The phrase was still not acceptable to those who thought human life should be taken only if necessary to save human life. But there was a concerted effort of the congressional leadership to get the House to accept this modification of principle.

In a revealing outburst on December 7, 1977, Chairman Mahon asked the House, "Is it not delightful to contemplate that we might dispose of this thing and not have to confront it month after month as we go campaigning next year?" [41] Facing the threat that the Senate would not compromise further, and that failure to agree would produce a payless Christmas for the employees of Labor and HEW, a weary House voted 187 to 161 to accept the compromise on "severe and lasting" injury to health.[42] With this result, which pleased neither those who believed that the funding should be coextensive with the constitutional liberty nor those who stood on the principle of a life only for a life, the funding battle came to an end for 1977–1978 appropriations. But there was almost no likelihood that the congressmen could go campaigning in 1978 with "this thing" disposed of.

The beginning of 1978 saw two sequelae to the great division, both likely to stir controversy. President Carter and HEW Secretary Califano had indicated their opposition to the federal financing of abortion, but the Administration with cool prudence had refrained from intervening in the congressional debate. Now Secretary Califano issued regulations interpreting the ambiguous phrase in the sense the pro-abortion Senators had insisted on: "medical procedures" included "abortions," so the government would provide Medicaid in the case of pregnancies resulting from rape and incest.[43] Congress had left the issue to the Carter Administration; the Administration had discretion to exercise; and, backed by an opinion from Attorney General Griffin Bell, the Administration tilted toward the pro-abortion side.[44]

At the same time there was a move by supporters of the pro-choice cause to make sure that no new Hyde Amendment would trouble them in 1978. They proposed to amend House Rule XXI. That rule, the "Holman Rule," permits amendment to appropriations acts that are germane to the law and "retrench expenditure." It was proposed to prohibit amendments retrenching expenditures.[45] A Hyde Amendment would thereby be made impossible.

Would the House abandon a device that had served the liberals as recently as 1973 as a way of checking the Nixon Administration's war-making power in Vietnam; that conservatives had used to express disapproval of federal employees' taking part in riots; that labor had used to protect domestic industries; and that conservationists had used to conserve oil? [46] The germane rider reducing expenditures was an established part of congressional legislation. To propose its elimination was to say that the conflict on abortion had become intolerable.

The means by which the conflict was to be suppressed was strikingly reminiscent of another legislative maneuver when another intolerable conflict had led the leadership to devise an effectual way to end discussion of it: the famous "Gag Rule," which the pro-slavery forces first imposed upon the House in 1836 to prevent the presentation of petitions seeking the end of slavery in the District of Columbia.[47] The response to that effort to impose silence could also be recalled. Spurred on by the women of Dorcester, Dover, Weymouth, and Braintree, Massachusetts, John Quincy Adams had fought back. The antislavery cause prospered from being linked to the cause of free petition. When eight years later the Gag Rule was repealed, Adams's fight against the procedural barrier had solidified the opposition to the forces that had imposed it.[48]

Abortion was bound to be an issue in each appropriation for Medicaid. It could become an issue wherever—say, in the Department of Defense—federal money or federal personnel were used for abortion. The tax treatment of abortion payments offered another broad area for legislative policymaking, where division was certain to occur. It could not be avoided as the Administration prepared a national health insurance bill.

The protracted battle had made clear that there were skilled political leaders for the anti-abortion cause in the Congress. These leaders, the target of the pro-abortion media and the heroes of the grass-roots anti-abortion movement, had welded an effective coalition. There was no reason for that coalition to dissolve. Behind it could be inferred a constituency spread throughout the nation, larger than any party, unconfined by religious bias, sectional grouping, or existing political loyalty. Congress had not sought a say on abortion. But when the issue had been put to it, Congress had responded in a fashion comprehensible only if the congressmen subject to reelection in 1978 saw commitment on the issue to be a necessity of political existence.[49]

In the 1978 elections, support for abortion funding was a major charge against Senator Brooke and Representative Fraser, against Senators Case of New Jersey, Clark of Iowa, Haskell of Colorado and McIntyre of New Hampshire, and against Governor Dukakis of Massachusetts. Dukakis and Fraser were beaten in the Democratic primaries, Case in the Republican primary; the rest lost in the general election. Defeats mysterious to a press used to concealing the revulsion against both abortion and the coercion of conscience needed to pay for it were explicable in terms of these issues. The House became even more strongly anti-abortion. The Senate shifted by a net seven senators to the anti-abortion camp.

In the face of this massive political fact, the description of abortion as a "private choice," as though the abortion decision was without social underpinnings and consequences, became ironic. The issue had come to stay in national politics.

Inquiry 13
On the Logic of the Liberty

Vis-à-vis the childbearing woman who wanted an abortion, the unborn child was valued by *The Abortion Cases* at zero before viability and as less than a whole human being after viability. Did this valuation give the child's carrier the power to consent to experimentation on the unborn child if the experiment carried substantial risk of harm to the child? Did the childbearer have this power if she had already agreed to the child's abortion? *The Abortion Cases* did not address these questions. The answer the cases implied became a matter of debate.

The American spokesman for "situation ethics," Joseph Fletcher, expressed succinctly one inference that could defensibly be drawn from the Court's action: "Only the pregnant patient is a 'human subject' to be protected in clinical experimentation and research; the fetus is an object, not a subject—a nonpersonal organism. A fetus is 'precious' or 'has value' when its potentiality is wanted. This means when it is wanted by the progenitors, not somebody else." Fletcher reached the conclusion, "It is justifiable, depending on the clinical situation and the design, to make any use of live fetuses *in utero,* if survival is not purposed or wanted, and if there is maternal consent." [1] With the unborn child viewed as object, "any use" appeared open to an investigator who could secure the mother's consent.

Fletcher used the two-valued logic characteristic of much legal thinking. There are in this logic only two boxes in the law, one marked "Persons" and one marked "Things." If you are not a person, you are a thing; and if you are a thing, your rights are nothing. In this way, exactly as the lawyers creating the slave system had reasoned, Fletcher put the unborn in the box marked "Things." [2]

The situation that was perceived to exist was summed up by

119

David Nathan, a professor of pediatrics at Harvard Medical School, himself engaged in research on the unborn: "The possibility that investigators might perform or tolerate some ghastly intrauterine intrusions prior to abortion because they do not think of the fetus as a person, creates deep moral and ethical concerns. Indeed, a few of my colleagues lend some credence to that fear by referring to the fetus as just 'a piece of tissue.' Obviously the fetus is not just any piece of tissue." [3]

If "some credence" to fear of abuse of the unborn was lent by the attitudes of some of Dr. Nathan's colleagues, additional credence was lent by what had actually happened in England. After a permissive abortion law had been enacted in 1967, the purchase of babies delivered by abortion and sold at a profit for experimentation had generated a national scandal. A governmental committee under Sir John Peel had been created to investigate the traffic and in 1972 had recommended a code of practice to eliminate abuses. The Peel Advisory Group had found it necessary to say, "It is unethical to administer drugs or carry out any procedures during pregnancy with the deliberate intent of ascertaining the harm that they might do to the fetus." [4] It also had to declare, "In our view any charges made are acceptable only if they do no more than meet the necessary costs in administering these services, such as those provided by the Royal Marsden Hospital. In no other circumstances should there be monetary exchange for fetuses, fetal tissue or fetal material." [5]

In these circumstances, where ethicians could think the law had turned the unborn into objects, and researchers could regard them as tissue, and "monetary exchange" had gone on for them abroad, it was not surprising that, in the year following *The Abortion Cases,* Congress placed a ban on the federal funding of nontherapeutic research on the human fetus until an American "Peel Commission" could recommend the proper limits of research. A new National Commission for the Protection of Human Subjects of Biomedical and Behavioral Research was assigned responsibility for making these recommendations to HEW. [6]

The commission created by Congress was chosen by negotiation between HEW and interested congressmen. The department had already indicated its position by drafting regulations permitting experimentation on the unborn who were about to be aborted. [7] The congressional ban overrode the regulations temporarily and the commission's recommendations were meant to supersede them permanently, but the department took charge of the commission. Of its eleven members, five held appointments in institutions doing medical

research, and only a single member was chosen who was publicly opposed to the liberty of abortion.[8] A ratio of ten to one was the department's view of fair representation on that question.

The executive director of the commission was Charles U. Lowe, a
pediatrician who had been with the National Institutes of Health
since 1968 and was now a "Special Assistant" for "Child Health
Affairs" in HEW. A man agile in the technical language of his subject, adroit in his command of committees, adept in containing congressmen, bureaucratic superiors, presidents and the press, and determined in his objectives will often become "the department" where
his subject is concerned. Such a man was the department's man who
became the commission's executive director. The sardonic spirit of
Dr. Lowe and his disdain for lay supervision are captured in his article "On Legislating Fetal Research" in which he describes the genesis
of the commission:

> Somehow certain legislators seemed to become convinced that fetal
> research encouraged abortion, and that curtailing fetal research
> would diminish the number of abortions. Fuel for the legislative
> fire was provided by publicity of a single fetal research project
> conducted by an American investigator in Finland, in which heads
> were removed from dead aborted fetuses for isolated perfusion
> studies. This research, in combination with the temper of the
> times, resulted in the passage of a notable piece of legislation
> affecting fetal research, the National Research Act.

If the irony of "a notable piece of legislation" resulting from a mis-
apprehension and a grotesque experiment was not evident, Dr. Lowe
made it clear four paragraphs later by observing, "Many of the laws
proposed before the Congress failed to realize that the fetus spent a
period of nine months of vulnerability in the uterus and, therefore,
did not address research on the pregnant woman." [9] Only Congressmen uninformed enough not to know that a fetus lived in the womb,
he gently implied, could have attempted by law to control the discretion of HEW in its funding of research.

A prime issue for the commission to decide was: Who can give
consent to nontherapeutic experiments on the unborn? One guide to
ethical conduct was a set of principles known as the Nuremberg Code
of Ethics in Medical Research, framed by the American judges trying
German researchers for experimenting on human subjects during the
Hitler regime. The heart of the case against those researchers had
been that the subjects had not consented to the experiments. The
response of the researchers was that, most of the time, anywhere in
the world, consent either was not given or was illusory; so they had

acted like other medical scientists. To that contention the American court had replied with a formulation of ethical principles of research. The code began with the words, "The voluntary consent of the human subject is absolutely essential." It continued with the words, "This means that the person involved shall have legal capacity to give consent." [10] The Nuremberg Code excluded nontherapeutic experimentation on those without capacity to consent.

The World Medical Association at Geneva, after hearing more information on war crimes, had formulated a new Hippocratic Oath. As a standard of conduct for doctors the Oath of Geneva included the pledge: "I will maintain the utmost respect for human life, from conception." [11] In a subsequent code, the 1964 Declaration of Helsinki, the World Medical Associations invoked Geneva's words, "The health of my patient will be my first consideration." Apparently the patient referred to was one existing from conception. The association then cited the International Code of Medical Ethics: "Any act or advice which could weaken physical or mental resistance of a human being may be used only in his interest," and went on to set standards for nontherapeutic research. Such research, it said, cannot be undertaken "on a human being" without his consent.[12] Read together, Geneva and Helsinki appeared to foreclose utterly any experiment on a child of tender years or a child in the womb. Like Nuremberg they appeared absolute in requiring "voluntary consent."

A loophole, however, existed. In law, parents and guardians are able to perform various acts on behalf of children. They are said sometimes to "consent" on behalf of the child for whose benefit they act. Could a parent or guardian "consent" in such a way for a child subjected to nontherapeutic experiment? The Declaration of Helsinki expressly accepted the possibility of using this kind of fiction.[13]

The leading American medical and research societies were subscribers to the Declaration of Helsinki; but Helsinki was a code of ethics, not American law. Whether American law actually permitted a parent or guardian to give consent on behalf of a child to an act that was not for the child's own benefit was unclear. No statute provided for such consent, and no court had ever decided the issue. In the opinion of some lawyers, such consent was legally inoperable.[14] As Warren Burger had put it before he was Chief Justice,

> No *adult* has the legal power to consent to experiments on an infant unless the treatment is for the benefit of the *infant* . . . .
> It is the lamentable use in experiments of such subjects as infant

children, incompetents in mental institutions, unconsenting soldiers subject to military discipline—as has been done—that is indefensible; and no rational social order will or should tolerate it.[15]

It was argued by others that, if the risk of harm to the child from the experiment was not "discernible" and the experiment promised great good for society, it was morally right to let the parent consent on the child's behalf.[16] In practice, many parents did consent to various tests on their children that were without therapeutic value to them, threatened them with no discernible harm, and were of benefit to society. This practice and the moral argument supporting it were foundations of a legal argument that proxy consent to nontherapeutic experiments might be lawful. But the argument restricted that kind of consent to low risk experiments, and it was premised on the assumption that a parent by nature and affection and a guardian by law would have the child's interest at heart. No ordinary mother or father would put their child at serious risk to benefit an anonymous group of other children. But did this presumption hold where a mother had decided her child must be aborted? In that case she had renounced the ties of biology and affection. Was there a basis in reality for accepting the fiction that the child consented when the consent actually given was that of the person who had already authorized the child's death?

The issue seemed even sharper when it concerned consent on behalf of children who had been delivered by abortion, who were in ordinary medical usage "preterm infants," [17] but who were not expected to live for long. Not only had their mothers abandoned them, but they were no longer within their mothers' bodies. Could their mothers give "free consent" on their behalf?

One solution to these questions was to give up the term "nontherapeutic." A medical researcher, Robert Levine of Yale Medical School, was to argue that such was the course the commission should have taken. The distinction between therapeutic and nontherapeutic, he argued, was blurred in some cases and "embarrassing" in others: In the case of children it opened research to a charge of proceeding without consent. Therefore, "nontherapeutic" should be dropped.[18] The difficulty, which he scarcely acknowledged, was that the Declaration of Helsinki had stated that the distinction between therapeutic and nontherapeutic was "fundamental." [19] The distinction had been intended to embarrass researchers doing nontherapeutic research without their patient's consent.

A second strategy to facilitate research was hinted at in Joseph Fletcher's testimony to the commission. The Declaration of Helsinki required respect for life from conception. But, observed Fletcher, this left open what " 'respect' and 'conception' are to mean." [20] If Fletcher's meaning was spelled out, "conception" could be defined as "survival for a year after birth," and "respect" could be given a Pickwickian definition such as "decent burial." Broadly reinterpreted, Helsinki could mean that respect was required only after a baby was a year old, or it could mean that the patient was treated with respect when he was buried with reverence. It was up to the commission to fill in the meanings of "conception" and "respect." The commission in fact followed that strategy in its rules on newborn infants with very short life expectancies. They could be experimented on, the commission determined, but "out of respect for the dying subjects" nontherapeutic experiments should not be permitted to alter the duration of their lives.[21] Respect, in this sense, meant respect for their life span but not regard for the pain the newborn would feel.

A third approach was to treat the unborn who were about to be aborted and the newborn after an abortion as simply objects beyond the protection of the Declaration of Helsinki and the other medical codes. This was Joseph Fletcher's main recommendation to the commission.[22] If such an approach were taken, consent on their behalf was unnecessary. The difficulty was that this approach treated the subjects of abortion as nonhuman. Yet Congress had created the commission as a commission on "the protection of human subjects." The unborn were not within its jurisdiction if they were not human.

Beyond this technical legal consideration, the entire argument for permitting experimentation on the unborn rested on the contention that they were members of the human species. A survey of research on the unborn prepared for the commission observed, "In spite of the enormous data base that exists regarding fetal well-being in the sheep and other laboratory animals, little of this is directly applicable to the human situation. Anatomical peculiarities and physiologic differences have meant that these models do not provide sufficient data to answer these questions in the human situation." Again, the commission's experts observed, "Because of important biological, anatomical, and physiological differences, no animal species has proven ideal as a model for human amniocentesis studies." [23] A HEW statement in 1974, arguing in favor of experiment, put it this way: "The opposition to research involvement of the fetus and the abortus appears to be based in part on the assumption that the needed research can be obtained through research with animal species or with adults. Unfortunately these assumptions are not valid." [24] It was because the unborn were human beings that the researchers wanted to experiment upon them.

How necessary was nontherapeutic research on the unborn who were about to be aborted? For the utilitarians on the commission, this was the key question. The Battelle-Columbus Laboratories were commissioned to do a "retrospective" study of certain medical advances that might have depended on fetal research—amniocentesis, rubella vaccine, Rh vaccine and therapeutic transfusions, and the management of respiratory distress syndrome. If "research on living human fetuses" was defined broadly to mean "any experimentation that could perturb the living fetus or its environment," the Laboratories reported, all four areas of advance had depended on "fetal research." [25] But this broad definition, provided by Charles Lowe's staff, ignored the fundamental difference between direct and indirect harm to the unborn. Almost any experiment affecting a pregnant woman affected the being within the womb and that being's environment. Under criticism by Commissioner Robert Cooke, himself a medical researcher, the Batelle-Columbus group admitted that, if fetal experimentation were defind in terms of direct action upon the unborn, their conclusions were "drastically altered." [26] Virtually no medical advances of the past were known to have been necessarily dependent on nontherapeutic experimentation of this kind. [27]

It was still true that there were medical advances that could conveniently be made by risking harm to the unborn who were about to be aborted. [28] It was also true that medical advances could be conveniently made by experiments on the brains of the senescent. [29] No one advocated the latter kind of experiment on the basis of utility. Why was utility an argument to justify experiments on the unborn who were about to die? The commission answered: "the dying fetus cannot be 'harmed' in the sense of 'injured for life.' " [30] The same observation, however, could be made of any dying adult.

In the end the commission gave no answer based on principle. It attempted no distinction between the unborn slated for death and other human subjects. It did not attempt to explain how those who had abandoned their unborn or delivered children could consent on their behalf. It put the Nuremberg Code, the Declaration of Geneva, and the Declaration of Helsinki in an Appendix and neglected to explain how it reconciled its own position with any of those codes. It declared that, if "important biomedical knowledge cannot be obtained by alternative means" and the mother had consented and the father "not objected," the unborn about to undergo abortion or suffering abortion could also be subjected to nontherapeutic experiment.[31]

The commission added one further proviso: that "no intrusion into the fetus [be] made which alters the duration of life." [32] In the case of an unborn child aborted by a curettage or by saline injection in the womb, the proviso had no possibility of being operative. It was apparently intended to cover cases of infants delivered by hysterotomy or prostaglandins who were not expected to survive. The proviso was apparently intended to prevent the shortening or lengthening of the lives of such infants for experimental purposes. Within its restrictions, such preterm infants could be made to submit to nontherapeutic invasions that did not affect the duration of their lives. The commission added, however, that they must be under twenty weeks gestational age (five lunar months, four and one-half calendar months).[33]

Two commissioners thought fetuses should not be experimented on if they could feel pain, while the other commissioners by their silence appeared indifferent to this aspect of the subject. The only biologist to present a paper to the commission, Marc Lappé, had referred to "a potentially sensate fetus" as present "around 20–22 weeks of gestation." No biologist or psychologist gave the commission any written report on the capability of newborn infants to experience pain. Dispensing with investigation of this sensitive subject, the commission majority gave no weight to the risk that it was approving the infliction of suffering on sentient beings.[34]

One Commissioner, David W. Louisell, Boalt Professor of Law at Boalt Hall, the Law School of the University of California at Berkeley, dissented from the commission's recommendations on the unborn. "For me," he wrote, "the lessons of history are too poignant, and those of the century too fresh, to ignore another violation of human integrity and autonomy by subjecting unconsenting human beings, whether or not viable, to harmful research even for laudable scientific purposes." In Louisell's judgment, "All infants, however premature or inevitable their death, are within the norms governing human experimentation generally." The unborn were within the human family. *The Abortion Cases* themselves had established no liberty to kill them if they could be delivered alive. The "mere youth of the fetus" did not take away the human right to live and the protection of the law.[35]

The logic of *The Abortion Cases* was too strong for this powerful dissent to sway the department. After receiving the commission's recommendations, HEW even eliminated the specific limit of gestational age, permitting experiment on any "nonviable fetus." [36] HEW eliminated as well the commission's gesture of respect for "dying subjects" and permitted experiments altering life duration if intended "to develop new methods for enabling fetuses to survive to the point of viability."[37] Otherwise, HEW adopted the recommendations of the majority of the commission.

In effect, although not in words, the commission and HEW had made the subjects of abortion, whether in the womb or actually born, objects that could be used. In treating the unborn within the womb in this way, the agencies of government had accepted the logic of the liberty of abortion. In extending the treatment to the dying baby outside the womb they had reached the frontier of the liberty.

Inquiry 14
On the Frontier of the Liberty

Did the liberty of abortion entail a liberty to cause the death of a child who was born alive? The question itself might be understood in two ways. Did the liberty include a liberty to inflict injuries within the womb that would be the cause of death after the baby's birth? Did the liberty include a liberty to abandon a baby delivered alive after an abortion so that the baby would die from not being cared for like other newborns? *The Abortion Cases* did not answer these questions expressly. The cases focused on the privacy of the childbearing woman. What happened after she was rid of her unwanted offspring was not their concern. But if the liberty was to expand, it was necessary that those questions be resolved.

Late in the first year after *The Abortion Cases,* an investigation was conducted into experiments on unborn children believed to have been carried out at Boston City Hospital. In the course of the investigation the body of a black baby male was discovered in the Southern Mortuary. The medical examiner reported the cause of his death to be anoxia, or lack of oxygen.[1] Dr. Kenneth Edelin, chief resident in obstetrics and gynecology at Boston City Hospital, was identified as the doctor who had delivered the baby. On January 7, 1975, Dr. Edelin went on trial for manslaughter.

The case was tried before a jury and, as is usual in jury trial cases, involved conflicts of testimony and evidence which it would be the duty of the jury, acting under the court's instructions, to resolve. In the next seven paragraphs the case most favorable to the prosecution is summarized; this is followed with a summary of defendant's case:

The evidence most favorable to the prosecution showed that a junior resident had estimated the age of the unborn child to be twenty-four weeks; that a senior doctor had estimated the age to be twenty-one or twenty-weeks; and that Dr. Edelin himself had estimated his age at twenty weeks to twenty-two weeks.[2] In the definition of medically permissible "abortion" by the American College of Obstetricians and Gynecologists, an abortion took place only if the infant expelled weighed 500 grams (1 lb. 2 oz.) or less and was under twenty completed weeks of gestation; that is, the infant had to be under four and one-half calendar months or five lunar months.[3] Even by Dr. Edelin's lower estimate the child was not "under 20 completed weeks of gestation"; and his weight was to turn out to be at least 693 grams (1 lb., 8½ oz.).[4] The child's mother, however, had come for an "abortion," and after three attempts at saline abortion had failed, Dr. Edelin decided on "abortion by hysterotomy."[5]

The incision into the womb was made. The doctor detached the unborn child's placenta from the womb. According to his assistant at the operation, the doctor kept his hand in the womb for at least three minutes by the clock.[6] He then pulled out the baby and placed him in a stainless steel basin held by the scrub nurse. In the course of passing him to the nurse, he felt the boy's chest with his rubber-gloved hand for three to five seconds and noticed no heartbeat.[7] The nurse took the basin, which was emptied into the container in "the back room."[8] According to the Commonwealth's experts, examination of the baby's lungs showed he had been born alive.[9] He indubitably was dead at some point before his body was taken to the morgue.

Some infants require stimulation to breathe air after birth, and this is especially so if the mother has been under general anesthesia. The baby's mother had been under general anesthesia for almost forty minutes, and the anesthesia would have made the baby drowsy. Dr. Edelin did nothing to help the baby breathe air.[10]

What did Dr. Edelin do? "After the fetus was removed, I observed it, and in the process of passing it from the operative field to a stainless steel basin . . . I also checked it for a heartbeat by touching the anterior chest . . . looking for a sign of life." This summary of his testimony is taken from his brief on appeal, with the omissions made by his lawyers of what they thought irrelevant. According to this summary, Dr. Edelin's check took "a couple of seconds" or "between three and five seconds."[11] His counsel argued this conduct was not wanton or reckless. But they admitted that one of Edelin's own experts, Dr. Pritchard, had testified that it would take up to ten seconds "to be absolutely certain there was no heartbeat."[12] The Commonwealth produced testimony that "the proper way to determine whether the child had a heartbeat and circulation is to palpate both its chest and the stump of the umbilical cord (*Transcript* 26, p. 58), that the proper way to palpate its chest is with a stethoscope (*Transcript* 12, p. 140; *Transcript* 23, p. 165; *Transcript* 26, p. 58), and that, in any event palpation of its chest should continue for at least 20 seconds in case the child's heart is intermittently stopping and starting (*Transcript* 26, p. 58)." [13] Dr. Edelin had only felt the chest with his hand for no more than five seconds.

For all deliveries of preterm infants, the standards of the American Academy of Pediatrics require notification of a pediatrician, the provision of nursing care, and immediate delivery of the baby to intensive-care facilities.[14] In particular, the academy's standards prescribe the following treatment for "infants of low birth weight":

> Even the smallest infants should be held head down after delivery to promote drainage of amniotic fluid, blood and vaginal mucus from the infant's oropharynx. During or promptly after birth, the mouth and throat should be aspirated gently with a 2-hole Rausch catheter; an ear syringe which can be autoclaved between patients may also be used. . . . Procedures such as rapidly drying the infant must be made available in the delivery room to minimize heat loss, which may lead to a fall of the infant's body temperature. Infrared thermal protection must be provided for the infant. . . . The survival, or ultimate functional integrity, of infants admitted to the intensive care room requires highly specialized facilities. . . . Some infants will require the full-time attention of one nurse.[15]

Dr. Edelin did not drain the baby, aspirate him, syringe him, dry him, or give him thermal protection. He did not notify a pediatrician. He did not send the baby to the intensive-care room. The only nurse he provided was the one who deposited him in "the back room." [16]

To prove Dr. Edelin guilty of involuntary manslaughter, the Commonwealth had to prove him guilty of "wanton or reckless conduct," causing death. Such conduct, as the jury was instructed by the trial judge, consisted in "indifference to or disregard of the probable consequences to the rights of others" by one who had a duty to those affected by his indifference.[17] It was the Commonwealth's contention that such conduct could be considered before the baby's birth if it affected the baby after birth. Concretely, if the judge accepted this view of the law, it appeared that the Commonwealth could prevail by satisfying the jury that Dr. Edelin had held the fetus in the womb for three minutes after the placenta had been disconnected, for that action, depriving the unborn child of oxygen from the placenta and keeping him from oxygen in the air, would have been a grave injury capable of causing his subsequent death.[18] Dr. Edelin might be found reckless or wanton in causing such injury. Alternatively, or cumulatively, the Commonwealth could prevail if the jury accepted its contention that Dr. Edelin had been indifferent to the baby after birth. To fail to take the proper steps to determine if life continued to exist after delivery; to fail to aid the baby to breathe; to fail to drain, syringe, aspirate, and warm the baby; to fail to provide facilities and nursing—all of these omissions indispensable to the survival of a preterm infant might be judged as indifference to the baby's rights, as wanton and reckless conduct.[19]

The defendant's case was this: He denied that he had delayed three minutes in extracting the baby, and his experts denied that the three-minute delay would have killed the baby.[20] On this issue the jury was left to choose between conflicting witnesses. As to his conduct after the baby's birth, he testified that he believed the baby was dead; hence there was no need for the procedures appropriate for a live birth.[21] He was supported in this belief by the testimony of his assistant, who saw the baby and thought him dead.[22] On this issue, his experts also challenged the Commonwealth's expert testimony that the baby had been born alive.[23]

On the law, the defendant asked the trial judge to charge the trial jury that it must acquit him "if you find that the fetus in question died in the course of a lawful abortion"; or if you find that he was not born alive as indicated by a functioning circulatory system or by the breathing of air through the lungs; or, "even if you find that the fetus breathed for a moment or moments or had the signs of life," you do not find beyond a reasonable doubt "that the fetus was capable of meaningful life." [24] All of these requested instructions were on the theory that *The Abortion Cases* immunized what Dr. Edelin had done and not done during and after the delivery. The defense also asked the judge to define abortion to be any medically accepted procedure that would "result in the termination of pre-natal life of the fetus or of the fetus' potentiality for life." [25]

The trial judge did not adopt any of these requests but ruled that *The Abortion Cases* had made the Massachusetts abortion law "null and void" for the entire term of pregnancy; that "abortion" under *Roe* v. *Wade* was the termination of pregnancy during the entire term of pregnancy and "that the abortion process and its effectuation must be left to the medical judgment of the pregnant woman's attending physician"; that a person existed only "after birth" and that the jury could convict Dr. Edelin only if "satisfied beyond a reasonable doubt" that he had caused "the death of a person" born alive outside the body of his mother.[26]

By these instructions the judge answered one question not resolved by *The Abortion Cases*. He decided that an injury inflicted in the womb during an abortion that caused the death of a child after the child's birth was not a prosecutable offense. The result was contrary to the English common law and to the rulings of four out of the five American jurisdictions that had considered the matter in the context not of abortions sought by the mother but of injuries inflicted on a fetus against the mother's will.[27] In 1889 Holmes had uttered a dictum that such injury was not manslaughter, but he had spoken in a Massachusetts civil case in which he took the ancient Roman law view that the unborn child was part of the body of his mother.[28] The usual understanding of the common law had been voiced by a commission on Massachusetts law in mid-nineteenth century: "If a child be born alive and then die, in direct consequence of potions administered, or violence done before its birth, or during its birth, it is the killing of a human being." [29] So little doubt existed on the point that the impartial expert for the National Commission for the Protection of Human Subjects advised the commission in 1975 that, if parents consented to, or a physician inflicted, injuries on the unborn child during an abortion and the child was born and died of the injuries, "[T]he most dire consequences for the parents or physician would come under the criminal law, which regards it as murder or manslaughter if prenatal injuries bring about postnatal death." [30] After the trial judge's instructions, no dire consequences could follow for Dr. Edelin because of his conduct prior to the boy's delivery.

With these instructions limiting it to the facts following the baby's birth and requiring that it determine that the baby was actually born alive, the jury returned a verdict of manslaughter. The judge imposed a sentence of probation.

Appeal lay to the Supreme Judicial Court of Massachusetts, a tribunal known for the excellence of its judgments and distinguished at the time of the appeal by numbering among its members two former professors of law at Harvard (Robert Braucher and Benjamin Kaplan) and a judge accorded national recognition as the best appellate judge in the country (Paul Reardon). Those familiar with the court and the Boston–Cambridge ambiance surrounding it predicted in advance where the two Cantabrigians plus Herbert Wilkins, a more recent Harvard graduate, would stand. No good judge can be completely pigeonholed, and Benjamin Kaplan in particular was distinguished by his erudition and his humane sympathies. But no judge is totally immune from his social surroundings. Harvard University is an academic institution whose individual scholars are remarkably free from bias and the highest institutional value is truth, while the community centered on Harvard is dominated by fashionable liberal clichés, and those who live in it are apt to believe the clichés partake of the verities established by scholarship. Those who knew the sympathies and antipathies, the assumptions and fashions of this community could scarcely doubt that the defendant would have at least three friendly hearers of his plea. The votes of the other three (Chief Justice Edward Hennessy, Francis Quirico, and Reardon) could not be so easily guessed. As a seventh judge to fill a vacancy was not appointed in time to hear the argument, a tie was conceivable.

Inferably, a struggle did go on within the bosom of the court—the appeal was argued on April 5, 1976; the court said nothing during the election months when abortion was a national issue; and the opinion, or rather opinions, were handed down only on December 17, 1976. When they finally came, they had the bleak and angry character of a New England winter.

The defense had claimed throughout the case that it was an "abortion case"; that under *The Abortion Cases* Dr. Edelin should not be prosecuted at all; and that his prosecution was an attempt to discourage abortion.[31] The media had played the case as an abortion case.[32] On appeal, the defense argued that Dr. Edelin's conviction would have a "chilling effect" on the abortion liberty.[33] Eighteen groups filed briefs supporting Dr. Edelin's main contentions. They ranged from the American Ethical Union to Planned Parenthood, and they all put their concern for Dr. Edelin into the context of their concern for the liberty of abortion.[34]

It became plain then what the frontier of the abortion liberty was —liberty of action that went beyond the "privacy" of the pregnant woman on which the liberty of abortion had been grounded in 1973. It was not enough that the gravida be free to "terminate her pregnancy." Her physician must be free to bring about "the termination" of the life of the fetus. He must even be free to abandon the unborn child after birth if that child was not "capable of meaningful life" outside the womb. As the defendant's appeal put it, "prosecution of a physician's judgment in authorizing and effectuating an abortion strikes directly and destructively at the woman's right to have an abortion." [35] The defendant had been convicted of causing the death of a person already born. The defense was determined that he should be freed because all he was convicted of was an act that the abortion liberty should encompass.

Three judges—Braucher, Kaplan, and Wilkins—found that the trial court's instructions excluding testimony on Dr. Edelin's conduct in the womb before delivery had been required by the Constitution as interpreted in *The Abortion Cases*. Writing for the three, Benjamin Kaplan said that after the Supreme Court's decisions, "the manslaughter statute could take hold only after a live birth and only with respect to acts of the physician in the postnatal period." [36] The trial court had rightly directed the jury to look only at the evidence of what Dr. Edelin had done after the delivery.

As to what happened after birth, the three judges observed that it was essential to the Commonwealth's case to prove that the victim had been born alive. To prove live birth, the Commonwealth had to show more than "some kind of breathing," something more than "fleeting respiratory efforts or gasps." [37] Not finding proof of more than gasps, they voted to acquit Dr. Edelin on the ground that no person had been killed.

Justice Kaplan scarcely disguised where his sympathies lay. He thanked the eighteen organizations submitting briefs on behalf of the liberty of abortion.[38] He dismissed the common law on manslaughter subsequent to an abortion as something for "the curious" to pursue "in the learned briefs of counsel." [39] He took at face value Dr. Edelin's testimony that "he had a personal scruple against abortion of a viable fetus." [40] He consistently referred to the victim as a "fetus," once even describing the subject of an abortion as "the products of conception." [41] He found it prejudicial error to let the jury see a black-and-white photograph of the deceased,[42] which, defense counsel had contended, was "both striking and deceiving" in its resemblance to "a baby which had been born and died." [43] He reweighed the evidence that it was the jury's normal function to weigh and treated the prosecution's case with sharpness and scorn. In the view of Justice Kaplan, the defendant was a reputable physician brought into the criminal court by persons disrespectful of the new liberty decreed by the Supreme Court. Beneath the surface of his elegant and ironic summation against the Commonwealth of

Massachusetts, a quiver of anger against the prosecution was detectable.

Different notes were struck by Justice Reardon, writing for himself and Quirico, and by Chief Justice Hennessy. None of them thought that *The Abortion Cases* immunized Dr. Edelin's conduct in the womb before birth. The Chief Justice did not believe the charge to the jury precluded consideration of evidence bearing on this period. But Reardon and Quirico found that the trial judge, bending over backward to be fair, had created what had to remain as "the law of the case" by his instructions to the jury. As the jury had been told it could not convict on the basis of prenatal conduct, so Dr. Edelin's conviction could not be sustained on that ground on appeal.[44] There were thus five votes for acquittal on the actions occurring before birth.

Justices Reardon, Quirico, and Hennessey, however, all said that the Commonwealth had provided ample evidence from which the jury could conclude the baby was born alive.[45] The autopsy had showed "what was in all respects a normal child with a body weight which was small, to be sure, but with which other children have survived."[46] There was "evidence of respiratory activity" and "of a fetal age which would indicate viability."[47] On the question of a live birth the court divided three to three. A tie meant the conviction was affirmed.

That was not the end of the opinions. There was still the question whether, even if the baby had been born alive, Dr. Edelin could have been found indifferent to his rights. The Chief Justice said that Dr. Edelin's failure to aid or stimulate the child in its weakened condition after birth could have been found by the jury to have been the cause of death and that a finding of recklessness on his part could have been sustained. Reardon and Quirico, however, joined Kaplan, Wilkins, and Braucher to declare, "There should be caution and circumspection in the interpretation of a criminal statute which, as employed here, must necessarily touch on professional practice and constitutional freedoms."[48] Showing such caution and circumspection, this majority of five accepted as a defense to the charge of reckless or wanton conduct Dr. Edelin's "good faith" belief that the baby was dead.[49] That his way of determining this crucial fact might itself have been reckless or wanton was not discussed by the court except for the Chief Justice's comment that Dr. Edelin regarded the death of the fetus as "presupposed." The Chief Justice himself was not satisfied that the jury was properly instructed on Edelin's state of mind, so he was for reversal but not acquittal.[50]

In the narrow terms in which *Commonwealth* v. *Edelin* was able to command a majority of the Supreme Judicial Court of Massachusetts, the case stands only for this proposition: When a physician in good faith believes that the baby he has delivered is dead, he has no duty to care for him. In practical terms the case absolved the doctor doing an abortion at any time in pregnancy of any serious obligation to determine whether the baby delivered needed care—a passing glance and a five-second feel were enough to constitute "good faith." The standards of an abortion-oriented delivery became different from those of a delivery directed to normal childbirth.

In ideological terms the case was a great victory for the pro-abortion party. The frontier of the liberty—liberty to commit infanticide—had been almost reached.

Inquiry 15
On the Liberty Taken Further

In the summer of 1974, Jesse T. Floyd, a doctor in Columbia, South Carolina, who "did abortions," was visited at his clinic by a young woman, identified in the records of the subsequent criminal case only by her Christian name, Louise. She said her last menstrual period had been in February. Dr. Floyd found her to be five months pregnant. She was twenty years old, unmarried, black, and hoping to enter a technical school in the fall. Her child would have been born sometime in the middle of the fall semester. She did not want the child; the father did not even know of the pregnancy. On September 4, five weeks after her first examination by Dr. Floyd, she entered Richland Memorial Hospital, paid $250, and waited to be aborted.[1]

The preoperative procedure called for a saline abortion, but Dr. Floyd performed the abortion by the injection of prostaglandins, powerful compounds derived from the human seminal vesicles, whose pharmacological and physiological impact on the human body has only recently become the subject of intensive exploration. They could affect both the body of the mother and the body of her unborn child.[2]

Following the dosage of prostaglandins, Louise went into labor and continued in labor for more than twenty-four hours. Early in the morning of September 6, alone in her hospital room, she gave birth to a son. He weighed 1,049 grams, or 2 pounds, 5 ounces. A nurse who saw him shortly after delivery exclaimed that he was "a seven-months baby." In the neonatal-care unit, his age was registered at over twenty-eight weeks.

Thirteen minutes after birth, the boy was examined by a doctor, who noted that the child was suffering from acidosis, or alkaline blood, affecting his respiratory tract; hypothermia, or a subnormal temperature; and the effects of being born in an unsterile environment. The child was placed in the neonatal intensive-care unit of the hospital, which was itself the regional center for the care of premature infants. He was given the usual care provided for "preemies." In the evening of his birthday a pediatrician prescribed that he remain on a ventilator to treat his breathing problem. He was found to be normally responsive to tactile stilumation.

Dr. Floyd was not present at the birth but visited Louise the following day and informed her that the boy had "a slight chance" of living. Louise left the hospital on September 8, leaving the child still in the intensive-care unit. He was not nursed by his mother, but the hospital provided his nourishment. On September 13 his breathing improved dramatically. Respiratory problems returned with a deterioration of blood gas values. On September 19 the boy's abdomen was extended and there were no bowel sounds. A preliminary laparotomy found the distal ileum, or small intestine, to have a one-inch tear. The surgical procedure known as "a Bishop-Koop stovepipe exteriorization of the ileum" was performed, repairing the tear and a small laceration in the liver. The child's condition improved, but two days later the heart rate had increased and the child was "doing poorly." On September 26, he died.

The pathologist, who performed an autopsy the same day, put under "Final Pathological Diagnosis," the following:

Premature infant.
Perforation of ileum secondary to meconium ileus. (Status post-operative Bishop-Koop ileostomy.)
Peritonitis, right subdiaphragmatic due to above #2.
Thrombocytopenia with cerebral intraventricular, intramyocardial, interstitial nephritic hemorrhages.
Hyaline membranes, intra-alveolar hemmorrhage, interstitial edema and aspiration of lungs.
Marked thymic lymphocytic depletion.
Multiple recent cutdown incisions and lancet wounds.

In the vernacular, the boy had been premature; his small intestine was perforated and it had been operated on; he had peritonitis and hemorrhaging in the lungs and kidneys; his thymus gland was depleted; and he had suffered many cuts. The death certificate completed at the hospital said, under the heading "Death Was Caused By," the following:

Preterm newborn 26–28 weeks gest. age.
Electively induced abortion.

The effect of the prostaglandins on the baby was not specifically described. Much depended on the specific prostaglandin employed and the method of ingestion. Prostaglandins are used to induce labor in wanted pregnancies without normally inflicting injury on the child. They are also used in abortions where a birth is not desired, and their application then may be fatal to the child in the womb or cause severe damage to the body of the child. For example, research using ultrasound has shown that, where the prostaglandin PGF^2 was applied intra-amniotically, the fetal heart, in a majority of cases, stopped in from ninety to one hundred twenty minutes. A dosage of twenty milligrams of PGF^{2a} has been hypothesized to decrease the functional capacity of the placenta, impairing the oxygen supplied to the fetal bloodstream and constricting the fetal blood vessels. Although the prostaglandins in abortion are designed to produce labor, they frequently depend for their efficacy upon their effect on the fetus. For example, when extra-amniotically administered, PGF^2 or PGF^{2a} resulted in incomplete abortions in 40 percent of the cases, so that the extraction of portions of the dead child had to complete the operation.[3]

It remained to be investigated in this case what prostaglandin Dr. Floyd had used and how he had injected it. Dr. Floyd was alleged to have used a dose of forty milligrams. This allegation remained to be proved. The correctness of the autopsy, and in particular its reported diagnosis of meconeum ileus, had to be tested. Had meconeum ileus, a bowel condition usually due to cystic fibrosis, mortally affected the baby's health; or had meconeum ileus been mistakenly diagnosed where necrotizing enterocolitis—a common sequel to prematurity and respiratory distress—had actually been at work? Only when these and similar questions were answered could it be determined beyond a reasonable doubt whether or not Dr. Floyd had inflicted great injury on the child before birth. Since, as it turned out, no trial took place in the courts of the state, nothing in the present discussion of the case should be taken as implying criminal guilt of any character on Dr. Floyd's part.

The hospital reported the boy's death to the county prosecutor, who took no action. Seven months later, in April 1975, a follow-up by the hospital's lawyer, led a new county prosecutor, James C. Anders, to investigate. On August 28 he presented a case against Dr.

Floyd to the Richland County Grand Jury, which promptly indicted the doctor for abortion and for murder.

The abortion statute that Dr. Floyd was alleged to have violated had been fashioned by the South Carolina legislature in 1974 in the wake of *The Abortion Cases*. It created a statutory presumption that an unborn child was not viable "sooner than the twenty-fourth week of pregnancy." The following section of the statute, apparently intended to be read with this definition in mind, provided that abortions "during the third trimester of pregnancy" could be performed if two doctors certified that the abortion was necessary to preserve the life or health of the mother. Otherwise, the statute appeared to proscribe third-trimester abortions as felonies.[4] Anders, the county prosecutor, acted on the basis that the baby in this case had been clearly viable—he was, in the words of *Roe* v. *Wade* "potentially able to live outside the mother's womb" [5]—and Dr. Floyd had apparently made no effort to comply with the statute requiring that the abortion be certified as necessary for the mother's health.

The murder indictment was based on the general South Carolina statute on homicide, interpreted with the aid of Anglo-American common law.[6] As far back as Sir Edward Coke in the seventeenth century, it had been murder at common law to inflict injuries on an unborn child from which the child died after delivery.[7] In Blackstone's classic presentation of the law, "[T]o kill a child in its mother's womb, though a felony, is no murder; but if the child be born alive, and die by reason of the potion or bruises it received in the womb, it may be murder in the wrongdoer." [8] The theory of the law was that the intentional infliction of severe bodily harm on anybody, which brought about that person's death, was murder. That the harm was done in the womb was an irrelevant justification or defense when the child was born alive and died of the injuries he had received. In an analogous way, a number of courts later permitted anybody born alive to sue in tort for the injuries they had received before birth.[9]

The common law had been applied. In 1832 in *Rex* v. *Senior,* a male midwife had been found guilty of manslaughter when with gross negligence he broke the skull of an unborn child he was attempting to deliver, and the child died shortly after birth. The crime was manslaughter, not murder, because the injury inflicted in the womb had not been intentional. The crime was not merely abortion, the killing of a fetus, but manslaughter, the killing of a person born alive. All the judges of King's Bench approved the charge of the trial judge instructing the jury that it should find the defendant guilty of the death of such a person if it found that the blows in the womb caused the subsequent death.[10]

In 1848 the causing of a premature birth by a criminal abortion was itself made the basis for a charge of murder when "the death of the child was occasioned by its premature birth," and it was contended that "the premature delivery was brought on by the felonious act of the prisoner." [11] In that case the jury did not convict.

The chief American cases restating the rule—in New Jersey in 1849, in Iowa in 1856, in Alabama in 1898, in Tennessee in 1923,[12]—involved assaults on the mother that resulted in the premature birth and subsequent death of the child. The principle of those cases did not depend on whether the born child's death was produced against the mother's consent. The charge of murder in those cases was not for a gross attack upon the mother; it was for intentionally causing grave bodily harm which resulted in the death, after birth, of a child. It was this law which had been kept out of the *Edelin* case by the trial judge—erroneously, in the opinion of half the Massachusetts Court.[13]

It was, of course, possible that the state courts of South Carolina would adopt the old dictum of Holmes in the civil case of *Dietrich* v. *Northampton,* invoked by Justice Benjamin Kaplan in his opinion in *Edelin;* or the South Carolina courts might follow the lead of Justice Kaplan and his two colleagues who believed that *The Abortion Cases* themselves shielded an act done in the cause of an abortion from being regarded as homicidal. Until the evidence in the case was laid out at the trial and until the South Carolina courts had ruled, it could not be said with certainty that causing the death of a person by a prenatal act was murder in South Carolina.

Dr. Floyd, aware that he was about to be charged with a serious crime, had been making his own preparations. The day before the grand jury voted the indictment, he filed a complaint in the federal district court in Columbia asking the federal judge, Robert Chapman, to enjoin any state criminal proceeding against him. The next afternoon, the grand jury having voted in the morning, Judge Chapman heard Dr. Floyd's claim that prosecution for his act would violate the constitutional liberty created by *Roe* v. *Wade* and immediately issued a temporary restraining order against the prosecutor.[14] As the constitutionality of two state statutes was drawn into question, a three-judge federal court was then convened by Chief Circuit Judge Clement Haynsworth to try the federal claim of Dr. Floyd.

The three-judge court had to surmount three convergent policies before it could act on Dr. Floyd's request to enjoin his prosecution permanently: the policy of "our federalism" as enunciated by Justice Black in a 1971 decision of the Supreme Court, *Younger* v. *Harris;*[15] the policy against courts deciding controversies "in the air" without much factual information about the matter in controversy; and the policy against a court's easy use of the extraordinary power of an injunction.

Once a state criminal prosecution was under way, Justice Black had held in *Younger,* a federal court should respect the state proceedings and not use federal power to cut them off. This restraint arose from "a proper respect for state functions, a recognition that the entire country is made up of a Union of separate state governments, and a continuance of the belief that the National Government will fare best if the States and their institutions are left free to perform their separate functions in their separate ways." [16] Sensitivity to state courts was called for by the federal nature of our system.

For the Court speaking through Justice Black this duty was also founded on the nature of the judicial power itself. That power was meant to be exercised in judging concrete cases. But if a federal court passed on the abstract constitutionality of a state statute without having before it the concrete circumstances of a case, the federal court gave a kind of advisory opinion and engaged in what was "rarely if ever an appropriate task for the judiciary." [17] Dr. Floyd's claim appeared to be precisely this kind of abstract request, because until the prosecution developed its evidence as to his knowledge of the baby's condition, the action of the prostaglandins, and the precise cause of death, and until the Supreme Court of South Carolina had decided whether South Carolina followed the common law on murder in these circumstances, the federal court had only abstract statutes to examine and pass on.

The teaching of *Younger* v. *Harris* was technically applicable only if the state criminal prosecution had "begun." [18] It could be argued by Dr. Floyd that until the grand jury's indictment was read in open court, the state prosecution had not begun. The temporary restraining order of the federal judge had been handed down before the grand jury's indictment had been read out. Consequently, the state proceedings had not "begun" before they were enjoined.

There was, however, an answer to this contention. The prosecutor could observe that the key question was whether "substantial proceedings on the merits" had taken place in the federal court before the state proceedings had begun. Only if such substantial federal proceedings "on the merits" had occurred before the state proceedings had begun was the federal court justified in acting. The hearing on the temporary restraining order was not "on the merits" but a mere determination whether to attempt to preserve the status quo, pending a decision on the merits of Dr. Floyd's claim. Under existing precedents of the Supreme Court, proceedings "on the merits" only came later, before the three-judge court, and by the time such proceedings occurred there, the grand jury indictment had been read and the state case unquestionably begun.[19]

Still, *Younger* might be avoided by Dr. Floyd if he could show "extraordinary circumstances" or "bad faith" by the prosecutor. As a precedent cited by *Younger* had said, "It is of course conceivable that a statute might be flagrantly and patently violative of express constitutional prohibitions in every clause, sentence and paragraph, and in whatever manner and against whomever an effort might be made to apply it."[20] It was clear that the ordinary South Carolina *murder* statute was not such a statute—it was like the murder statute of every other state. It was arguable that the South Carolina *abortion* statute was not such a statute when it was applied to the abortion of a viable fetus. Neither statute appeared to violate "express constitutional prohibitions."

Nor was this a case where there had been constant harassment of Dr. Floyd, unlike a New Hampshire case when the Supreme Court had approved the federal court's intervention to prevent the fifth state criminal prosecution in five weeks.[21] On the contrary, Anders had proceeded slowly, had acted only after prodding by the hospital, and had charged Dr. Floyd with responsibility for a single action committed almost a year before the prosecution started.

Again, this was not the kind of case where an exception to *Younger* could be found in "the breakdown of the state judicial system."[22] Dr. Floyd had been about to be given full opportunity to litigate his constitutional claims in the courts of South Carolina. In the language of Justice Rehnquist, explaining *Younger* in another case, he was to be afforded "a concrete opportunity" to present his constitutional defense.[23] In such circumstances there was no occasion for the federal court to supplant the state tribunal.

Finally, for any court to exercise the equity power of issuing an injunction, there was the traditional equity requirement that "irreparable injury" to the plaintiff be threatened if the court failed to act.[24] Although it might seem otherwise to a layman, it had been authoritatively established by the Supreme Court that the anxiety, inconvenience, and expense of defending a criminal suit did not constitute "irreparable injury."[25] This was the kind of injury that threatened Dr. Floyd if he went to trial; and by established precedents it seemed insufficient to justify equitable intervention by the federal court even if considerations of federalism, of the appropriateness of judging in the abstract, and of the actual holding in *Younger* did not command abstention.

None of these reasons swayed Judge Haynsworth and his colleagues. For a surprising length of time they left the temporary injunction in effect. Then, after more than two years had passed, on November 4, 1977, they issued an opinion in favor of Dr. Floyd and soon afterward made the injunction permanent. Whatever the outcome of the case would be on appeal—for the state had a direct appeal to the Supreme Court and exercised it—no trial could take place before the autumn of 1978 or, more probably, the spring of 1979. The Supreme Court might summarily affirm Judge Haynsworth and uphold his new encroachment on the laws protecting life, or it might find his intervention unjustified as an interpretation of *The Abortion Cases* or as an interpretation of *Younger*. But if the Court did send the case back, four or five years would have elapsed since the time Dr. Floyd had performed the abortion. Witnesses would be dispersed. Evidence would be stale. Whatever the Court decided, Judge Haynsworth had disrupted the state's case.

Judge Haynsworth held that the "bad faith" exception to *Younger* applied. Anders, he found, should have known that, under *Roe* v. *Wade*, "there was no possibility of his obtaining a conviction that could have been constitutionally sustained."[26] The state abortion statute, he held, was "flagrantly and patently violative of express constitutional prohibitions"—that is, violative of the prohibitions laid down in *The Abortion Cases*. If the abortion statute was so obviously bad, then the indictment for murder, too, was "clearly foreclosed by *Roe* v. *Wade*."

At the heart of Haynsworth's opinion was this extraordinary passage:

> Until the child is viable, the mother's constitutionally protected right to choose to terminate her pregnancy or not to do so must be allowed by the state to prevail over any interest it may have in

the preservation of fetal life. Indeed, the Supreme Court declared the fetus in the womb is neither alive nor a person within the meaning of the Fourteenth Amendment.

To confirm that what he said here was not by accident, he added, "The fetus in this case was not a person whose life state law could legally protect." [27]

These statements were remarkable for their unarticulated assumption: that the boy born alive, left by his mother in the hospital, treated as a separate human being for twenty days, had not been a "viable fetus." Judge Haynsworth had replaced the Supreme Court's test of "potential ability to live" with a new test of "actual ability to live indefinitely." He also had spelled out what was implied in *Roe* v. *Wade* but never actually stated there: For the American legal systems the fetus in the womb was not alive.

As a result of these conclusions, Judge Haynsworth held Dr. Floyd innocent without a trial: He could not be convicted of anything for which he had been indicted. Judge Haynsworth reached this judgment merely by looking at the South Carolina law and at the Constitution as interpreted by the Supreme Court. What Dr. Floyd had done or not done had not been determined. There had been no trial. Before the law and before the public he was and is an innocent man. But his case had become a means for expanding the abortion liberty to its limit.

The Abortion Cases had left open the question whether the liberty of abortion implied that a physician might assure the post-abortion death of a viable child he was aborting. The common law had held such action homicidal. The *Edelin* court had divided on the issue. *Anders* v. *Floyd* eliminated the issue by treating a child who did not survive an abortion for more than twenty days as non-viable, whatever act had made the child's life so short. In effect, Judge Haynsworth declared constitutionally dead the common-law rule. He advanced beyond *The Abortion Cases* to invalidate an ordinary homicide statute as "flagrantly and patently violative" of the liberty of abortion.

Inquiry 16
On the Language of the Liberty

For the pro-abortion party, to expand the law was only to win a political victory. What was necessary to establish the liberty in its full dimensions was to change the language. Only then would the liberty be secure in the popular consciousness.

At one level, the change in language was made self-consciously and openly. An instance is afforded by the interpretation of the Social Security Act. Prior to *The Abortion Cases,* "a child" under the Social Security Act, eligible for assistance as a dependent, was a child, whether born or unborn. If a mother on welfare became pregnant, she received aid not only for herself but for her unborn dependent. For more than thirty years this had been the interpretation of the Social Security Act by HEW.[1] In this respect the department had acted like the state courts, which, interpreting the term "child" in statutes requiring fathers to support their children, had ruled that fathers must support children unborn as well as born.[2] In the light of *The Abortion Cases,* HEW decided that "child" no longer meant "unborn child."

As aid under the Social Security Act depended in part on state interpretations of the act, twenty-five federal courts heard litigation on the meaning of "child." Six of the courts held that "child," as used by Congress in the act, did not include the unborn. Nineteen courts held that it did. The conflict forced the Supreme Court itself to resolve the matter. The issue reached the Court one year after *The Abortion Cases.*[3] On the one side was the weight of thirty years' administrative interpretion of the law, the opinion of nineteen lower courts, and the meaning of "child" in common speech. On the other was the new interpretation of HEW, the opinion of six courts, and the psychological difficulty for the Justices of treating as persons entitled to government aid those very beings they had a year before treated as zeros. In this intolerable conflict, it was not difficult to predict how the Court would act, and the Court behaved as might have been predicted. It redefined "child" in the Social Security Act to exclude the unborn.[4]

Here, tangibly, *The Abortion Cases* transformed legal language. At a more fundamental level they affected how the act of abortion itself was to be described. In an unusually forthright way, *California Medicine,* the voice of the California Medical Association, described what was being done as early as 1970: "Since the old ethic has not yet been fully displaced, it has been necessary to separate the idea of abortion from killing."[5] A language code in which the concept of killing disappeared became after 1973 a legal and societal necessity.

How was the being eliminated by an abortion to be referred to? Preferably, not at all, for any reference raised questions about the being's status. In the ideal reduction achieved by the *Journal of Marketing,* discussing the proper pricing of abortion for a profit, there were only "producers," "suppliers," and "consumers." Producers performed the abortion; suppliers provided the necessary equipment; consumers were the mothers of the unborn.[6] Could abortion be described without mentioning its object? Yes, by referring only to the condition of the mother. For this reason, *termination of pregnancy* was a favored nounal phrase of the pro-abortion party, and to *terminate a pregnancy* a favored verbal locution. The object of the action became the mother's state. The other object was dropped from view.

There were, however, circumstances in which it was important to mention the being who was being aborted. Justice Blackmun had generally avoided the problem, but even he had been compelled to refer to the being who was affected in the last stage of pregnancy. His choice of a term for this stage was "potential life." It was an oxymoron. If the being was life, how was it potential? What is living is alive. It is not potentially alive. Only by expanding the phrase to "potential human life" was the evident contradiction avoided. But the defenders of the abortion liberty had no desire to introduce "human" into the definition. A term more neutral, more technical, more impersonal, was needed.

An ancient word, *embryo* had some serviceability. Its derivation from the Greek for "to swell inside" suggested a mere protuberance. It had a definiteness that suggested there was a significant line between an embryo and a more developed being. "Embryo," indeed, indicated only a being in the first two months of intrauterine life, according to the definition adopted by the American Academy of Pediatrics.[7] But there was no significant biological line at two months, so that this usage was arbitrary. For legal purposes it was awkward to have a term that applied only to pregnancies aborted early, when under the new law of *The Abortion Cases* any pregnancy might be aborted.

Only slightly more useful were *ovum* and *products of conception*. *Ovum* was used by some authors of medical textbooks to describe the entity being aborted.[8] In their usage it was not confined to the early stage of development but could be applied to any object of a medical abortion. It had the advantage of assimilating the object to the several hundred thousand unfertilized eggs in the female body, so that the fetus seemed almost nothing. It had the peculiarity of making no distinction between an unfertilized and a fertilized egg, thereby failing to acknowledge the male contribution to conception. It was not widely adopted.

Products of conception was another term from medical textbooks, used to describe the growing entity at any stage of intrauterine growth. The term was impersonal. It suggested that the entity was a type of natural object. It had one drawback: It was plural. The plural was used to cover two other occasional results of conception: hydatidiform mole and choriocarcinoma.[9] No doubt context would usually distinguish whether the mole, the malignant tumor or the unwanted conception itself was meant. As an appropriate description of the entity being aborted, the term was actually employed in Justice Kaplan's opinion in *Edelin*.

Far more widely used was the term *fetus,* whose usage for intrauterine existence was approved by the American College of Obstetricians and Gynecologists.[10] The term, derived from the Latin for "offspring," was used in biology where research on the offspring of various animals could generally be designated as "research on the fetus," leaving it to context whether the offspring was that of a sheep or a woman. The term had the great advantage of sharply distinguishing the intrauterine being from the human being after birth. The term had the additional advantage of requiring an impersonal pronoun—a fetus was "it" or "which," not "he" or "she." "Fetus" became the term of choice for defenders of the liberty of abortion when they had to discuss its object.[11]

Prior to *The Abortion Cases,* statutes against abortion often identified the beneficiary of their protection as "the unborn child." [12] The terminology corresponded to usage in other branches of law. In tort, when recovery of damages was allowed for negligent injury to the unborn, the damages were for injury to a "child," not a "fetus." [13] When a will was drafted giving property to unborn descendants, they were regularly called "children" not "fetuses." A future beneficiary of a trust was a "child," not a "fetus." [14] These usages were now to be expelled from the field governed by the liberty of abortion.

The only real drawback with the term, from the perspective of the pro-abortion party, appeared when the liberty of abortion was to be expanded to include disposition of a living child after birth. "Fetus" by every definition—biological, medical, and legal—designated the unborn.[15] But once it was established that a fetus was an object that could be disposed of, it was convenient to use the same word for the infant to be disposed of. The National Commission for the Protection of Human Subjects responded to the need. It created the *"fetus ex utero."* [16]

The fetus *ex utero* was a fetus who was no longer a fetus, who was born but who was not expected to live. The fetus *ex utero* had formerly been described in the 1973 standards of the American Gynecologists and Obstetricians as a *preterm infant,* defined as anyone "born at any time through the 27th completed week of gestation." [17] The new language of the commission defined one type of preterm infant as "the fetus ex utero which, although it is living, cannot possibly survive to the point of sustaining life independently, given the support of available medical technology." [18] Charles Lowe of HEW had laughed at congressmen who did not know that a fetus inhabited the womb. In the end it was he who was to defend the oxymoron fetus *ex utero.* The phrase at first sight was as intelligible as "the living dead." Its operational significance in facilitating the treatment of dying newborns as objects could not be doubted.

When an abortion was successful, the result was a *dead fetus,* an *abortus,* or *fetal wastage.* The first two were interchangeable synonyms, although specific medical usage had restricted "abortus" to a dead fetus of less than three months' gestation.[19] Both of the first two terms had a certain macabre quality, emphasizing the existence of an identifiable entity. Some kinds of abortion left no identifiable entity. The most comprehensive term was the third. It conveyed the notion that the abortus was a by-product of the action of abortion, and a valueless by-product. It suggested that the abortus was like other excreta of the body. It was capable of being applied to the parts of a single dismembered fetus or being used as a plural to indicate thousands of abortuses.

Abortion itself, as the term used to designate the liberty, had a number of advantages. They stemmed from its ambiguity, for in 1973 it had four meanings:

1. an "involuntary miscarriage"
2. an "expulsion of a human fetus during the first twelve weeks of gestation"
3. the "expulsion or extraction of the placenta or membranes without an identifiable fetus or with a live or stillborn infant weighing 500 grams (1 lb., 2 oz.) or less, under 20 completed weeks of gestation"
4. extraction of a child at any time before the normal completion of pregnancy [20]

In the first sense abortion was not at issue when the liberty was discussed. Nonetheless, use of the word assimilated voluntary extraction to involuntary expulsion. It facilitated a type of natural law argument: "As nature produces abortions, why not man?" The ambiguity was an advantage in defending the liberty.

The second sense was one definition provided by Webster's *Third International Dictionary* (1969). The term was not used in this sense in either medical or legal parlance. The ambiguity was again an advantage. It permitted the uninstructed listener to suppose that the liberty granted was for a comparatively short period. It is even possible that such ambiguity contributed to the persistent understanding of the liberty by the press as being of only three months' duration.[21]

"Abortion" in the third sense was the definition of the American College of Obstetricians and Gynecologists and of sundry standard medical textbooks. It was the current medical meaning. The constitutional liberty, which was far more extensive, was often confused with this medical meaning.

The fourth and final meaning was the meaning of "abortion" in *The Abortion Cases,* where the term was applied to extraction of the unborn at any time before normal childbirth.[22] This was the language of the Constitution as read by Justice Blackmun. The triumph of the liberty meant that this meaning would in law supplant the meanings afforded by Webster's and by medical practice. Popular acceptance of the liberty would be aided by the ambiguities arising from the other meanings.

"Abortion" had only one distinct disadvantage: its metaphorical meanings. "Abortion" meant "something that fails to attain full development"; "arrest of development of an organ so that it remains imperfect"; a "misshapen thing or person"; a "monstrosity." [23] For the full vindication of the liberty it became desirable to infuse more positive meanings into the term. HEW set out to do so.

On June 30, 1974, HEW issued regulations against sex discrimination in higher education. The regulations provided definitions. Section 86.47c read: "For the purpose of this part, 'pregnancy' means the entire process of pregnancy, childbirth and recovery therefrom, and includes false pregnancy, miscarriage and abortion." Wherever in this subpart one read "pregnancy," one was also to read "abortion." [24]

That such a metamorphosis of language should have been attempted by bureaucratic fiat was instructive. That when its oddity was noted it should be defended drove the lesson home. Senator James Buckley pointed out to the Secretary of Health, Education, and Welfare that HEW's definition did violence to ordinary language. The Secretary replied:

> The government may not now, as I am advised, treat those who terminate their pregnancy in one way, by abortion, any differently from those who terminate it any other way. . . . Of course I did not intend to suggest that abortion is a natural result of pregnancy. It is, as you say, an end of the process of pregnancy initiated from the outside. The problem again is, however, that the distinction did not impress the Supreme Court as constitutionally significant.[25]

It was pleasant to know that the Secretary did not intend to suggest that abortion was the natural result of pregnancy. It was startling to learn that a distinction which was not constitutionally significant was not linguistically significant. The Secretary conceded to the Court power to reshape the language. Naive and even comic as his response appeared, its message was profoundly serious. To make the abortion liberty stick, the language would be revised. The unborn "children" of the law of torts and of wills and of trusts had become the "fetuses" of the law of abortion. The "child" of the Social Security Act no longer meant "unborn child." The dead unborn child had become "fetal wastage." A living baby not expected to live had become a "fetus *ex utero.*" Now "pregnancy" must include "abortion."

In this last transformation a term was turned into its grisly opposite. The attachment of friends of the liberty to this dialectic has already been observed with "Parents Aid," the nonprofit abortion clinic that wanted to aid parents by aborting their daughters without their knowledge and to aid parents-to-be by eliminating their off-spring.[26] On the grander governmental scale of HEW, this tendency had the quality of slogan-making by the bureaucracies of Orwell's *1984,* in which it will be recalled that the Ministry of Love is "the really frightening one" and that its slogans include "War Is Peace," "Freedom Is Slavery," "Ignorance Is Strength." [27] Why not "Abortion Is Pregnancy"? The linguistic triumph of the liberty was almost complete.

The supreme linguistic accomplishment, however, was reserved to the federal judiciary. It took place in Clement Haynsworth's understanding of *The Abortion Cases* to mean that for the law the unborn child was not alive.[28] When first read, his opinion in *Floyd* v. *Anders* calls to mind all that has been said in derogation of law and lawyers, beginning with Mr. Bumble's, "The law is a ass, a idiot," [29] and all that has been said about making words mean what one pleases, beginning with Alice's reply to Humpty Dumpty: "The question is whether you *can* make words mean so many different things." [30] In what sense could a reasonably intelligent adult in the year 1977 understand the child in the womb not to be alive? What does "alive" mean? It means "not dead," and if the child is not alive, not "not dead," how can an abortion be performed upon it? Would Judge Haynsworth understand and obey if the Supreme Court told him that, according to the Constitution, all children under five were not alive, or that all Christians were not alive, or that all persons over eighty were not alive? Would there not be some point at which his common sense and humanity would rebel and lead him to say, "The Supreme Court treats these beings as though they were not alive; it has coined the oxymoron 'potential life' to describe them; but it is wrong." And if Judge Haynsworth could reach that point for the children or the Christians or the octogenarians, what kept him from saying something like this on behalf of the unborn? The answer must lie in his appreciation of the societal necessity to which the Court was responding. He understood that the language of Justice Blackmun was intended to fashion a linguistic mask as real, as durable, and as deliberate as any iron mask pressed upon a prisoner's face. That mask was intended to fit the face of the fetus. The language was designed to foreclose debate. It was meant to eliminate from human discourse the living nature of the beings who were aborted.

Inquiry 17
On the Masks of the Liberty: The Object

It is a propensity of professionals in the legal process to dehumanize by legal concepts those whom the law affects harshly. No more attention need then be paid to them. On a grand scale the masking of humanity by legal concepts went on for more than two hundred years when English and American judges, legislators, and lawyers created and sustained the legal system of human slavery. They eliminated embarrassment for themselves, and made the system work, by never letting themselves, as judges or lawyers, consider the human beings they were affecting. These human beings became "property." In the words of George Wythe, the first American law professor and Chancellor of Virginia, they were things to be transferred under the law "with as little judicial ceremony as a single quadruped or article of house or kitchen furniture." [1]

That is the way these human beings were transferred by judges as intelligent as George Wythe. That is the way such human beings were governed by a legislator as enlightened as Thomas Jefferson. That is the way they were claimed in court by a lawyer as liberal as Abraham Lincoln.[2] It was difficult for participants in the legal process to think they acted badly when they applied the mask the law provided to hide humanity. It was difficult for anyone in their society to think that what such intelligent, enlightened, liberal men were doing was wrong.

So it is in our society. It is difficult to believe that what so many intelligent, enlightened, liberal men have done as judges is wrong. Their respectability, their reasonableness, their care for the rights of citizens assure us that what they have done is only what the law requires. If we recall Wythe, Jefferson, Lincoln, and a hundred leading American lawyers like them who cooperated in creating the slave system, we can be certain that the assurance is misplaced. Respectability, reasonableness, care for the citizenry are not guarantees that a judge will not commit an atrocity.

There is no question here of subjective guilt. Wythe, Jefferson, and Lincoln acted as they thought they had a right to do, as do our judges. To question them is not to question their intelligence, their sincerity, or their good intentions. It is to ask if they have not put masks upon a portion of humanity.

The mask in law is a social construct willingly used by a lawyer or a judge to permit him to suppress a human being without guilt. The lawyer or judge suffers a "willing suspension of disbelief," analogous to that undergone in entering the world of the literary imagination. His mind attends to the fiction and is untroubled by what the fiction may hide.

How far can the masking that suppresses guilt be carried? The slaveholders went so far as to speak of the slaves as transferable, no less so than kitchen furniture, but as a rule they never denied that they were alive. How far the masking goes depends on what there is a social imperative to conceal. In the case of abortion, the social pressure has been enormous and the need for socially acceptable sponsorship has been proportionately high. The famous editorial on the new ethic in *California Medicine* described the masks and their sponsors in these terms: "The very considerable semantic gymnastics which are required to rationalize abortion as anything but taking a human life would be ludicrous if they were not put forward under socially impeccable auspices." [3] The semantic solutions have not been ludicrous because of the high social status of those issuing them, and the sponsors' high social status has been a necessity for their constructions to be received as adequate cloaks.

The authors of *Techniques of Abortion*, a medical handbook on how to perform the abortion operation, observe, "Nobody wants to see or handle the fetus." [4] The observation has a general truth beyond the context of the saline method of abortion they are describing: Nobody wants to see the being who is the object of the operation. The starting point for inquiry here must be that being. Is "it" a zero, potential life, an embryo, an ovum, a product of conception, a fetus, or something else?

What is common experience on the point? *Baby* is the most usual way to refer in ordinary speech to the being a particular woman is carrying. "How is your child?" is slightly jocular. "How is your embryo" will not be asked. "How is your fetus?" is absurd. "How are your products of conception?" is beyond absurdity, as is a similar question about "your ovum." "How is your baby?" is the way a relative, a close friend, or even a doctor will inquire about the mother's perceptions of the being within. "How is my baby?" is what a mother will ask when the physician listens to the new heartbeat within her.

In law *baby* has not been generally used to designate the unborn. It has seemed, perhaps, too informal and familiar a term. In law, *child* or *unborn child* have been the expressions adopted to reflect what is most often perceived by most people if there is injury to a woman "with child" or if a bequest is willed to an unborn descendant. The vocabulary of the law prior to *The Abortion Cases* was testimony to the common understanding of the nature of the unborn.[5]

"Baby" or "child" denotes the distinctively human, and this denotation is true to reality. From the beginning of the new being there are regularly present the forty-six chromosomes that constitute the human karyotype and distinguish the human being from fish, fowl, and beast. Packed in any single set of these chromosomes is the information that makes any particular human being what he or she is in sex, pigmentation, facial structure, body height, and a thousand other details of individuation as a man or woman.[6] The information is a program not for vegetable or animal existence, but for a human life. There seems to be no reason in ordinary discourse to distinguish the embryonic stage of this program's development from the fetal stage.

As a contemporary biologist, David Epel, puts it:

> The interaction of a sperm and an egg marks a dividing line between life and death. If the two cells interact successfully and fertilization occurs, their nuclei (each containing half of the full complement of chromosomes) will combine, and the development of a new individual will begin. If successful interaction does not occur, the two cells will die within hours or at the most a few days.[7]

A leading zoologist, P. S. Timiras, writes a standard textbook, *Developmental Physiology and Aging*. She declares, "This book deals fundamentally with the physiologic changes that occur during the human life-span," and she begins with an account of the human embryo.[8] Three leading psychologists, Paul Mussen, John Congar, and Jerome Kagan, do a standard text, *Child Development and Personality*. They declare, "The life of each individual begins when a sperm cell from the father penetrates the wall of an ovum, or egg, from the mother." They compliment the wisdom of the Chinese in treating each child at birth as one year old; for, they say, the child at birth has already had many important experiences as an individual.[9]

Alan Guttmacher, before his duties as president of Planned Parenthood had altered his perspective, published an account of the process of birth, emphasizing the difference between the unborn and their mothers. The old belief that the fetus had the mother's blood, he observed, was wrong: It was "no more true than that his mother's tears fall from his eyes." Guttmacher eloquently described "the positions that the child assumes *in utero*." In his revision of the work in 1947, he spoke of "the fetus," "the human fetus," and "the child" interchangeably; he had no suspicion then that "child" needed to be purged from the language appropriate to uterine life. His book was about "creating a baby," and he wrote that "the exact moment" of such creation was fertilization.[10]

The genetic material is in interaction with its environment, affecting thereby the development of the human species. As Waddington observes, "Man in the world is like a caterpillar weaving its cocoon. The cocoon is made of threads extruded by the caterpillar itself, and is woven into a shape in which the caterpillar fits comfortably. But it also has to be fitted to the thorny twigs—the external world which supports it." As this imagery indicates, evolution does not prevent identification of caterpillar or of man.[11]

Further development will occur after birth, as development occurs in each of us until we die. The potential is mixed with the actual; but there is nothing about this kind of combination that sets off the youngest human being from the most mature. "They and they only," exclaims Coleridge, "can acquire the philosophic imagination . . . who can interpret and understand the symbol that the wings of the air-sylph are forming within the skin of the caterpillar. They know and feel that the potential works in them, even as the actual works on them!" [12] A philosopher, as much as a person of common sense, understands that life in the human womb is partly promise, partly actuality, but the promise is contained in what is already actual.

There is no reason to denominate the active new individual as pure "potential." If Mozart's entire musical corpus were put on the magnetic tape of a tape recorder, the information contained on the recorder would be the kind of information contained in a DNA molecule.[13] If all the scores and other records of Mozart's work were destroyed except for the single tape, the information on the tape would then be unique, as is the information in a DNA molecule. If someone proposed to destroy the tape, observing that, until it was played, the tape was only "potential," the linguistic ploy would scarcely be acceptable to anyone. The ploy is no more tolerable when the unique information that will be played by a new human individual is destroyed. And in the case of DNA, development does not depend upon an external stimulus; the new individual is actively organizing his or her own development.

Not only does the womb carry the uniquely human genetic program, but at a very tender age the being within has features and functions that are recognizably those of children. When, on March 6, 1978, CBS Television presented a movie of a forty-day-old heart, it was natural that the narrator should describe it as "a human heart," observe that it was already pumping blood in the body it inhabited, and remark that that heart would last as long as that individual would live. When, on May 11, 1978, CBS Television presented a movie of a seventy-day-old brain, it was natural that the narrator should describe it as "a human brain," observe that it was already in command of the body it inhabited, and remark that it would serve that individual for all of life. Before the viewer's eye was "that rarest of all things for confused and frightened human nature —the obvious." What was on the television screen were not pictures of the body of the baby's mother. Naked and visible, the human heart of the child beat to its own rhythm, and the human brain of the child made its own vital connections.

At twenty-four days the heart has regular beats or pulsations; at twenty-eight days, muscles are developing along the trunk and arms and legs are forming; at thirty days there is a regular flow of blood— the child's—within the vascular system; at forty-two days the skelton is complete; at forty-three days electrical brain impulses can be recorded; at forty-nine days there are fingers, toes, and ears.[14] At fifty-five to sixty days the child is less than one thumb's length, but everything—hands, feet, head, organs, brain—is in place.[15] As Jérome Lejeune has expressed it, "Each of us, once, was Tom Thumb in our mother's womb. We each existed in this miniature form at two months." [16]

The development continues without cease and without great

gaps. Between days sixty-three and seventy the child swallows, the lips part, the brow furrows. The child moves to avoid light or pressure. The sex of the genital tract becomes visible.[17] At seventy-five days the palms of the hands become sensitive to stimulation, as do the soles of the feet. At day seventy-seven the eyelids squint, affording protection against an outside stimulus.[18]

Until the 1970s "it was uncertain whether the child in the womb breathed." The competence of the breathing system at birth was well-established. But fetal pulmonary fluid was more viscous and dense than air. Did the child breath it? Now, through the use of ultrasound, movements of the fetal chest can be detected. It has been established that a movement like breathing is normal after four and one-half months. Such movement has been detected as early as three and one-fourth months.[19]

The child has been moving about in the womb since about eight weeks. There is room enough in the womb during the first half of pregnancy for this motion to be relatively unconstrained. Later, as the child grows, movements become more restricted.[20] By the 180th day the child in the womb has been swallowing, feeding, and urinating—the whole cycle of ingestion and excretion has been going on for weeks.[21] The child has been sleeping, moving, kicking—the whole cycle of rest and motion has begun.[22] The child if removed from the womb will weep.[23]

Summing up a lifetime of study of the unborn, Sir William Liley, a leader in modern fetology, wrote:

> The opportunity to invade fetal privacy allows an exploration of the fetal physical and sensory environment, and it is apparent that the traditional picture of a fetus as living in a dark and silent world, with blindly maturing structures in anticipation of life and function to begin at birth, is far from the reality. The development of structure and the development of function go hand in hand. Fetal comfort determines fetal positions, and fetal movement is necessary for a proper development of fetal bones and joints. The fetus is responsive to light and sound, and the inside of the uterus is far from silent and not completely dark.[24]

Do the unborn also experience pain? In a society with strong humanitarian instincts this question has a special weight and deserves special consideration. In California, for example, a newborn kitten cannot be put to death except by legislatively specified means that will spare the animal all suffering; the use of nitrogen gas to kill a cat is regulated in terms of an oxygen reduction to be reached within sixty seconds; cattle may be slaughtered for meat only if "rapid and effective" measures are taken to render them insensible before their death.[25] All of these measures of kindness are premised on the belief that even very young and even very passive animals experience pain and should, if possible, be spared it. Few, it may be presumed, would wish less for the unborn human child if that child had the capacity for suffering of a cow or a kitten.

The problem of knowing whether an animal, a baby, or an unborn child can suffer is basically the same. We cannot experience anyone else's pain. We know it only by empathy. We must be led to identify enough with the other to feel the pain. In the case of adults, language is the chief means by which we learn what they are experiencing. We are told, "I am in pain." We see that the other looks like us, we believe, and we sympathize. With babies and with animals who can scream we do not depend on language but learn to discriminate cries of fatigue or rage from cries of pain and empathize accordingly. With animals who do not scream and with the unborn, we must interpret other signs, such as wriggling, and by the context in which the sign occurs infer that pain is present. The changes in position of a baby in the womb can be interpreted, as Liley interprets them, as changes in response to discomfort. The avoidance of light by the fetus can be seen, once the pain connections are present, as a response not only of vision but of pain. Thumb sucking can be interpreted as comfort seeking. When the unborn responds, as Liley reports, to differences in the taste or flavor of amniotic fluid, we are faced with conduct which, observed in an infant after birth, would lead us to say, "The baby doesn't like the medicine." Liley himself concludes from such evidence: "The fetus is responsive to touch, pain, and cold." He means that "the fetus responds violently to painful stimuli or should I say stimuli which you and I would agree were painful, which children tell you are painful and which the newborn to judge from his responses finds painful." [26] Applied to the unborn who have reached the age of about three and one-half gestational months, his conclusion appears probable.

In each case in which we empathize we assume the presence of the physical organs necessary to apprehend pain. How these organs operate is a matter of hypothesis and not free from controversy. According to the most persuasive theory, there are a large number of sensory fibers that are receptors and transmitters, receiving information about pressure, temperature, and chemical changes at the skin and transmitting the information to the spinal column and the brain. These transmissions have both temporal and spatial patterns. They will be perceived as painful at certain levels of intensity and and duration when they are uninhibited by any modulation from the spinal column or brain. Interaction between stimuli and inhibitory controls determines what is experienced as painful. Pain itself is not a specific sensation but includes a multitude of different events with a variety of sensory and affective differences.[27]

For the unborn to experience pain, there must be sensory fibers capable of receiving and transmitting information as to temperature, pressure, or chemical change, and central connections in the nervous system capable of registering and responding to the information. Between the third and fourth month the cerebral cortex is 30 to 40 percent complete. By that time a standard authority on human developmental physiology notes the differentiation of sensory transmitters of pain. By then it may be concluded that pain can be experienced by the unborn.[28] It would be rash to deny the possibility that even much earlier, as soon as the brain is able to function at all, the unborn can know pain.

We do not remember what we felt in the womb: The nonexistence of memories can be argued to indicate either the lack of anything memorable or the suppression of what is intolerable to recall. Who can remember being born? Babies outside the womb react to all painful stimuli with about the same intensity: The uniformity of response can be argued to show that their consciousness of pain is not very discriminating or to show that many things are equally painful for them. The same alternatives exist as to the unborn. In adult pain, a large part is played by memory and interpretation and understanding of the pain's cause. These factors may magnify the pain or diminish it. For any adult, inhibition of pain by the brain has a substantial role in making it bearable. For babies, and a fortiori for the unborn, memory, anticipation, and understanding cannot affect the experience very much, and the inhibitory input will be smaller the less developed the cerebral cortex is. Babies, and a fortiori the unborn, will have a shorter range of pain but also less control of the sensory information that is perceived as painful. We cannot dismiss what babies feel. By the same token, we must conclude that the unborn, once sense transmitters are in place and central nervous connections made, are capable of pain experiences, just as are animals and other human beings.[29]

When Clement Haynsworth gave his memorable opinion in 1977

that, according to the Supreme Court, a fetus was not alive, it was the public facts of zoology and psychology which, unmentioned by him, he subordinated to the teaching of Justice Blackmun.[30] New life, different from the parents', has been there from the conjunction of chromosomes from the father and the mother. Is there any reason to deny such a living sentient creature conceived by our species a name that identifies the creature with the species? By the same token, is there reason to call such a creature "it," as if a neuter were being described? Chromosomal constitution determines sex. A fetus may be an "it." A child is a boy or a girl, and so from the beginning.

We should, it has been argued, banish "humanity" from discussions about abortion because it is "confusing terminology," and in its place we are to put "reasons to preserve life." To find humanity in a fetus, we are told, is to engage in "misplaced abstraction." [31] But humanity is a concept that causes confusion only when one does not want to face the object of an abortion, and far from being abstract, it evokes what is most concrete in the situation, the moving, sentient child. Predication of humanity is also a precondition of moral reasoning. Perception of the humanity of others is the precondition of discourse with them and about them. You cannot reason why your life should be preserved, or why another's should be. To all such thin attempts, Lear gives the only answer possible:

> O reason not the need. Our basest beggars
> Are in their poorest things superfluous.[32]

Perception of the humanity of the unborn is affected by the perspective of the perceiver. David Nathan, the medical researcher, a person of great moral sensitivity, attempting to understand the objection to experiments on the unborn undergoing an abortion, acknowledges that the objectors "believe that the fetus *is* a person"; but, although he italicizes "is," he does not keep his focus on this point. He continues, "The possibility that investigators might perform or tolerate ghastly intrauterine intrusions prior to abortion because they do not think of the fetus as a person, creates deep moral and ethical concerns." [33] Suppose the "ghastly intrauterine intrusions" were the abortions themselves? He is himself an investigator. He does not entertain the thought.

In contemporary American literature, John Updike's *Couples* catches the shift in perspective that permits even the mother of a baby to shield herself from recognizing what she is carrying:

Piet Hanema, married to Angela, has promiscuously pursued other married women, among them Foxy Whitman, who is now pregnant by him. They have this exchange:

> "All I know is what I honestly want. I want this damn thing to stop growing inside me."
> "Don't cry."
> "Nature is so stupid. It has all my maternal glands working, do you know what that means, Piet? You know what the great thing about being pregnant I found out was? It's something I just couldn't have imagined. You're never alone. When you have a baby inside you, you are not alone. It's a person." [34]

To procure the abortion it becomes necessary for Piet to surrender his own wife, Angela, to Freddy, who has access to the abortionist. Embarked upon his course Piet does not stop at this act, which destroys his own marriage irretrievably. Foxy's feelings at the time of the abortion are then described through Piet:

> Not until days later, after Foxy had survived the forty-eight hours alone in the house with Toby and the test of Ken's return from Chicago, did Piet learn, not from Freddy but from her as told by Freddy, that at the moment of anesthesia she had panicked; she had tried to strike the Negress pressing the sweet, sweet mask to her face and through the first waves of ether had continued to cry that she should go home, that he was supposed to have this baby, that the child's father was coming to smash the door down with a hammer and would stop them. [35]

The sweet, sweet mask which covers the face of the mother is necessary for the anesthesia. It is symbolic of the mask that is necessary for the mother to conceal from herself the nature of her act. At the moment when her act takes effect, she sets the mask aside and sees. The mother's masking is the counterpart of that legal mask which is necessary to disguise the identity of the being who is aborted and which, when it is removed, leaves in naked humanity the object of the operation.

On the Masks of the Liberty: The Operation

The difficulty for professionals of grasping that what they do for professional reasons may be evil is extreme. It is even difficult for them to understand that it is their own conduct which is questioned. The readers of Orwell do not suppose that they are the ones making the linguistic changes necessary for an Orwellian society.

Among the German researchers convicted at Nuremberg of experimenting on human beings without their consent was Gerhard Rose, described by the American court that convicted him as "a physician of large experience, for many years recognized as an expert in tropical diseases." [1] The research for which other German physicians were punished by the American tribunal included work to develop a vaccine for typhus, work on a vaccine for malaria, work to test a vitamin compound designed to make sea water usable in emergencies. [2] In each of these instances the research design, which included experiments on human subjects, was not framed in wanton cruelty but composed to further highly humane purposes. The principal defendant, Karl Brandt, could exclaim, "Here I am, a subject of the most frightful charges, as if I had been a man without heart or conscience. . . . Every patient was to me like a brother." [3] Gerhard Rose could observe that all medical advance depended on experiment on human beings and that in the majority of cases there was no true consent but an "exploitation of ignorance, frivolity, or economic distress." [4] He could say in good faith that he had only done what other researchers did, "to serve the good of humanity." [5] The defendant Wilhelm Beiglbock was able to invoke the words over the entrance gate of the General Hospital in Vienna, *"Saluti et solatio aegrorum*—To the health and consolation of the sick." These words, he could say, "demand the highest accomplishments of a doctor's duties" and are "the motive for the most successful work in the large field of medical work." [6] It was with this motive, he would tell his judges, that he had worked on the vitamins to transform sea water and had used human beings in his experiments. These were professional men carrying out professional tasks. They were unwilling to believe that what they had done was evil.

In our society the auspices of abortion have been "socially impeccable." Joseph Fletcher, a leading American ethician, sees as the primary objection to fetal research that it "would have a brutalizing effect on us" but answers that it has already been done "without that effect." [7] In November 1978, the *Chicago Sun-Times* published the results of an investigation the newspaper and the Better Government Association had made of abortion clinics on Michigan Avenue, in the heart of the Chicago shopping district.[8] Four of these clinics—Water Tower Reproductive Center, Biogenetics, Chicago Loop Mediclinic, and Michigan Avenue Medical Center—did over 60,000 abortions in 1977, over one-third of the abortions done that year in Illinois. Their patients included grandmothers and ten-year-olds. At the Michigan Avenue Medical Center an investigator saw an abortion performed on a screaming woman without anesthetics; in interviews "all [of these doctors' patients] recounted stories of excruciating abortions." At Biogenetics the investigators reported abortions performed by doctors who had been drinking and by moonlighting residents without experience in abortion. In the four clinics, the investigators reported, there were "dozens of abortions" performed on women who were not pregnant. Pregnancy tests had not been done or else the results had not been given the patient. Twelve percent of the abortions at Water Tower Reproductive Center, in the two months one undercover investigator observed the clinic from within, were done on women with negative pregnancy tests. "He gave me no anesthesia, not even a local. I had tears running down my cheeks. And then right in the middle of performing the abortion, he yelled to the nurse, 'This lady is not pregnant.' " So reads one victim's account. The focus of these clinics was money. (One doctor billed Medicaid in a single year for $792,000 worth of abortions.) The doctors performed abortions rapidly. A safe and relatively painless abortion requires at least fifteen minutes; postoperative recovery time should be about an hour. In these clinics, however, abortions were sometimes actually done in two minutes; recovery time, before the women were told to dress and leave, was ten to fifteen minutes. The vital signs of the women about to be operated on were sometimes not taken, sometimes faked. "Make it up," an undercover investigator was told at Michigan Avenue Medical Center. Because of "unsterile conditions and haphazard clinic care," an "alarming number of women" were found who had suffered "debilitating cramps, massive infections, and such severe internal damage that their reproductive organs had to be removed." Dead tissue left within the womb, perforated bowels, punctured uteri—these were among the ravages effected by the clinics on the patients who, unlike the objects of the operation, could speak and had come to them voluntarily. Shall one not call those who did these things brutalized?

Fletcher's claim, however, is empty not only because of these squalid medical practices. Fletcher looks for some further consequence, some further reason. He is unwilling to face the fact that abortion itself is a brutal act. Those who perform it are already brutalized as Jefferson and Wythe were brutalized in their acceptance of slavery—inured to it, willing to have it continue, able to mask it. Brutalization increases with the degree of absence of conscious guilt.

If we look at "that rarest of all things for confused and frightened human nature—the obvious," the unborn child is the object of an abortion. If the masks are to be removed, we must ask what an abortion is. Three methods are usual:

In the first trimester, dilation and curettage (D and C) is most common. The cervix is dilated and the unborn child is the subject of the curettage. The curettage is either "sharp" or "suction." Sharp curettage is by a stainless steel scraper called a curet or curette, wielded by hand. Suction curettage is by a vacuum pump with a curet attached.[9]

The method of operation in sharp curettage may be gleaned from this technical evaluation in a standard textbook, *Williams' Obstetrics,* edited by Louis Hellman, later the Deputy Assistant HEW Secretary for Population Affairs: "It is our opinion that a sharp curette is more efficacious and that its dangers are not greater than those of the dull instrument in the usual therapeutic abortion. Perforations of the uterus rarely occur on the downstroke of the curette, but may occur when any instrument is introduced into the uterus; since the knife edge of a sharp curette is directed downward, it can have no bearing on this hazard." [10] A curettage, then, is a form of cutting. If improperly used, the knife will cut the mother. Properly used, the knife will cut the unborn child.

The curet used in suction is set in a hollow tube with a moderate-size opening near the top. A glass trap is interposed between the curet and a vacuum pump. Curets used in suction can be either stainless steel or plastic. They are often sold under the name "Vacuettes." The pumps employed are specifically designed for this kind of vacuuming; a popular model is "the Berkeley aspirator." Curettage by suction is a relatively recent invention, having first been developed for use in Communist China. [11]

Here is how the process is currently practiced at the Concord Medical Center, a private outpatient clinic in Chicago:

> After anesthetic and dilation of uterus, the uterus was evacuated with a rigid plastic suction curet attached to a Berkeley aspirator. After completion of the suction curettage the uterus cavity was gently explored with a sharp curet and suction was reapplied. All tissues were sent to the pathologist for examination. [12]

Another standard medical work, *Techniques of Abortion,* may be used to supplement this description of an early abortion:

> The suction machine is turned on, and a finger is used to block the handle until a small amount of suction is obtained. . . . A vacuum is created in the uterus. [The curet is rotated.] At any point that material is felt flowing into the tube, motion is stopped until the flow stops. Then the slow up-and-down gradual rotation pattern is continued. Bloody fluid and bits of pink tissue will be seen flowing through the plastic tubing during the entire suction curettage. However, the procedure should be continued until the entire endometrial cavity is covered at least twice. . . . If no more tissue is obtained and the endometrial surface gives a consistently gritty resistance to the sharp edge of the curet, the procedure is finished. [13]

This method has not been so common in the second trimester, but it is now being used with success as this description of current practice at Detroit Memorial Hospital indicates: "The cervix was then dilated with Pratt dilators to No. 39 or No. 43. A No. 12 or No. 14 section cannula was inserted to remove the amniotic fluid and a ring forceps was used to extract fetal parts. With a sharp curet, the placenta and any additional fetal parts were removed from the uterine cavity." [14] The fetal parts referred to are the dismembered portions of the body of the unborn child, who has been cut up and vacuumed.

The most common method in the second trimester is what is known as intra-amniotic instillation. Water with a salt solution is injected by catheter into the amniotic fluid which surrounds the unborn child. The precise way in which death is then caused is not known, but two specialists in abortion offer this theory:

> In all probability, 20% sodium chloride is a chemical poison. If by accident it is injected subcutaneously, intraperitoneally, or intramyometrially, it produces exquisite and severe pain. If it is injected into the amniotic cavity, and the membranes rupture at the end of the procedure, the abortion usually still occurs on schedule. In general, no fetal heart sounds are detectable one or two hours after the procedure. Some patients begin to experience painful uterine contractions at the end of the instillation, indicating the onset of labor. . . . Intra-amniotic hypertonic saline probably exercises its effect by chemically stopping fetal and placental function and thereby initiating labor.[15]

In layman's language, the fetus is poisoned, dies within two hours, and is expelled.

Does the fetus feel the "exquisite and severe pain" which the childbearing woman may feel if an accident occurs? When the body of the child is expelled, it will be "acid-soaked." [16] Given that the saline method of abortion is typically used in the second trimester, it is not unlikely that the individual subjected to it is developed enough to feel pain.[17] Although the appreciation of sensation will not be that of a developed nervous system, it may be inferred that what is exquisite and severe for the childbearing woman will also have painful consequences for the child.

An older method for abortion, still medically sanctioned if the fetus has not reached twenty weeks, is a hysterotomy, or incision of the uterus and removal of the unborn child. The action following the incision is described in a medical textbook of the 1960s in these terms: "The index finger [the doctor's] is inserted between the sac or placenta and the uterine wall and the membranes and placenta gradually and carefully separated. The finger is not removed until it is felt that the sac and placenta are entirely free in the uterine cavity. . . . The fetus in the sac and placenta should then be spontaneously expelled in toto." [18] The death of the unborn child is caused by exposure to an environment he or she is not developed enough to function in. Death by exposure was a Greek and Roman way of killing infants. The method is here applied to the delivered child.

Current medical works do not recognize as "abortion" any method of disposing of the fetus who has reached five months. But a hysterotomy can be done. When it is performed at this age, it is not properly a hysterotomy at all, but a Caesarean delivery. It differs from such a delivery only if the continued life of the child is not desired.[19] For that result to be achieved, the child at birth must not be given the ordinary medical treatment of a preterm infant. If not given aid, he or she will choke to death, suffocate, or freeze.

The sensitivity of the pro-abortion party to language accurately reflecting these realities has been extraordinary. As was acutely observed, "Nobody would mind if you were to speak of having your appendix cut out. But they'd flinch if you spoke of having your fetus cut out. The locution would offend both reason and moral sense." [20] To avoid such offensive facing of reality, the pro-abortion party has preferred "procedures terminating a pregnancy."

A piece of research on the use of prostaglandins for abortion reflects the language preferred by workers in the field. Reflecting the joint effort of doctors at Washington University, St. Louis; at Turku University in Finland; and at Semmelweis University and Debrecen University in Hungary, encouraged by Dr. Ravenholt of AID, and "generously" supplied with the PGF^{2a} by the Upjohn Company, the experiments were a work of cooperation between an international team of medical biologists, the United States Government, and an American drug company. They were aimed at perfecting abortifacients which could be used as late as the second trimester.[21] With such sponsorship it would have been abhorrent to all involved to have reported the results under the title, "Ways of Killing Live Second-Trimester Fetuses." The title the researchers chose was "Termination of Pregnancy with Double Prostaglandin Input." Where possible they blurred the existence of the fetus by terminology such as "the fetalplacental unit." [22] They explained that, to avoid side effects to "the patient," it had seemed preferable to "use the marketed compound PGF^{2a} and focus instead on improving its delivery to the target organs." [23] That the fetus was the ultimate target organ was not stated. A military abstractness permitted the researchers to discuss lethal preparations with the coolness of Graham Greene's Dr. Percival preparing the poisoned peanuts.

But to describe abortion as killing is accurate. The verb "to kill" is universally employed to indicate intentional destruction of a living animal. One kills a chicken, a bear, a man, an infant. One also kills an unborn child.

This kind of language is uncomfortable for those who practice and those who support abortion. In their view they are already being charged with murder or complicity in murder. *To kill* evokes the soldier, the hunter, the executioner. It is difficult to imagine professional medical publications such as the *American Obstetrical and Gynecological Journal* publishing articles on "Second-Trimester Killings." By the same token, physicians performing abortions do not want to describe the use of the curet as *knifing* or the use of the saline solution as *poisoning*. These ways of killing have vivid associations with the methods of killing other living things. It is true that killing an unborn child is not *infanticide, manslaughter,* or *murder,* all terms that law and usage reserve for acts of destroying a human being who has been born. These emotional epithets are usually employed either by opponents of abortion who exaggerate the gravity of the act or by proponents of abortion caricaturing their critics, although they have also been used by such eminent authorities as Barth and Bonhoeffer, and they are appropriate to describe the acts of infanticide to which the liberty of abortion has led. Properly, they have no place in characterizing abortion itself. *To kill* is accurate and not exaggerated.

Those who have watched abortion operations and reported what they saw confirm this conclusion.

Richard Selzer, a surgeon and medical writer at Yale Medical School, had never seen an abortion. He decided to observe and describe one performed through the injection of prostaglandins into the amniotic fluid surrounding an unborn child twenty-four weeks old. His account begins with the doctor reassuring the adult patient that there will only be "a little pinprick" without further pain. A needle has been inserted. The doctors and nurses are busy. Then:

> I see something! It is unexpected, utterly unexpected, like a disturbance in the earth, a tumultuous jarring. I see something other than what I expected here. I see a movement—a small one. But I have seen it.
>
> And then I see it again. And now I see that it is the hub of the needle in the woman's belly that has jerked. First to one side. Then to the other side. Once more it wobbles, is tugged, like a fishing line nibbled by a sunfish.
>
> Again! And I know! . . .
>
> I close my eyes. I see the inside of the uterus. It is bathed in

ruby gloom. I see the creature curled upon itself. Its knees are flexed. Its head is bent upon its chest. It is in fluid and gently rocks to the rhythm of the distant heartbeat.

It resembles . . . a sleeping infant . . .

What I saw I saw as that: a defense, a motion from, an effort away. And it has happened that you cannot reason with me now. For what can language do against the truth of what I saw? [24]

The linguistic mask put aside, Selzer saw. The observations of a woman, Magda Denes, a psychologist who herself had had an abortion and later decided to study life in a New York City abortion clinic, are not dissimilar. She describes what she saw at the end of an abortion: "I look inside the bucket in front of me. There is a small naked person in there floating in a bloody liquid—plainly the tragic victim of a drowning accident. But then perhaps this was no accident, because the body is purple with bruises and the face has the agonized tautness of one forced to die too soon." She continues: "Death overtakes me in a rush of madness." She will not deny her consciousness that a life has been taken. She will not suppress her reflection that "the agony of an early death is the same anywhere," whether it is a "death factory" in Europe or an abortion clinic in New York City.[25]

Bernard Nathanson, the director of an abortion clinic in New York City, came to the same conclusion as to what was occurring in the establishment he headed. Nathanson had been a founder of the National Association for the Repeal of Abortion Laws; he had welcomed the legalization of abortion in New York; and for a year and a half he was the director of the largest abortion clinic in the world. When he resigned, he reported the impact the work had had on him and on his staff. The constant immersion in the clinic's business, he observed, had been demoralizing for the people engaged in it: "I was seeing personality structures dissolve in front of me on a scale I had never seen before in a medical situation. Very few members of the staff seemed to remain fully intact through their experiences." [26] As for himself, he declared, "[I] was deeply troubled by my own increasing certainty that I had in fact presided over 60,000 deaths." [27] Those terminations of pregnancy, which he judged as deaths, came from 60,000 acts of killing. His responsibility, which he did not evade, was for presiding over the taking of 60,000 lives.

In the fall of 1976, shortly after the events involving Dr. Floyd in South Carolina, an old and famous pediatric surgeon received the highest award in the power of his colleagues to give him, the William E. Ladd Medal for pediatric surgery of the American Academy of Pediatrics. The recipient, Everett Koop, the co-author of the Bishop–Koop operation used in the surgery attempting to save Louise's boy, chose the occasion to speak not of the death of the small black boy in South Carolina, unknown to him, but of what he did know of current medical practice in the great university teaching hospitals of the country, the hospitals that had pioneered in the care of babies prematurely born. He called his speech "The Slide to Auschwitz." [28]

"You all know," Dr. Koop said to his colleagues in the American Academy of Pediatrics, "that infanticide is being practiced right now in this country." You all know, he continued, "it is being practiced by that very segment of our profession which has always stood in the role of advocates for the lives of our children." [29] Refusing to go along, painfully recalling the silence of German scientists in another era, Dr. Koop attacked the sophistry of language that papered over what was done. "I don't mean ever," he said, "to use the words 'care' and 'kill' as being synonymous." [30]

When the mask of property was lifted from the slave, it was found that the constitutional right of property so often asserted in "its" regard was the right to sell, lend, work, mistreat, and generally dispose of a human being no different from his or her owner or the judge whose decree made this treatment possible. When the mask is lifted from the liberty of abortion, it is seen that the liberty consists in a freedom to knife, poison, starve, or choke a human being differing only in his or her degree of helplessness from the one who kills and the judge whose decree makes the killing possible.

Inquiry 19
Why the Liberty May Be Limited

Has the liberty so recently created become such a part of the American way of life that it must remain undisturbed? Have so many practices and institutions sprung up in the last five years in dependence on the liberty that they can never be uprooted? Have language and concepts been so altered by the liberty that they can never be the same? Are *The Abortion Cases* irreversible?

What the controlling language and concepts should be is still in contention. The practice of medical schools and hospitals has not changed beyond recognition. Abortion clinics, the most public manifestation of the liberty, are isolatable and could easily be closed.

If *The Abortion Cases* were put to popular vote, it is probable that they would be reversed.

One foundation of the liberty is the privacy of the carrier. The other foundation is the insubstantial character of the being trammeling the liberty. Life, Justice Blackmun informed his readers, does not begin until birth, according to the Stoics, the "predominant" attitude of Jews, and a "large segment" of the Protestant community. Life in the womb he termed "potential life." Life before seven months of pregnancy he termed a theory.[1]

When Justice Blackmun wrote his decision in January 1973, as Inquiry 5 has shown, exactly half of American women polled thought that human life began at conception. By the time an unborn child was viable and so merely "potential life" to Justice Blackmun, more than 75 percent of American women and men believed human life existed; less than 14 percent agreed with him that human life began at birth, and about 10 percent were "don't-knows."

Two years later, after Justice Blackmun's teaching had been disseminated, there had been some shifts in public opinion: 15 percent of the women and men now believed that life began at birth, but 58 percent of American women now believed human life began at conception, and 79 percent of American women *and* men thought human life existed by the time of viability. In other words, the number of "don't know" responses had been reduced, with a slight increase in the number placing the start of life at birth, and a large increase in the number of women placing it at conception.[2] As Judith Blake reported these changes, "In short, most men and women place both 'human life' and personhood early in the gestational process, and," she delicately added, "this public definition of the situation may be important in coloring attitudes toward the timing of abortion. Moreover, it is a view that is both at odds with that of the Supreme Court and at variance with what the Supreme Court believed public opinion to be."[3]

As to the abortion liberty itself, where 84 percent of married women under the age of forty-five were reported to be against it in 1970 when it was criminal, 72 percent were reported to be against it in 1975 when it was a constitutional liberty.[4] While men were less opposed to late abortion, 58 percent of all men and 61 percent of married men under forty-five were opposed to "a law which permits a woman to have an abortion even if she is more than three months pregnant."[5] Three years after *The Abortion Cases,* the great majority of the people had not accepted the liberty conferred by them.

In 1972, 67 percent of women and men opposed "elective abortion." Surveyed by Gallup in 1977 on "elective abortion"—"Do you think abortion operations should or should not be legal where the parents simply have all the children they want although there would be no major health or financial problems in having another child"— almost two-thirds (63 percent) of the women and men responding answered "No."[6] Not only did this response reject abortion on demand, it rejected abortion as favored by Planned Parenthood as a technique of population control. Not only did this response reject law permitting liberty of abortion, it rejected the American Constitution as interpreted by *The Abortion Cases:* For those cases, permitting abortion for the woman's well-being, psychologically determined, did not confine abortion to major health reasons but made it legal electively.[7]

The foundation of this solid opposition to the liberty was the experience of abortion. In a strict sense only the victim has the experience of rape, and only the unborn have the experience of abortion. Human judgment of such events, however, does not depend

on such a narrow concept of experience. By sympathetic identification with others we are able to understand the quality of an act
affecting them. By empathy we understand the suffering of others.
To have the experience of abortion you need not be aborted.

Once the characteristics of the object of an abortion are grasped
—once it is seen that the being who is destroyed is a living member
of our species—it is not hard to empathize with the unborn. They
cannot tell us what they feel, as a dog cannot speak our language.
But we are able to guess what a dog feels when he is kicked, or what
a five-month-old fetus experiences when he is soaked in acid. Empathy with the immediate sensations is the way to empathy with
the fundamental position of the small creature awaiting death.
Whether it is accompanied by physical torment or comes very early,
before sensation is developed, death itself is the fundamental experience of the unborn who are aborted. We who have been fetuses
and who will someday die can intuit what the coming of death is to
any living creature: There is, among physical evils to be suffered,
none more evil.

The experience of having an abortion can be undergone only by
a fraction of the human race, a fraction in other times and places
regarded as extraordinarily fortunate in being able to bear children;
and only a fraction of this fraction, a fraction who have given birth
and who also have undergone abortion, can speak with the authority
of those who have known both. Some women experiencing an abortion have found it "a good thing," a "relief," a "joy." [8] For some
women, even in the best hospital conditions, an abortion has been
a depressing event, "lousy," attended with deep emotion and filled
with anguish.[9] The essence of any testimony to a concrete event is
that it is personal. It is what a particular witness with particular
sensibilities has experienced from a particular perspective. Testimony as to clinical experience will always be of this anecdotal, partial, personal character. If only the testimony of women who have
undergone the experience counted, the judgment on abortion would
be in doubt, although what is strikingly apparent in a nation with
more than one million abortions a year is that only a very small
number of those having the experience are articulate in its defense.
But beyond the subjective sensations of the happening, the "experience" of an event is its meaning as it is integrated into a broader
culture.

The integration of the abortion experience into the moral culture
is the point where the battle over language becomes critical. If all

that has happened may fairly be described as "termination of a pregnancy" with "fetal wastage" the outcome, abortion may be accepted without break with the larger moral culture. If, however, such a description is a mask, if the perceptions of observers like Richard Selzer, Bernard Nathanson, and Magda Denes are accurate, if the life of an unborn child is being taken, it is difficult to reconcile the acceptance of abortion with the overarching prohibition against the taking of life.

If all that is done may fairly be described as the removal of a portion of a mother's body of no more distinctive nature than tonsils or an appendix, abortion may be accepted as another medical operation. Tonsillectomies and appendectomies involve no moral issues and no challenges to our culture. But a mother's love for her child is a central paradigm of human fidelity. If the object of the operation is her child and the end of the operation is the child's death, it is hard to reconcile what is done with the basic cultural norms of love and fidelity.

In the art of the Western world, birth has been a symbol of creativity and of hope. Central to the story of the Nativity of Jesus, it has been celebrated by artists in this context with a power that does not depend on acceptance of the Nativity story. Every human being in our culture can grasp its joyful meaning. The cultural evaluation of abortion has always been negative, in direct contrast to the evaluation of birth. In an extraordinary mural by José Orozco in the Hopkins Library at Dartmouth College, the symbolic sense of abortion, as it has been understood in common experience, has been evoked. The mural is a satire on academic pedantry. Professors, clothed in their black academic gowns, are depicted as obstetricians delivering Truth from a patient, who is Knowledge. Each child is stillborn. The collection of fetuses underlines the incompetence and the futility of the faculty. The abortuses function as the symbol of the sterility of academe. Orozco assumes that everyone understands abortion to be deathly failure.

The use of abortion as an event and a symbol is found in American literature. The symbolism reflects the judgments of a culture that finds life good, childbearing good, fidelity good. The outlook is that of Jewish thought as it is reflected in the Bible and of Christian thought as it is reflected in the Gospels and their later theological development. The values cherished—human life, childbearing, maternal fidelity—are values with religious origins, sustained by religious commitment; but they also exist, detached from their beginnings, in the assumptions and attitudes of American humanism. Although there are dark currents in this culture in the 1970s—streaks of Sartrean absurdity and Manichean hatred of procreation—the mainstream carries these values. The difficulty of reconciling them with abortion assures the eventual defeat of the abortion liberty.

The way in which abortion is regarded in this culture may be gauged by looking at those works of literature where the abortion event is central because its symbolic significance is assumed to be obvious to everyone. In Eugene O'Neill's *Abortion* the actual abortion accurs offstage with fatal consequences to child and to mother. But the focus of the play itself is upon what participation in these acts means to Jack Townsend and his family. The title *Abortion* comprehensively extends to the destruction of the family's hopes and the suicide of Jack. The failure of fruition is the meaning of the physical event and the meaning of its consequences.[10]

In Ernest Hemingway's "Hills like White Elephants" the title points to a vision of the world that cannot be recaptured after the abortion to which Jig is being pushed by her man, who doesn't "want anyone else" in addition to her. The loss of her child is a symbol for Jig of a larger loss. They can no longer have "the whole world. . . . Once they take it away, you never get it back." [11] She will never get back the aborted child, she will never get back the destroyed vision.

In Joan Didion's *Play It as It Lays,* Maria Wyeth's abortion is central to a story of human desolation. Bullied by her husband to take the life of the child who is not his, she undergoes the doctor's scraping. Later she tries "to stop thinking about what he had done with the baby. The tissue. The living dead thing, whatever you called it." She dreams of a "business proposition" involving the use of a house which will "in no way concern her." She need only supply certain information on the house's plumbing. But in the nightmare she cannot call the plumber, for she knows "all along what would be found in the pipes, what hacked pieces of human flesh."

Maria's private choice leads to a recurrent dream evoking the largest social evil of the twentieth century: " 'This way to the gas, ladies and gentlemen,' a loudspeaker kept repeating in her dreams now, and she would be checking off names as the children filed past her, the little children in the green antechamber, she would be collecting their lockets and baby rings in a fine mesh basket. Her instructions were to whisper a few comforting words to those children who cried or held back, because this was a humane operation." [12]

In John Updike's *Couples* the abortion itself is obtainable only through the crudest kind of bargained infidelity. Foxy Whitman struggles with her feelings that "it's a thing," "it's a person." The sweet, sweet mask is pressed down as she calls out that the child's father is coming. In retrospect, Updike as the author permits himself one comment: "Death, once invited in, leaves his muddy bootprints everywhere." [13]

Functioning as a symbol of sterility, of infidelity, of destruction, the killing of an unborn child is understood as evil. Its consequences are "muddy bootprints." It becomes death personified. Our writers tell us that this is the experience of our culture. Because this is our experience, in our culture the liberty can be limited.

Inquiry 20
How the Liberty May Be Limited

The most obvious way for the liberty to be limited would be for the Supreme Court, which made the error, to correct its mistake. The Court has often reversed itself, even on points where it had proclaimed its teaching to be the Constitution's. It would violate no rule, subvert no constitutional authority, create no revolutionary precedent, if the Court should simply say, "We were wrong. The Constitution does not forbid the states to protect the unborn." *Roe* v. *Wade* would go the way of *Lochner*.[1]

The difficulty is that, given the present composition of the Court, such a confession of error is unlikely to occur. In *The Abortion Funding Cases*, Justices Blackmun, Brennan, and Marshall indicated a deep, even passionate, attachment to the abortion liberty. Outvoting them on funding, the majority affirmed that the liberty itself still stood.[2] No one on the Court disagreed with Justice Powell's statement of this position. Time is necessary for adherence to the decisions of 1973 to weaken. It is unlikely that in, say, the next five years the liberty will be limited by the action of the Court itself.

The only way that the popular view of the liberty can take effect is by amendment to the Constitution. The Court has grossly misinterpreted the Constitution. As now constituted, it will not correct itself. Its error can be corrected only by an amendment restoring the power to protect unborn life.

Four times in the history of the country it has been necessary to reverse decisions of the Supreme Court by amendment of the Constitution. The first occasion was a mere decade after the adoption of the Constitution itself: In 1798 the Eleventh Amendment overruled the Court's holding in *Chisholm* v. *Georgia* [3] that a state could be sued in the federal courts by the citizen of another state.

The second time was in 1868, when the Fourteenth Amendment, providing that "all persons born or naturalized in the United States are citizens," corrected the *Dred Scott* decision of eleven years earlier denying that a slave or a slave's child could ever be an American citizen.[4] The third time, in 1913, the Sixteenth Amendment gave Congress ability to tax income, a power which the Supreme Court in *Pollock* v. *Farmers Loan and Trust Company* had denied to Congress eighteen years earlier.[5] The fourth time was within this decade, in 1971, when the Twenty-Sixth Amendment giving eighteen-year-olds the right to vote overrode *Oregon* v. *Mitchell*,[6] decided the year before. The longest time taken to correct the Court has been eighteen years, the shortest, one year. Three of the amendments restored to government powers or immunities that the Court had denied it; one amendment restored a whole class of human beings to the full protection of the laws. Each time the method of amendment operated as it had been intended by the founders to operate. Mistakes by the Supreme Court were treated as not immune from correction when "the general liberty or security of the people" was seen to be at stake.[7]

For an amendment to become law, Article V of the Constitution has provided two routes: Either two-thirds of the Senate and the House must propose the amendment, which must then be ratified by three-quarters of the states; or two-thirds of the states must make "application," upon which Congress "shall call a Convention for proposing Amendments," and any amendment proposed must then be ratified by three-quarters of the states. If the second way is taken, the "convention call" of each state need not be identical in wording or in its proposed action, but the call of each state must be on the same subject.[8] The states, in ratifying an amendment, may then act either by their legislatures or by conventions, as Congress in each case determines. The signature of the President is unnecessary for Congress to propose an amendment. The signatures of the state governors are unnecessary for the legislatures to ratify one.[9]

The first way is the way in which every amendment has in fact been adopted. The second way has never been used. It is reasonable to conclude that what has not been used in two hundred years will not be used. The second way, nonetheless, has a function. It assures that congressional indifference to an issue troubling the public can be overcome. If a number of states apply to Congress for a convention, Congress is put on notice that there is a strong popular demand for consideration of an amendment. An issue may be bottled up in a congressional committee. But when Congress sees that the operation of the second method of amendment will leave it without a say, Congress can take the issue from the committees, frame its own amendment, and put the matter to the states. The most striking instance of the process occurred in the adoption of the Seventeenth Amendment on the direct election of United States Senators. This amendment was a direct challenge to the interests of Senators elected by legislatures. Between 1893 and 1911 thirty-one States made application for a convention to propose direct election.[10] In 1911, when the number was one short of two-thirds, Congress proposed the Seventeenth Amendment. In this fashion, the second method of amendment functioned to spur a retrograde Senate to act.

The second method has become of great importance in the struggle over abortion. Two committees—the Subcommittee on Constitutional Amendments of the Committee of the Judiciary of the Senate, and the Subcommittee on Constitutional and Civil Liberties of the Committee of the Judiciary of the House—held hearings on constitutional amendments in 1975. Both committees failed to report out an amendment for action by Congress. Anti-abortion groups turned in 1977 to the states. By July 1978, thirteen states—Arkansas, Indiana, Delaware, Kentucky, Louisiana, Massachusetts, Missouri, Nebraska, New Jersey, Pennsylvania, Rhode Island, South Dakota, and Utah—had adopted resolutions calling for a convention to adopt an amendment on abortion.[11]

The diversity of the petitioners was striking evidence of the strength of the dissatisfaction with the Court—two New England states which in their regular voting were heavily Democratic and socially liberal; three mid-Atlantic states, of which two were urban, politically divided, and socially progressive; two populous Midwestern states considered to be centrist in political philosophy; one deeply Republican farm state and the farm state that had produced George McGovern; one Southeastern state, one Southwestern state; and one Southern state; and one Western state. Given the variety of political, ethnic, religious, and cultural factors reflected in these thirteen states, there was reason to think that if the call to a convention on abortion appealed to them, it would appeal to the requisite two-thirds of the states. Such was the determined opposition (the proposal did not have the untroubled sailing of the eighteen-year-old vote), that adoption by thirteen states in less than two years was a rapid response; and because the opposition was articulate, congressmen from the petitioning states could scarcely doubt that the will of their states had been elicited on *The Abortion Cases.* As this book went to press, action was pending in a dozen other states.[12] The desired effect upon Congress was in range of accomplishment within four years.

The major grassroots organization against abortion, the National Right to Life Committee, did not at first support the convention drive. It believed that the effort was diversionary and that it distracted attention from Congress where the main action had to be accomplished. But in July 1978, responding to the success of the strategy and seeing its tactical value, Right to Life endorsed this approach.

The pro-choice adherents fought the movement with determination. Conscious of the unpopularity of their position, they devised a strategy of fear. A convention, they contended, would be a Pandora's Box that could cause the whole Constitution to be looked at and revised. The Bill of Rights, they cried, was itself in jeopardy.[13]

Although the press proved willing to repeat and to support this argument, it was hard for any serious student of the Constitution to believe. The states were given power to make application for a convention. Their applications specified the subject. It was unreasonable to say that the convention could be held on subjects which they had not mentioned. The classic explanation of Article V was James Madison's: "It guards equally against that extreme facility which would render the Constitution too mutable; and that extreme difficulty which might perpetuate its discovered faults." [14] If the only way of correcting an error by the application of the states was a convention capable of changing the whole Constitution, then Article V had "that extreme difficulty" which would perpetuate discovered faults. As Madison noted, the article "equally enables the general and the state governments to originate the amendment of errors as they may be pointed out by the experience on one side or the other." [15] If the state governments could "originate the amendment of errors" only by asking to alter the entire document, their power of amendment was almost illusory. A special committee of the American Bar Association, appointed to examine Article V conventions, unanimously reported in 1973 that a convention could be limited to a single topic.[16] The contention that the Constitution was in danger when an error was addressed in this way was little better than a hoax.

A much more substantial question was, How should an amendment read? It was this fundamental question that required serious attention and the concentration of the most disinterested thought.

In framing an amendment, several principles and their consequences are evident. First, the Constitution is not a criminal code. Therefore, neither the detail nor the preciseness appropriate to a criminal code are appropriate to it. The great phrases of the Constitution, "due process of law," "equal protection of the laws," "freedom of speech, or of the press" would not pass muster in a criminal statute. Their amplitude is suited to the basic charter of our government.

Second, the Constitution is not addressed to persons of bad will, but to persons—judges, legislators, officeholders, citizens—who want to abide by its provisions. Therefore, it is neither necessary nor desirable to draft with an eye to silly, sophistical, or evasive interpretations. No language can be made foolproof. There is no language that cannot be distorted by evil men or inverted by clever men. It is not hard to show the vulnerability of any form of words to ingenious and unsympathetic interpretation. As the Constitution is not addressed to the wicked or the foolish, so it is not addressed to the sophistical. The Constitution, and any amendment to it, speak to the understanding of those who with good will seek to comprehend the purposes of its framers.

A third principle is this: The Constitution is not self-executing. It sets a framework in which power may be exercised. Therefore, it is wrong to suppose that any controversy is settled by the Constitution. The Constitution must be executed by the government, observed by legislators, interpreted by judges, and responded to by the people. In these acts of interpretation and response to the written document, the document gives direction, but the addressees as living human beings have power and will, responsibility and discretion. Opponents of abortion have hoped that, once an amendment was enacted, their work would be done and the status of the unborn forever put beyond the vicissitudes of political debate and judicial interpretation.[17] But whatever form the amendment takes, its enactment would be only a first step—a momentous step—toward limitation of the liberty of abortion. Ahead would lie a thousand problems of implementation. It would be a mistake to seek an amendment so absolute that these problems could be eliminated. No language is capable of achieving a result that depends not only on the communication but on the persons addressed.

One approach, adopted by Senator James Buckley and eight other Senators, was to propose an amendment defining "person" as it is used "with respect to the right to life" in the Fifth and Fourteenth Amendments. Their draft provided that "person" in these contexts "applies to all human beings, including their unborn offspring at every stage of their biological development, irrespective of age, health, function, or condition of dependency." [18] The intent was to give the unborn equality with adult human beings so far as protection of their lives under these amendments was concerned.

Justice Blackmun had treated the unborn as zeros prior to viability and as "potential life" thereafter, and he had balanced the liberty of the gravida against these non-beings. If the Constitution itself defined the unborn as persons, the proposers of the amendment thought, the Court could not strike a balance that put their right to live below the convenience of the childbearer. In addition, their draft gave Congress and the states "power to enforce this Article by appropriate legislation within their respective jurisdictions." And it provided one exception when the article would not apply: "when a reasonable medical certainty exists that continuation of the pregnancy will cause the death of the mother."

The difficulty with this approach was that it remitted to the Supreme Court, initially likely to be unsympathetic to its purpose, the striking of the appropriate balance between the unborn and the childbearer. Neither the Fifth nor the Fourteenth Amendment as affected by the proposed Amendment would itself outlaw abortion. If a state did restore its old abortion law, the proposed amendment would compel the Supreme Court to uphold the law. But if a state did choose not to restore its old law or did choose to enact a lax abortion statute, then a court, and ultimately the Supreme Court, would have to be resorted to by a guardian for the unborn objecting to the absence of full protection for his wards. Assuming good faith implementation of the amendment by the Court, the task of remedying this situation was left to the Court. Would it, could it, order a legislature to pass a criminal abortion statute and prosecutors to prosecute under it? Would it simply enjoin all abortions except those necessary to save the mother's life? The proposed amendment, if it were to work, required a Court at least as determined to prevent evasion as the Court had been in enforcing desegregation. Given the composition of the Court, this was not a very realistic requirement.

The difficulty could be met by an additional section, which other congressmen in fact proposed: "No person shall take the life of any other person." [19] The supplement would have an effect analogous to that of the Thirteenth Amendment, which abolished slavery completely, except penal servitude for a crime, and gave Congress power to enact law operating directly on the acts of individuals.[20] With this addition Congress itself could outlaw abortion.

The advantage of this approach was that it offered a national solution for a national issue. If it were taken, Congress could enact an abortion statute. States could be prevented from turning themselves into abortion havens. The Supreme Court, having set a federal standard of unrestricted liberty in *The Abortion Cases,* would be answered, if Congress acted, by a federal standard of protection.

The difficulty with this approach was that, if a national standard of protection were enacted, the law would work a substantial change in duty and power within our federal system of government. The states have always had the responsibility of protecting life within their boundaries. Even in the 1930s, when lynching seemed capable of control only by federal law, the nation did not take from the states their duty to preserve life. Now, to correct a bad decision by the Supreme Court, it was proposed to disturb the fundamental distribution of power.

A corollary of this approach was that capital punishment by the states would probably be outlawed by the words, "No person shall take the life of any other person." The text defined "person" as "any human being" where the right to life was at stake. The words embraced the criminal as well as the child; and action by the state taking the life of either was forbidden. It was consistent for the defenders of life to oppose capital punishment; it was not clear that a single amendment should deal with subjects otherwise so diverse as capital punishment and abortion.

There was a further difficulty. The single exception for life-saving abortion was parallel to the single exception for imprisonment in the Thirteenth Amendment. But the recognition of any exception invited debate as to whether there should be more. Congress had written four exceptions into the 1977 law restricting the federal funding of abortion.[21] A draft amendment carrying one exception invited Congress to add the health, rape, and incest exceptions. Yet the Constitution did not seem to be the right place to draw such exact and particular lines.

There was a fourth difficulty, intimated already in the statement of the third. It was a matter of power. In the voting on federal funding of abortion, the Senate had shown itself strongly opposed to an almost absolute restriction on abortion funding. It was improbable that the Senate would be more amenable to an almost absolute restriction on the abortion liberty.

The Thirteenth Amendment was possible to enact after an actual war. One side no longer had effective representation. But now there had been and would be no war. There had been no substantial change in the power of the two sides in conflict. It would be remarkable if the opponents of abortion could achieve as sweeping a victory as the opponents of slavery. An amendment with hope of effect had to be framed so that it would have a hope of adoption.

If the path of an amendment defining "person" in the Fourteenth Amendment led back to interpretation by the Supreme Court, and if the path of empowering Congress to enact a national law was unlikely to be taken, one other path was open. It was to restore to both the national and the state governments the power taken from them by *The Abortion Cases*. An amendment to this effect read:

> The Congress within its jurisdiction, and the States within their respective jurisdictions, shall have power to protect life, including the unborn, at every stage of biological development, irrespective of age, health, or condition of dependency.[22]

Such an amendment was drafted by the author of this book, and submitted by Senator Burdick to the Senate Subcommittee on Constitutional Amendments of the Committee on the Judiciary. There it came to a tie vote, receiving the highest number of votes of any amendment but, by virtue of the tie, failing of adoption by the subcommittee.

From the perspective of the opponents of the unrestricted liberty there was one difficulty in this language. Under it, a state had no obligation to protect the unborn. A state legislature could enact a lax abortion statute. The absence of a national standard meant that the unborn would be more or less protected depending on the accident of jurisdiction.[23]

This difficulty could be mitigated. It could be mitigated by Congress exercising the power the amendment confers on it. That power extends to all matters within federal jurisdiction. The jurisdiction includes the territories, the military enclaves, the income tax, excise taxes, the mails, interstate commerce, and welfare. Exercising its power over these realms after adoption of the amendment, Congress would be in a position to impose formidable restraints upon, or disincentives to, abortion, without enacting a national abortion statute. The instinct of those who want a national approach is right in recognizing that, in modern America, there tends to be standard conduct throughout the country. It does not have to be achieved by a national criminal statute.

A more subtle difficulty remained. Did not the proposed Amendment reflect a kind of indifferentism regarding the fundamental issue, as though it did not matter whether or not a state chose to protect life? Was there not inconsistency in objecting to abortion as the taking of life and then proposing an amendment which let the people of a state take life if they voted to do so? These questions, hard to answer if abstracted from the context of American government, did not acknowledge the limitations intrinsic to the federal system. There was a great difference between a "don't care" attitude and respect for the distribution of governmental power made by the Constitution.

To be for federalism is not to be for the evils which federalism may leave untouched. The famous Lincoln–Douglas debates of 1858 illustrate the difference. Douglas was for states' rights on slavery, holding that the federal power should not override each state's own determination of whether it was free or slave. He also professed himself indifferent as to the choice each state made: In Lincoln's paraphrase of his position, "He cares not whether slavery is voted down or voted up." Lincoln had precisely the same view of states' rights on the issue: The federal power should not in peacetime determine the question for the states. But he was convinced that slavery was a "political, social, and moral evil" and that the right choice of each state would be to end slavery. Douglas's indifference, he observed, was equivalent to "blowing out the moral lights around us." [24]

Lincoln believed in the self-government of states within the federal system, but, trusting in the moral lights around us, he also believed it unnecessary for the national government to extirpate the evil of slavery in the states where it was established. Committed to the proposition that slavery was an evil, he saw that eventually freedom must spread throughout the land. His respect for federalism could never be confused with the "don't care" philosophy of Douglas.

The case is similar to that of abortion: Although it is a political, social, and moral evil, the federal system should not be distorted to overcome it. An amendment respecting the limitations of the system but restoring power to the states to act will be sufficient as long as our moral lights are not extinguished. No doubt, if an amendment were passed, there would be states where the liberty of abortion would exist largely undiminished. In the long run, if the opposition to abortion is grounded in human experience, those state legislatures that were lax in permitting abortion would be repudiated. Before January 22, 1973, no state granted the unrestricted liberty of abortion. If the people again had power to decide, it is highly probable that none of them would grant it now; and the people of the states that failed to give the unborn full protection would, eventually, come to see that they were tolerating the intolerable.

In the meantime, in such states the lives of the unborn would be taken. But if this kind of amendment is not adopted, the lives of the unborn will be taken in all the states. The opponents of the unrestricted liberty do not possess the power to pass a national outlawing of abortion. For them to insist on such an amendment is to accept the status quo created by Justice Blackmun.

A state court, under the proposed amendment, would be able to interpret any phrase in its own state constitution to outlaw abortion. No state court had done so before *The Abortion Cases,* but as some courts have shown a marked sympathy to abortion—e.g., the Supreme Judicial Court of Massachusetts—the possibility is a live one that a state constitution would be the last refuge of the abortion liberty.[25] It is therefore necessary to add a clause to the proposed amendment, so that it reads as follows:

"The Congress within its jurisdiction, and the states within their respective jurisdictions, shall have power to protect life, including the unborn, at every stage of biological development, irrespective of age, health, or condition of dependence, and notwithstanding any other state or federal constitutional provision."

The last additional eight words remove the danger, as well as removing any ambiguity that could be created by the adoption of the Equal Rights Amendment.

Such are the possible ways of limiting the liberty. While all the ways have difficulties, the last has the least. The proposed amendment overrules the holding of the Supreme Court in *The Abortion Cases.* Under the amendment, Congress in its jurisdiction, and the states within their borders, are empowered by the Constitution to protect life, born or unborn. No court can negate this negation by holding offspring of early gestational age to be "not unborn." There are only two classes of discrete life, the born and the unborn; the amendment embraces both.

The proposed amendment conforms to an established pattern in which a decision of the Supreme Court is overruled by constitutional correction. Empowering the law to protect life, it creates the expectation that life will be protected. Restoring to the states the power taken from them by the Supreme Court, it gives the state legislatures the opportunity to shape the protection of life. Denying that abortion is solely a private choice, it returns to the community the power to defend the family structure centered on the child. Returning to the people what was taken from them by the vote of seven men, it gives to all men and women the safeguarding of the lives of future generations.[26]

Inquiry 21
Why the Liberty Must Be Limited and Surpassed

Twenty inquiries have explored the nature of the liberty of abortion and its boundaries, its jurisprudential and constitutional context, its political constituencies, its legends, and its dynamism. Its impact on the legal structure of the family, on the practice of medicine, on the political process itself have been observed. It is time to gather in one place the conclusions these inquiries support.[1]

First. The liberty established by *The Abortion Cases* has no foundation in the Constitution of the United States. It was established by an act of raw judicial power. Its establishment was illegitimate and unprincipled, the imposition of the personal beliefs of seven justices on the women and men of fifty states. The continuation of the liberty is a continuing affront to constitutional government in this country.

No "discrete and insular minority" can feel secure when its constitutional existence may be affected by the exercise of such raw power. And we are all members of discrete and insular minorities, depending on the criterion employed to set up the categories. The population may be divided a thousand ways to suit the preferences of the judges, who have power to define who is a person, who have even power to declare who is alive. If it becomes settled that it is the Supreme Court's will that confers personhood and existence, no one is safe.

Second. The Abortion Cases rest on serious errors. They invoke history but mistakenly assert that the historical purpose of American abortion laws was the protection of the health of the gravida. They invoke medical standards but mistakenly treat abortion as a procedure medically acceptable after the fifth month. They appeal to Holmes's criterion of liberty and in fact apply the contrary criterion of *Lochner*. They invoke the freedom of women but ignore what American women believe and want. They claim not to decide when human life begins and in fact decide that human life begins at birth. Their multiple errors of history, medicine, constitutional law, political psychology, and biology require their erasure.

Third. The liberty established by *The Abortion Cases* is destructive of the structure of the family. It sets up the carrier as autonomous and isolated. It separates her from her partner in procreation. It separates her when she is a minor from her parents. It is destructive of the responsibility of parents for their daughters. It is destructive of a father's responsibility for his offspring. Its exercise is the reverse of a mother's care of her offspring. Its exercise is a betrayal of the most paradigmatic of trusts, that which entrusts to a mother the life of her helpless child.

Fourth. The liberty is oppressive to the poor. Its existence has led to depriving the pregnant poor of assistance for their dependent unborn children. Its existence has intensified the pressure on the poor to destroy their unborn children. The obligation of the government is to aid the disadvantaged by social assistance and economic improvement; the liberty transforms this responsibility to the poor into a responsibility to reduce poverty by reducing the children of the poor.

Fifth. The liberty violates the ethic of Western medicine from Hippocrates to the present. It narrows the service of the obstetrician from caring for two patients, mother and child, to caring for one. The doctor's duty to preserve every human life he touches is converted into a duty to take human lives. He is turned from a healer in all seasons to a bringer of death on occasion.

Sixth. The liberty divides the country. Never before has the nation been split on who shall live and who shall die. Only once before has it been split on who was to be respected as a person and who was not. The present division has not been brought about by the defenders of the lives of the unborn. They adhere to the law and traditions of our people as they were understood for almost two hundred years, until January 22, 1973. The division has been brought about by the abortion liberty and the aggressive actions on its behalf. It is the abortion liberty which has fanned religious animosity by setting Protestants against Catholics, secularists against believers. It is the abortion liberty which has assaulted the structure of the family, setting daughter against mother and father, wife against husband, mother against unborn child. It is advocates of abortion who have made the liberty of abortion part of the ideology of the emancipation of women. It is expounders of the liberty who say men and women are not partners in procreation and make a woman a solo entity and the sole judge of whether jointly conceived offspring shall live or die.

Seventh. The liberty encourages the coercion of conscience. Already it has led college administrators to force students to pay for acts the students believe to be the killing of human beings. Already it has led judges to order communities to pay for actions the communities believe are evil. Already it has permitted governors to disregard the consciences of their citizens and force them to finance abortions repugnant to their consciences. In the view of a philosopher of the pro-abortion party, a conscientious opponent of abortion should be made to perform an abortion with his own hands. In the view of the American Civil Liberties Union, that custodian of the American conscience, the hospitals of those who abhor abortion should be commandeered for their performance. In the view of the counsel for Planned Parenthood, a doctor who fails to advise an abortion is open to the charge of practising sectarian medicine. In the view of the counsel for an ACLU affiliate, a mayor who enforces a law regulating an abortion clinic may be personally liable in damages. The dynamism of the liberty does not allow for neutrality. He or she who does not conform must be made to cooperate.

Eighth. Implementation of the liberty has subverted other parts of the Constitution in addition to the Ninth and Fourteenth Amendments, which were specifically distorted by *The Abortion Cases*. The organic distribution of powers made by Article I has been violated. A federal court has ordered the federal government to pay money not appropriated by Congress, in violation of the constitutional command that "no money shall be drawn from the Treasury, but in Consequence of Appropriations made by Law." The Treasury has complied, paying out large sums for elective abortions for which no congressional appropriation existed.

Ninth. The liberty has fostered a sinister and Orwellian reshaping of our language in which "child" no longer means child in the womb; the unborn dead have become fetal wastage; a dying infant has become a fetus *ex utero;* pregnancy has come to mean abortion; and new human life within a mother has been officially declared to be not alive.

Tenth. The liberty has led to the use of the unborn child and the dying infant for experiments. The experiments have not been for their benefit. Without their consent, the unborn child and the infant dying after an abortion have been utilized for the benefit of others. In disregard of the great codes of medical ethics, the Nuremberg Code, the Oath of Geneva, and the Declaration of Helsinki, they have been treated as disposable; and the liberty has permitted their classification and use as things.

Eleventh. The liberty has diminished the care due a child capable of life outside the womb if the child is marked for abortion. The acts of the physician affecting that child's life before birth have been shielded from inquiry. Whether such child had been born alive has been made a matter of cursory examination. The practice in our great teaching hospitals has been denounced by a leading pediatric surgeon as the practice of infanticide. A philosopher has argued for the complete acceptance of infanticide. Lawyers and judges have assaulted the laws protecting the infant outside the womb.

Twelfth. The liberty of abortion has caused a very high loss of human life. The liberty of abortion is acting as its proponents expected it to act: It is reducing the birthrate by increasing the number of abortion deaths. The loss of human life now annually attributable to the liberty in the United States is in the hundreds of thousands. More than one million have died through the exercise of the liberty. No plague, no war has so devastated the land.

There must be a limit to a liberty so mistaken in its foundations, so far-reaching in its malignant consequences, and so deadly in its exercise. There must be a surpassing of such liberty by love.

Notes

Inquiry 1. On the Nature of the Present Conflict and Its Resolution

1. Alexis de Tocqueville, *Democracy in America,* trans. Francis Bowen, rev. trans. Philippe Bradley (New York: Knopf, 1945), v. 1, 280.
2. Walter Jackson Bate, *Samuel Johnson* (New York: Harcourt Brace Jovanovich, 1977), 405.
3. André Malraux, *The Voices of Silence,* trans. Stuart Gilbert (Garden City, N.Y.: Doubleday, 1953), 74–75.

Inquiry 2. On the Creation of the Constitutional Liberty of Abortion

1. William Blackstone, *Commentaries on the Laws of England* (London, 1765) book 1, ch. 1, 125–126, and book 4, ch. 14.
2. Robert A. Destro, "Abortion and the Constitution," *California Law Review* 63 (1975): 1250, 1267–1273. See also Inquiry 15.
3. James C. Mohr, *Abortion in America: The Origins and Evolution of National Policy, 1800–1900* (New York: Oxford University Press, 1978), 200.
4. *Ibid.,* 301. A peculiarity of Mohr's *Abortion in America* is to speak at times as though "laws" in the United States did not include the common law—e.g., "In the period from 1880 to 1900 the United States completed its transition from a nation without abortion laws of any sort to a nation where abortion was legally and officially proscribed" (226). In fact, as he says on the opening page of his book, page 3, abortion after quickening, "late in the fourth or early in the fifth month," was a common-law crime in the United States.

5. *Ibid.,* 200.

6. Destro, "Abortion and the Constitution," 1273–1278.

7. See David W. Louisell and John T. Noonan, Jr., "Constitutional Balance," in John T. Noonan, Jr., ed., *The Morality of Abortion* (Cambridge: Harvard University Press, 1970), 225.

8. *Red Lion Broadcasting Co.* v. *FCC,* 395 U.S. 367 (1969).

9. *Gideon* v. *Wainwright,* 372 U.S. 335 (1963).

10. *Lochner* v. *New York,* 198 U.S. 45 (1905).

11. *Bunting* v. *Oregon,* 243 U.S. 426 (1917).

12. *Roe* v. *Wade,* 410 U.S. 113 at 153 (1973).

Inquiry 3. On the Full Dimensions of the Liberty

1. *Roe* v. *Wade,* 410 U.S. 113 at 153–154.

2. See *ibid.* at 153, where the liberty is described as "a woman's decision."

3. *Ibid.* at 163. At 164 the Court phrased the liberty in terms of "the medical judgment of the pregnant woman's attending physician," but this way of putting it seems to mean no more than that a woman could not make a doctor perform an abortion against his medical judgment; she had to find a physician willing to act.

4. *Ibid.* at 164.

5. *Ibid.* at 162.

6. *Ibid* at 163.

7. *Ibid.* at 163.

8. *Ibid.* at 164.

9. *Doe* v. *Bolton,* 410 U.S. 179 at 192.

Inquiry 4. On the Jurisprudence of the Liberty

1. Hans Kelsen, *The Pure Theory of Law,* trans. Max Knight from 2d ed. (Berkeley: University of California Press, 1967), 95.

2. *Ibid.,* 94.

3. *Ibid.,* 95.

4. *Ibid.,* 113.

5. See John T. Noonan, Jr., "Virginian Liberators," in *idem, Persons and Masks of the Law* (New York: Farrar, Straus & Giroux, 1976), 46–64.

6. *The Antelope,* 10 Wheat. 66 (1825). Key's argument is at 70–79. For

a full discussion of the case, see John T. Noonan, Jr., *The Antelope* (Berkeley: University of California Press, 1977).

7. *Ibid.* at 121.

8. *Dred Scott* v. *Sanford,* 19 How. 393 (1857).

9. *Meyer* v. *Nebraska,* 262 U.S. 390 (1923).

10. *Ibid.* at 402.

11. *Pierce* v. *Society of Sisters,* 268 U.S. 510 (1925).

12. *Ibid.* at 535.

13. *Skinner* v. *Oklahoma,* 315 U.S. 535 (1942).

14. *Ibid.* at 541.

15. *Ibid.* at 546.

16. *Griswold* v. *Connecticut,* 381 U.S. 479 at 485.

17. *Ibid.* at 486.

18. *Loving* v. *Virginia,* 388 U.S. 1, 12 (1967).

19. *Byrn* v. *New York City Health and Hospitals Corp.,* 329 N.Y.S. 2d 722 (1971).

20. *Byrn* v. *New York City Health and Hospitals Corp.,* 31 N.Y. 2d 194, 286 N.E. 2d 887 (1972); appeal dismissed, 410 U.S. 940 (1973).

21. *Ibid.* at 889.

22. *Ibid.* at 893.

23. See the classic essay by Edward S. Corwin, "The 'Higher Law' Background of American Constitutional Law," *Harvard Law Review* 42 (1928): 149, 365.

24. *Roe* v. *Wade,* 410 U.S., 113, 162.

25. See *Doe* v. *Israel,* 358 F. Supp. 1193 (D.R.I., 1973).

26. *Ibid.* at 1197.

27. On appeal, the case was affirmed by the First Circuit Court of Appeal, 482 F.2d 156, and certiorari was denied by the Supreme Court, 416 U.S. 993 (1974).

28. William Blackstone, *Commentaries on the Laws of England* (London, 1765), book I, ch. 14, 411–412.

29. *United States* v. *Carolene Products Co.,* 304 U.S. 144 at 152, n. 4 (1938).

Inquiry 5. On the Constitutional Foundation of the Liberty

1. Philip B. Heymann and Douglas E. Barzelay, "The Forest and the Trees: *Roe* v. *Wade* and Its Critics," *Boston University Law Review* 53 (1973): 765, 769.

2. *Meyer* v. *Nebraska,* 262 U.S. 390 (1923).

3. *Pierce* v. *Society of Sisters,* 268 U.S. 510 (1925).

4. *Skinner* v. *Oklahoma,* 315 U.S. 535 (1942).

5. *Griswold* v. *Connecticut,* 381 U.S. 479 (1965).

6. *Loving* v. *Virginia,* 388 U.S. 1 (1967).

7. *Eisenstadt* v. *Baird,* 405 U.S. 438 (1972).

8. Heymann and Barzelay, "The Forest and the Trees," at 772.

9. See Inquiry 10.

10. 381 U.S. 479 at 485 (1965).

11. 405 U.S. 438, 453 (1972).

12. Laurence H. Tribe, "Foreword to the Supreme Court—1972 Term: Toward a Model of Roles in the Due Process of Life and Law," *Harvard Law Review* 87 (1973): 20–23.

13. *Ibid.,* 21.

14. Laurence H. Tribe, *American Constitutional Law* (Mineola, N.Y.: Foundation Press, 1978), 928.

15. Michael J. Perry, "Abortion, the Public Morals, and the Police Power: The Ethical Function of Substantive Due Process," *U.C.L.A. Law Review* 23 (1976): 689, 706.

16. *Ibid.,* 735.

17. *Ibid.,* 721.

18. *Ibid.,* 726.

19. *Ibid.,* 728.

20. *Ibid.,* 730, 731.

21. *Lochner* v. *New York,* 198 U.S. 45 (1905).

22. *People* v. *Lochner,* 177 N.Y. 145, 69 N.E. 373 (1904).

23. *Lochner* v. *New York,* 198 U.S. at 53 and 61.

24. *Ibid.* at 57.

25. *Ibid.* at 76 (dissenting opinion).

26. *Baldwin* v. *Missouri,* 281 U.S. 586, 595 (1930).

27. *Adams* v. *Tanner,* 244 U.S. 590 (1917).

28. *Burns Baking Co.* v. *Bryan,* 264 U.S. 504, 517 (1924).

29. Felix Frankfurter, "Mr. Justice Brandeis and the Constitution," *Harvard Law Review* 45 (1931): 33 at 58.

30. *Ferguson* v. *Skrupa,* 372 U.S. 726 (1963).

31. *Dandridge* v. *Williams,* 397 U.S. 471, 484 (1970).

32. Archibald Cox, *The Role of the Supreme Court in American Government* (New York: Oxford University Press, 1976), 113, 114.

33. Alexander M. Bickel, *The Morality of Consent* (New Haven: Yale University Press, 1975), 28.

34. *Ibid.,* 29.

35. *Ibid.,* 27.

36. Richard Epstein, "Substantive Due Process by Any Other Name: The Abortion Cases," *Supreme Court Review* (1973), 159 at 162.

37. *Roe* v. *Wade,* 410 U.S. 113 at 148–149, 151. On the history involved, see Inquiry 7.

38. Epstein, "Substantive Due Process," at 168.

39. *Ibid.* at 175–176.

40. *Ibid.* at 176–177.

41. *Ibid.* at 182.

42. *Ibid.* at 184.

43. Harry Wellington, "Common Law Rules and Constitutional Double Standards," *Yale Law Journal* 83 (1973): 221 at 301.

44. *Ibid.* at 301.

45. *Ibid.* at 302.

46. *Ibid.* at 303.

47. *Ibid.* at 311.

48. John Hart Ely, "The Wages of Crying Wolf: A Comment on *Roe* v. *Wade,*" *Yale Law Journal* 82 (1973): 920 at 947.

49. *Ibid.* at 946.

50. The strongest modern expression of this viewpoint is Raoul Berger, *Government by Judiciary* (Cambridge: Harvard University Press, 1977). Berger, however, does not deal with *Roe* v. *Wade* explicitly. His criteria are applied to *The Abortion Cases* by Robert A. Destro, "Some Fresh Perspectives on the Abortion Controversy", *Human Life Review,* Spring 1978, 27–32.

51. For other keen criticism, see Joseph O'Meara, Jr., "Abortion: The Court Decides a Non-Case," *Human Life Review,* Fall 1975, 17; Joseph W. Dellapenna, "Nor Piety nor Wit: The Supreme Court on Abortion," *Columbia Human Rights Law Review* 6 (1974): 379; Charles E. Rice, "Dred Scott Case of the Twentieth Century," *Houston Law Review* 10 (1973): 1059; Robert M. Byrn, "Wade and Bolton: Fundamental Legal Errors and Dangerous Implications," *Catholic Lawyer* 19 (1973): 243.

52. See *Roe* v. *Wade,* 410 U.S. 113 at 222 (White, J., dissenting).

Inquiry 6.   On the Political Constituencies of the Liberty

1. Finley Peter Dunne, *Mr. Dooley on Ivrybody and Ivrything,* ed. Robert Hutchinson (New York: Dover Publications, 1963), 160.

2. Alaska, Arkansas, California, Colorado, Delaware, Georgia, Hawaii, Kansas, Maryland, Mississippi, New Mexico, New York, North Carolina, Oregon, South Carolina, and Virginia changed their laws by legislation. Charles H. Young, "A Survey of the Present Statutory and Case Law on Abortion: The Contradictions and the Problems," *University of Illinois Law Forum* (1972), 179. For the Washington action by referendum in 1970, see 181. For Massachusetts, see the dictum in *Kudish* v. *Board,* 356 Mass. 98, 248 N.E. 2d 264 (1964). *Alabama Code,* 14, sec. 9 (1958), permitted abortion for the health of the mother.

3. *Ibid.,* 179–180.

4. *New York Times,* May 14, 1972, 1.

5. Robert A. Destro, "Abortion and the Constitution," *California Law Review* 53 (1975): 1250, 1337–1338.

6. E.g., *Georgia Statutes Annotated,* sec. 25–1202(c), 1972.

7. Judith Blake, "The Supreme Court's Abortion Decisions and Public Opinion in the United States," *Population and Development Review* 3 (1977): 52.

8. *Ibid.,* 52.

9. *Ibid.,* 54.

10. The present author writes from personal experience as a law student in the 1950s and a law professor in the 1960s. In the words of Robert E. Hall, President of the Association for the Study of Abortion, "A few years ago 'abortion' was a dirty word. Everyone knew it existed, but almost no one wanted to talk about it." Hall, "Commentary," in David E. Smith, ed., *Abortion and the Law* (Cleveland: Case Western Reserve University Press, 1967), p. 224.

11. Madeleine Simms, "Abortion—A Note on Some Recent Developments in Britain," *British Journal of Criminology* 4 (1964): 493.

12. American Law Institute, *Model Penal Code: Proposed Official Code* (1962), sec. 230.

13. E.g., Harold Rosen, "Psychiatric Implications of Abortion: A Case Study in Social Hypocrisy," in Smith, ed., *Abortion and the Law,* 72–106.

14. Alan Guttmacher, "Abortion Laws Make Hypocrites of Us All," *New Medical Materia* 4 (1956): 56; Robert E. Hall, "Commentary," 234; Frank Lorimer, "Issues of Population Policy" in Philip M. Hauser, ed., *The Population Dilemma* (Englewood Cliffs, N.J.: Prentice-Hall, 1969), 206.

15. American Civil Liberties Union, *Policy Number 247,* approved January 25, 1968 in ACLU, *1976 Policy Guide* (New York, 1976), 231.

16. See *Roe* v. *Wade,* 410 U.S. 113 at 115.

17. Margaret Sanger, *My Fight for Birth Control* (New York: Farrar & Rinehart, 1931), 133.

18. Alan F. Guttmacher, *Birth Control and Love: The Complete Guide to Contraception and Fertility* (New York: Macmillan, 1961), 12.

19. Alan F. Guttmacher, *Into This Universe: The Story of Human Birth* (New York: Viking Press, 1937), 46. This work was revised and issued as *Having a Baby: A Guide for Expectant Parents* (New York: New American Library, 1947). The creation of the new baby is referred to on page 15 of this version.

20. Kan Majima, "Induced Abortion Is No Longer a Crime in Japan," in Third International Conference on Planned Parenthood, *Report of the Proceedings* (Bombay: Family Planning Association of India, 1952), 156, and Hans Harnsen, "The Medical Evil of Abortion," *ibid.*, 153.

21. Andras Klinger, "Rapporteur's Summary: The World-Wide Problem of Abortion," *Proceedings of the Eighth International Conference of the International Planned Parenthood Federation* (London: International Planned Parenthood Federation, 1967), 153.

22. Alan F. Guttmacher, "Symposium: Law, Morality, and Abortion," *Rutgers Law Review* 22 (1960): 415, 416.

23. Text in American Friends Service Committee, *Who Shall Live?* (New York: Hill & Wang, 1970) 102.

24. Alan F. Guttmacher, *Birth Control and Love*, 2d rev. ed. (New York: Macmillan, 1969), 12.

25. On the side-effects of the 1960s: Sydney Ahlstrom, "National Trauma and Changing Religious Values," *Daedalus*, Winter 1978, 20–22. On the critique by Zero Populationists, see, e.g., Paul R. Ehrlich, *The Population Bomb* (New York: Ballantine Books, 1968), 81–95. Ehrlich drew on the criticisms of family planning programs by Kingsley Davis, "Population Policy: Will Current Programs Succeed?", *Science*, November 10, 1967. On the challenge to oral contraceptives, see, e.g., Morton Mintz, "Are Birth Control Pills Safe?—Some Doctors Doubt that the Drug Has Been Tested Well Enough for Possible Side Effects," *Washington Post*, December 19, 1965, E1 and E5. The doubts expressed as early as 1965 were to increase and to lead to Senate hearings, "Oral Contraceptives," *Competitive Problems in the Drug Industry*, Hearings Before the Subcommittee on Monopoly of the Select Committee on Small Business, United States Senate, January–March 1970, 91st Cong. 2d Sess.

26. Robert M. Sade, "Medical Care as a Right: A Refutation," *New England Journal of Medicine* 285 (1971): 1288. Cf. John T. Noonan, Jr., "The Case of the Talented Bakers," *Harvard Medical Alumni Bulletin* 47 (1972): 12.

27. "A New Ethic for Medicine and Society," *California Medicine,* September 1970, 67–68.

28. *Ibid.,* 68.

29. E.g., Erma Clardy Craven, "Abortion, Poverty and Black Genocide: Gifts to the Poor?" in Thomas W. Hilgers and Dennis J. Horan, eds., *Abortion and Social Justice* (New York: Sheed & Ward, 1972), 231–242. The author, a black person, had been a psychiatric social worker in New York and was currently chairman of the Minneapolis Commission of Human Rights.

30. See Gordon Chase, Health Services Administrator, City of New York, testimony before the Commission on Population Growth and the American Future, *Statements at Public Hearings of the Commission,* 181.

31. See *Bigelow* v. *Virginia,* 421 U.S. 809 (1975).

32. The first person I ever heard advocate liberal abortion laws was a white official of the city of Chicago in 1964. He referred to the black population of Chicago as a problem. Since that time, in a number of different contexts, I have heard well-to-do white males express hope that abortion would end pregnancies out of wedlock for black mothers on welfare. The expression of this hope was usually in coarse terms unsympathetic either to the babies or to the mothers.

33. Department of Health, Education, and Welfare, "Effects of General Provision 413 of the Labor–HEW Appropriation Act," memorandum to the Conference Committee on the Labor–HEW Appropriations Act (H.R. 16680), September 24, 1974, reprinted in *Congressional Record* 120 (November 20, 1974): 36695.

34. National Abortion Rights Action League to Senator James Buckley (form letter to Senators), September 1974, reprinted in *Congressional Record* 120 (November 20, 1974): 36695.

35. The theme has been taken up by Planned Parenthood. One recent estimate of savings put the "welfare cost" of mother and child at more than $6,000 as against $360 for an abortion, so that Medicaid in California in one year alone saved the taxpayers almost a half-billion dollars by funding 77,000 abortions. Planned Parenthood Affiliates of California, *Memo,* October–November 1977, 3. The financial argument is also pressed vigorously upon state legislatures. For example, on March 13, 1978, the author was present at a hearing before an appropriations subcommittee of the California Senate considering state funding of abortion. A county health officer speaking on behalf of all county health officers urged the funding on the ground of financial savings calculated by him at $4,061 per pregnancy times 70,000 pregnancies, or $284,270,000 a year. He observed, "That's

only one year's crop," and "We'll be supporting them [i.e., babies born on welfare] for the next eighteen years."

36. The coalition was first evident to me as a participant in 1967 in the legislative hearings on amendment of California's abortion law. The advocates of change were the ACLU and the California Medical Association.

37. John Mitchell, "Presentation of Presidential Commission of Harry Blackmun as an Associate Justice of the Supreme Court of the United States," 398 U.S., xii (1970).

38. *New York Times,* May 7, 1972, 1.

39. *New York Times,* May 6, 1972, 1.

40. Philip Roth, *Our Gang* (New York: Bantam Books, 1971), 10–23.

41. *New York Times,* August 4, 1970, 1.

42. William Safire, *Before the Fall* (New York: Ballantine Books, 1977), 724.

43. *New York Times,* March 2, 1974, 16.

44. *New York Times,* February 2, 1973, 12.

45. Richard M. Nixon, "Remarks of the President," December 2, 1969, White House Conference on Food, Nutrition, and Health, *Final Report,* 7–12 (1970).

46. Louis Hellman, testimony, January 22, 1970, "Oral Contraceptives" (n. 25 *supra*), 1, 6188.

47. *Ibid.* at 6205. At issue was whether the oral contraceptives could be ruled "safe" by the Food and Drug Administration. In determining that they were, Dr. Hellman weighed the risks to any given woman against the benefits to the American public in general and, finding that the general benefit outweighed the individual risks, advised that the pills were "safe." His interpretation was challenged by Senator Gaylord Nelson: "I would doubt whether anybody contemplated that you could put on the balance side on the scale the question of the fact that the control of the population is a benefit to that patient in any direct way" (*ibid.*, 6212).

48. *Ibid.,* 6212.

49. Thomas B. Littlewood, *The Politics of Population Control* (Notre Dame, Ind.: University of Notre Dame Press, 1977), 96.

50. Introductory matter, Sarah Lewitt, ed., *Abortion Techniques and Services* (Amsterdam: Excerpta Medica, 1972).

51. Louis M. Rousselot, Assistant Secretary of Defense for Health and Environment, to the Surgeons General of the Military Departments, July 31, 1970.

52. George J. Hayes, Principal Deputy of the Assistant Secretary of De-

fense for Health and Environment, to the author, October 29, 1970.
General Hayes speaks of "HEW," for which I read "Hellman."

53. Public Law 71–213 (1970).

54. Commission on Population Growth and the American Future, *Population and the American Future* (Washington: Government Printing Office, 1972), 5–6.

55. Robert E. Hall, ed., *Abortion in a Changing World* (New York: Columbia University Press, 1970), v–vi.

56. John D. Rockefeller III, "Abortion Law Reform: The Moral Basis," in *ibid.*, xix.

57. Commission on Population Growth, *Population and the American Future*, 103–104.

58. "Blackmun, Harry," *Who's Who in America* (1969).

Inquiry 7. On the Legends of the Liberty

1. E.g., "A Little Dearer than His Horse: Legal Stereotypes and the Feminine Personality," *Harvard Civil Rights–Civil Liberties Law Review* 6 (1971): 260 at 263. It has been characteristic of pro-abortionists to refer to their opponents as "the compulsory pregnancy movement," e.g., Lisa Cronin Wohl, "Are We 25 Votes Away from Losing The Bill of Rights. . .And the Rest of the Constitution?", *Ms.*, February 1978, 47.

2. See Inquiry 17.

3. Inquiries 6 and 19.

4. James C. Mohr, *Abortion in America: The Origins and Evolution of National Policy, 1800–1900* (New York: Oxford University Press, 1978), 113.

5. Horatio Storer, *Is It I?*, cited in Mohr, *Abortion in America*, 114.

6. E[lizabeth] C[ady] S[tanton], "Child Murder," *Revolution* 1 (March 12, 1868): 146–147, cited in Mohr, *Abortion in America*, 111.

7. Grace Olivarez, "Separate Statement," in Commission on Population Growth and the American Future, *Population and the American Future* (Washington: Government Printing Office 1972), 160–161. For further feminine crititcism of the pro-abortion movement, see Clare Booth Luce, "A Letter to the Women's Lobby," *Human Life Review*, Spring 1978, 5–10; Sally Helgesen, "Virtue Rewarded," *Harper's*, May 1978, 24–25; and Sandra Haun, head of "Women Exploited," whose testimony before the Pennsylvania legislature is quoted in Michael Novak, "The Murder Case of Dr. Waddill,"

Washington Star, April 1, 1978, reprinted in *Human Life Review,* Spring 1978, 93.

8. Judith Blake, "Abortion and Public Opinion: The 1960–1970 Decade," *Science* 171 (1971): 540–544.

9. *Ibid.,* 544.

10. Eugene O'Neill, *Abortion,* in O'Neill, *Lost Plays* (New York: Citadel Press, 1958).

11. Ernest Hemingway, "Hills Like White Elephants," in Hemingway, *Men Without Women* (New York: Scribner's, 1927), 72–73.

12. Joan Didion, *Run, River* (New York: Ivan Obolensky), 139.

13. *Ibid.,* 180–181.

14. See *New York Times,* March 31, 1968, 1; *Byrn* v. *New York City Health and Hospitals Corp.,* 31 N.Y. 2d 144, 286 N.E. 2d 887 (1972); Commission on Population Growth, *Population and the American Future,* 101; *Roe* v. *Wade,* 410 U.S. 112, 148–149.

15. Jerome, Letter 22, to Eustochium, *Corpus Scriptorum Ecclesiasticorum latinorum* 54, 160–161.

16. Mohr, *Abortion in America,* 30–31.

17. *Ibid.,* 18–19.

18. *Ibid.,* 31.

19. "A. M. Mauricean" [Charles R. Lohman], *The Married Woman's Private Medical Companion* (1847), 169, cited in *ibid.,* 65.

20. Edwin M. Hale, *On the Homeopathic Treatment of Abortion, Its Causes and Its Consequences* (Chicago, 1860), 5–15, cited in Mohr, *Abortion in America,* 173–174.

21. Mohr, *Abortion in America,* 234–240.

22. *Ibid.,* 239–240.

23. *Ibid.,* 165.

24. American Medical Association, *Minutes of the Annual Meeting, 1859,* 10.

25. Mohr, *Abortion in America,* 147–170.

26. Glanville Williams, *The Sanctity of Human Life and the Criminal Law* (1957), 193.

27. American Law Institute, *Model Penal Code: Tentative Draft No. 9* (1959), 148, n. 12.

28. See John T. Noonan, Jr., "An Almost Absolute Value in History," in *idem,* ed., *The Morality of Abortion* (Cambridge: Harvard University Press, 1970), 24.

29. E.g., Jane M. Friedman, "The Federal Fetal Experimentation Regulations: An Establishment Clause Analysis," *Minnesota Law Review* 61 (1977): 961 at 994–998.

30. John T. Noonan, Jr., *Contraception: A History of Its Treatment by the Catholic Theologians and Canonists* (Cambridge: Harvard University Press, 1965), 424.

31. Laurence H. Tribe, "Toward a Model of Roles in the Due Process of Life and Law," *Harvard Law Review* 87 (1973): 1 at 22.

32. *Commonwealth* v. *Edelin*, (Mass.) 359 N.E.2d 4 (1976), Defendant's Brief, 33–34.

33. *Houston Chronicle*, February 3, 1976. For the rationale of the Religious Coalition for Abortion Rights, see Religious Coalition for Abortion Rights, "The Abortion Rights Issue: How We Stand," reproduced in Subcommittee on Civil and Constitutional Rights of the Committee on the Judiciary, House of Representatives, 94th Cong. 2d Sess., *Proposed Constitutional Amendments on Abortion—Hearings* (1976) (hereafter *Hearings–Abortion*), part 2, 979. For the "Orange Card," see Winston Churchill, *Lord Randolph Churchill* (London and New York: Macmillan, 1906), v.2, 59.

34. The flyer is in my files, provided me by a professor of constitutional law who received it in the mails and was outraged by its appeal to religious prejudice. Another reference to the flyer: M. J. Sobran, "A Letter to a Friend," *Human Life Review* 4 (Winter 1978): 10.

35. On the bombings: *Cleveland Plain Dealer*, February 20, 1978, 1, quoting respectively William Baird, founder of the Abortion Freedom League, and Carolyn Buell, director of Preterm Clinic, Cleveland. On the cartoons, see letter dated April 7, 1978, sending them to newspaper editors, signed by Jan Brittain, Public Education Director, Planned Parenthood Association/Chicago Area. In addition to the cartoons on the bishop, others satirize, in gross terms, the religious beliefs and the sexual morals of Secretary Califano. The cartoons of the bishop and of Califano were criticized by Joan Beck, "A Tasteless Anti-Church Tirade—with Tax Support," *Chicago Tribune*, May 1, 1978, Section 5.

36. Plaintiffs' Amended Complaint, paragraph 91, *McRae* v. *Califano*, 76 Civ. 1804, E.D.N.Y. (1977).

37. See *Wall Street Journal*, January 26, 1978, 34.

38. *San Francisco Chronicle*, August 8, 1978, 3.

39. Akron City Ordinance, sec. 1870.06; for a similar state statute see the Louisiana law effective September 8, 1978, reported in the *New York Times* August 1, 1978, B6. The Louisiana law had been adopted 88 to 0 in the House and 35 to 1 in the Senate.

40. Plaintiffs' *Complaint* in *Doe* v. *Akron*, C78–155A N.D. Ohio (1978).

41. "A Call To Concern," *Christianity and Crisis*, October 3, 1977, 222.

42. Mohr, *Abortion in America,* 147–170.

43. See Noonan, "An Almost Absolute Value," 14–18. The New Testament references: Galatians 5:20; Apocalypse 9:21; 21:8; 22:15. See my exegesis of the Greek term *pharmakeia,* "medicine," in Noonan, "An Almost Absolute Value in History," 8–9; for *The Teaching of the Twelve Apostles* or *Didache* 2:2, and for the *Epistle of Barnabas,* 19:5, see *Doctrina duodecim apostolorum; Barnabae epistula,* ed. Theodor Klauser (Bonn, 1940).

44. Lindsay Dewar, *An Outline of Anglican Moral Theology* (London: A. W. Mowbrey, 1968), 85; George Hunston Williams, "Religious Residues and Presuppositions in the American Debate on Abortion," *Theological Studies* 31 (1970): 43–46.

45. John Calvin, *Commentarius in Exodum,* 21, 22, in *Opera,* ed. J. W. Baum (Brunswick, 1882) 24, 625; Benjamin Wadsworth, *The Well-Ordered Family* (Boston, 1712), 45; Benjamin Wadsworth, *An Essay on the Decalogue or Ten Commandments* (Boston, 1719), 89.

46. Quoted in Dewar, *An Outline of Anglican Moral Theology,* 85.

47. W. R. Inge, *Christian Ethics and Modern Problems,* 5th ed. (London: Hodder & Stoughton, 1932), 126.

48. Quoted in Richard M. Fagley, *The Population Explosion and Christian Responsibility* (New York: Oxford University Press, 1960), 208.

49. A Committee of the Church Assembly Board of Social Responsibility, *Abortion: An Ethical Discussion* (London: Church Information Office, 1965).

50. Dewar, *An Outline of Anglican Moral Theology,* 86.

51. Helmut Thielicke, *The Ethics of Sex,* trans. John W. Doberstein (New York: Harper & Row, 1964), 231.

52. Karl Barth, *Church Dogmatics,* authorized English translation of *Die Kirchliche Dogmatik* (Edinburgh: T. & T. Clark, 1961) v. 3, part 4, 415–422.

53. Dietrich Bonhoeffer, *Ethics,* ed. Eberhard Bethage, trans. from 6th German edition of *Ethik* (New York: Macmillan, 1965), 175–176.

54. Williams, "Religious Residues," 51. Eighth General Synod, United Church of Christ, "Freedom of Choice Concerning Abortion," excerpted in *Hearings–Abortion,* part 2, 993; 1972 General Conference, United Methodist Chuch, "Social Principles," excerpted in *Hearings–Abortion,* part 2, 994.

55. Paul Ramsey, testimony (1974) before the Senate Subcommittee on Constitutional Amendments, reprinted in *Hearings–Abortion,* part 2, 959.

56. Spencer W. Kimball, president, address at the General Conference, April 5, 1974, quoting the *Priestly Bulletin* for February 1973, *One*

Hundred Fortieth Annual Conference of the Church of Jesus Christ of Latter-Day Saints (Salt Lake City, 1974), 8.

57. *Ibid.,* 8.

58. Oholoth 7, 6, Seder Tohoroth, in *The Babylonian Talmud,* ed. I. Epstein (London: Soncino Press, 1959), 178.

59. Jair Hayyim Bacharach (1639–1702), *Responsa Havot Ya'ir,* no. 31, cited in Immanuel Jakobovits, "Jewish Views on Abortion," in David W. Walbert and J. Douglas Butler, eds., *Abortion, Society and the Law,* (Cleveland: Case Western Reserve University Press, 1973), 109. Rabbi Jakobovits, now Chief Rabbi of the British Commonwealth, repeated and expanded his presentation of Jewish condemnation of abortion in "Jewish Views on Abortion," *Human Life Review* 1 (Winter 1975): 74.

60. Unterman, 6 *No'am,* cited in Jakobovits, "Jewish Views," 109.

61. *Ibid.,* 118.

62. Statement of Association of Orthodox Jewish Scientists of America, 1971, quoted in *ibid.,* 118.

63. E.g., "A Call to Concern," *Christianity and Crisis,* October 3, 1977, 272.

64. *Roe* v. *Wade,* 410 U.S. 113 at 153.

65. For documentation, see Inquiries 8 through 12.

66. Alice S. Rossi in Alan Guttmacher, ed., *The Case for Legalized Abortion Now* (Berkeley: Diablo, 1967), 27; American Law Institute, *Model Penal Code: Tentative Draft No. 9* (1959), Comment, 146.

67. E.g., *Congressional Record* 123 (December 6, 1977): H. 12656 (Representative Fraser).

68. Christopher Tietze and Sarah Lewitt in *Scientific American* 220 (1969): 5.

69. The numbers reported are given by Christopher Tietze, "Induced Abortion: 1977 Supplement," *Reports on Population/Family Planning* (New York: Population Council, December 1977), v. 14, Supplement, 6. Tietze, an ardent supporter of abortion, had, as noted in the text, estimated the increase per year, as of 1975, at 250,000. Tietze, "The Effect of Legalization of Abortion on Population Growth and Public Health," *Family Planning Perspectives* 7, no. 3 (May–June 1975).

70. *Dandridge* v. *Williams,* 397 U.S. 471 (1970). Compare Blackmun's vote for *Dandridge* v. *Williams* with his dissent in *Maher* v. *Roe,* 45 *U.S. Law Week* 4787 (1977).

71. Edward C. Smith, "Abortion and Human Rights," *Human Life Review,* Winter 1978, 57.

72. *Burns* v. *Alcala,* 420 U.S. 575 (1975). On the evil of malnourishment

of the unborn, see George Moscone, "Unborn and Underfed," *Interim Report of the Subcommittee on Nutrition and Human Needs,* California State Senate, 1973.

73. Jesse Jackson, president of Operation P.U.S.H. (People United to Save Humanity), "Open Letter to Congress," September 6, 1977, quoted in Smith, "Abortion and Human Rights," 58.

74. Grace Olivarez, "Separate Statement," in Commission on Population Growth, *Population and the American Future,* 161.

75. Jérome Lejeune, "The William Allan Memorial Award Lecture: On the Nature of Men," *American Journal of Human Genetics* 22 (1970): 126.

76. *Ibid.,* 128.

Inquiry 8. On the Propagation of the Liberty by the Press

1. *New York Times Co.* v. *Sullivan,* 376 U.S. 255 (1964).

2. *New York Times Co.* v. *United States,* 403 U.S. 713 (1971).

3. *New York Times,* January 23, 1973, 1.

4. *Ibid.,* January 24, 1973, 40.

5. *Ibid.,* January 27, 1973, 14.

6. Penal Law 125.45, *McKinney's Consolidated Laws of New York.*

7. *Time,* February 3, 1973, 50.

8. Judith Blake, "The Supreme Court's Abortion Decisions and Public Opinion in the United States," *Population and Development Review* 3 (1977): 51–52.

9. Louis Harris, "Abortion Debate Continues," *Harris Survey,* August 18, 1977, 2.

10. Taylor to Dexter Duggan, November 25, 1977, copy in the files of the author.

11. Jon Swan to Dexter Duggan, February 3, 1976, and subsequent Duggan letters, copies in the files of the author.

12. Louis D. Boccardi, executive editor of the Associated Press, to Nancy Roach, undated, printed in *National Right to Life News,* October 1977, 7.

13. Decision of the National News Council, June 21, 1977, "National News Council Report," *Columbia Journalism Review,* September–October 1977, 90–91.

14. *New York Times,* November 1, 1977, p. 29; a comparable paragraph by Tolchin appeared in the *Times* on November 27, 1977.

15. This paragraph and what follows are based on notes I took while watching the program on Channel 5 in the San Francisco Bay Area.

16. Robert Chandler, vice president and director, Public Affairs Broadcasts, CBS News, to the author, May 17, 1978.

17. The presence of religious prejudice in the press's treatment of abortion has also been noted by a sociologist. Andrew M. Greeley, *An Ugly Little Secret* (Kansas City, Mo.: Sheed, Andrews & McMeel, 1977), 21–23.

Inquiry 9. On the Dynamism of the Liberty

1. See Ronald G. Walters, *The Antislavery Appeal* (Baltimore: Johns Hopkins Press, 1976), 178.

2. See the description of the community's response in *Ela* v. *Smith,* 5 Gray 121 (Mass., 1855).

3. See, e.g., Jefferson Davis, speech of February 13–14, 1850, *Appendix to the Congressional Globe,* 31st Cong., 1st Sess. 149–153.

4. *Dred Scott* v. *Sanford,* 19 How. 393 (1857).

5. Abraham Lincoln, speech at Springfield, Ill., June 17, 1858, in *The Works of Abraham Lincoln* (New York, 1905), v. 3, 7.

6. *Dred Scott* v. *Sanford* at 407 and 421.

7. Lincoln, Speech at Springfield, Ill., July 17, 1858, in *Works,* v. 3, 173.

8. Abraham Lincoln, Speech at Cooper Institute, New York, February 27, 1860, in *Works,* v. 5, 147. Italics in original.

9. My observations on California practice are based on experience gained through living in the state from 1967 to date. As Congressman Silvio Conte observed to the House, 92 percent of the California abortions in 1968 were done for "mental health reasons," *Congressional Record,* 123 (September 27, 1977): H 10130.

10. *United States* v. *Vuitch,* 402 U.S. 62 (1971).

11. *Roe* v. *Wade* and *Doe* v. *Bolton* were argued before the Supreme Court on December 13, 1971. *U.S. Law Week* 40, 3300. Barring some unusual difficulty, they should have been decided immediately and the opinion written and the decision announced some time in the spring of 1972. That spring was also the time when the Rockefeller Commission made its report recommending the end of all abortion laws. The opinion eventually issued in *The Abortion Cases* and the Rockefeller recommendation coincided; but in an election year the recommendation embarrassed the president. On June 27, 1972, the cases were set down for reargument. *U.S. Law Week* 40, 3617. The reasons for this delay are not known; maybe Blackmun was merely

having trouble with the writing; it can be thought that the relation of delay to the presidential election in November 1972 was coincidental.

In *Dred Scott*, Chief Justice Taney rationalized the reargument and consequent delay by observing, "After the argument at the last term, differences were found to exist among the members of the court; and as the questions in controversy are of the highest importance, and the court was at that time much pressed by the ordinary business of the term, it was deemed advisable to continue the case, and direct a reargument on some of the points, in order that we might have an opportunity of giving to the whole subject a more deliberate consideration." *Dred Scott* v. *Sanford,* 19 How. at 399–400. Abraham Lincoln skeptically suggested that political strategy had motivated the delay. After reading Taney's explanation, he asked, "Why was the court decision held up?—Why the delay of a reargument?" Lincoln, Speech at Springfield, June 17, 1858, *Works,* v. 3, 7–8. For a view taking Taney's explanation seriously and also questioning the "test case" theory of Dred Scott, see Don E. Fehrenbacher, *The Dred Scott Case* (New York: Oxford University Press, 1978), 275 and 290.

As to the "test case" character of *Bolton* and *Wade,* the original plaintiffs in *Doe* v. *Bolton* claimed to represent "pregnant women, single or married, wishing legal abortions" and physicians, nurses, ministers, and social workers desiring to aid or counsel abortions. *Doe* v. *Bolton,* 319 F. Supp. 1048 (N.D. Georgia 1970). Only the pseudonymous "Mary Doe," a pregnant woman, was found to present a real case, and of course her condition had changed by the time the Supreme Court acted in 1973. In *Roe* v. *Wade,* 314 F. Supp. 1217 (N.D. Texas 1970), the plaintiffs were a pseudonymous Jane Roe, John and Mary Doe, and a doctor, suing on their own behalf and for those similarly situated.

12. For an illuminating elaboration of the comparison between *Dred Scott* and *The Abortion Cases,* see James F. Csank, "The Lords & Givers of Life," *Human Life Review,* Spring 1977, 75–100.

13. *Doe* v. *Bolton,* 410 U.S. 179 at 197–198.

14. *Doe* v. *Brigeton Hospital Association,* 71 N.J. 478, 366 A.2d 641 (1976). See also *Greco* v. *Orange Memorial Hospital,* 374 F. Supp. 227 (E.D. Texas, 1974), a lawsuit brought by same Austin firm that brought *Roe* v. *Wade,* court holds private hospital need not permit elective abortion; *Doe* v. *Bellin Memorial Hospital,* 479 F.2d 756 (7th Cir., 1973), court holds private hospital need not permit elective abortions; *Doe* v. *Charleston Area Medical Center Inc.,* 529 F.2d 638 (4th Cir. 1975), the "National Health Law Program" filed a brief as *amicus curiae,* and the court held that a private hospital receiving federal money under the Hill-Burton Act must permit

elective abortions. Congress had sought to forestall the result of the third case in the Church Amendment of 1973, 42 U.S.C. sec. 300-7(a)(2)A, which permitted hospitals receiving Hill-Burton federal money to refuse abortions "on the basis of religious beliefs or moral convictions." Speaking for a panel composed of Clement F. Haynsworth, Harrison L. Winter, and himself, Judge J. Braxton Craven, Jr., could not find that the hospital had acted "on moral convictions." *Doe* v. *Charleston Medical Area Center,* at 642, n. 7. It is permissible to wonder if such a court would have recognized a "moral conviction" opposed to the abortion liberty.

15. Richard E. Flathman, "The Theory of Rights and the Practice of Abortion," American Political Science Association, *Proceedings— 1977.*

16. Harriet F. Pilpel, "A Non-Catholic Lawyer's View," in Robert Hall, ed., *Abortion in a Changing World* (New York: Columbia University Press, 1970) 1, 158.

17. Marc Stern, "Abortion Conscience Clauses," *Columbia Journal of Law and Social Problems* 11 (1975): 571, 573–585.

18. Harriet F. Pilpel and Dorothy E. Patton, "Abortion, Conscience and the Constitution: An Examination of Federal Institutional Conscience Clauses," *Columbia Human Rights Law Review* 6 (1974–1975): 278 at 303. For the contrary view, see Dennis J. Horan, "Abortion and the Conscience Clause," *The Catholic Lawyer* 20 (1974): 289, and Martin F. McKernon, Jr., "Compelling Hospitals To Provide Abortion Services," *The Catholic Lawyer* 20 (1974): 317.

19. Joseph Fletcher, "Fetal Research: An Ethical Appraisal," in National Commission for the Protection of Human Subjects, *Research on the Fetus: Appendix* (Washington: U.S. Department of Health, Education, and Welfare, 1976), 3–4.

20. *Ibid.,* 3–11.

21. Jane M. Friedman, "The Federal Fetal Experimentation Regulations: An Establishment Clause Analysis," *Minnesota Law Review* 61, (1977): 961 at 994–1005.

22. Laurence H. Tribe, Foreword to the Supreme Court—1972 Term," *Harvard Law Review* 87 (1973): 1 at 47.

23. Justice Thurgood Marshall dissenting in *Beal v. Doe,* 432 U.S. 438 (1977): at 455.

24. The students were Susan Erzinger, a freshman; Margaret Patton, a sophomore; and Albin Rhomberg, a graduate student. *Erzinger* v. *Regents,* Complaint No. 408559, Superior Court for San Diego, California, filed December 12, 1977. For the reply of the university, see Regents of the University of California, *Demurrers to Complaint,* February 15, 1978, in *Erzinger* v. *Regents,* 11–12.

25. E.g., Philip E. Young, M.D., Department of Reproductive Medicine, University of California, San Diego, to Michael Karos, November 2, 1977, copy in the files of the author. By letter of October 27, 1977, Dr. Karos had indicated to Dr. Young his interest in a residency but had stated, "I do have ethical convictions against performing abortions except in those infrequent cases where it would be indicated in order to preserve the life of the mother." See also Paul Ramsey, "Abortion After the Law," *Hearings—Abortion,* House of Representatives, part 2, 971–972, and Paul Ramsey, *Ethics at the Edges of Life* (New Haven: Yale University Press, 1978), 61–71.

26. S.784, 95th Cong., 1st Sess. (1977).

27. *San Francisco Chronicle,* September 25, 1978, p. 5.

28. Sarah Weddington, Banquet Address, February 28, 1976, in Warren M. Hern and Bonnie Andrikopoulos, eds., *Abortion in the Seventies: Proceedings of the Western Regional Conference on Abortion, Denver, Colorado* (New York: National Abortion Federation, 1977), 279.

29. *Wulff* v. *Singleton,* 508 F.2d 1211 (8th Cir. 1975), reversed *Singleton* v. *Wulff,* 428 U.S. 106 (1976).

30. *Singleton* v. *Wulff,* 428 U.S. 106, 122 (dissent).

31. For the cruelty of the saline method, see Inquiry 18, *infra;* on prostaglandins, see Inquiry 15, *infra.*

32. *Planned Parenthood of Missouri* v. *Danforth,* 428 U.S. 52, 98 (dissent).

33. See Inquiry 12.

34. *Framingham Clinic Inc.* v. *Board of Selectmen of Southborough* (Mass.), 367 N.E. 2d 606 (1977).

35. *Drake* v. *Covington County Board of Education,* 371 F. Supp. 974 (D. Ala. 1974).

36. Michael Tooley, "Abortion and Infanticide," *Philosophy and Public Affairs* 2 (1972): 37.

37. See Inquires 14 and 15.

38. See Lincoln, Speech at Cooper Institute, New York, February 27, 1860, in *Works,* v. 5, 138–140.

Inquiry 10.   On the Application of the Liberty to the Family

1. *Roe* v. *Wade,* 410 U.S. 113 at 165 (1973).

2. *Skinner* v. *Oklahoma,* 316 U.S. 535 (1942).

3. *Loving* v. *Virginia,* 388 U.S. 1 (1967).

4. *Armstrong* v. *Manzo,* 380 U.S. 545 (1965).

5. *Stanley* v. *Illinois,* 405 U.S. 645 (1972).

6. *Planned Parenthood of Central Missouri* v. *Danforth,* 428 U.S. 52 (1976).

7. *Smith* v. *Organization of Foster Families,* 45 *U.S. Law Week* 4638 (1977).

8. *Prosser on Torts* (St. Paul; West, 1971 ed.), sec. 18.

9. E.g., *Zoski* v. *Gaines,* 271 Mich. 1, 260 N.W. 99 (1935).

10. *Meyer* v. *Nebraska,* 262 U.S. 390 at 402 (1923).

11. *Pierce* v. *Society of Sisters,* 268 U.S. 510 at 534 (1925).

12. *Bellotti* v. *Baird,* 428 U.S. 132 (1977).

13. The corporate papers of the foundation identify it as Parents Aid without the apostrophe which a grammatically minded federal court added to Parents.

14. *Baird* v. *Bellotti,* 393 F. Supp. 847 (D. Mass. 1975).

15. For the figures, Parents Aid Society, Form 12, for 1973–1974, 1974–1975, 1975–1976, filed with the Division of Public Charities, Department of the Attorney General, Commonwealth of Massachusetts.

16. *Bellotti* v. *Baird,* 428 U. S. 132.

17. *Baird* v. *Attorney-General* (Mass.), 360 N.E. 2d 288, 301 (1977).

18. *Ibid.,* 293, 300–301.

19. *Ibid.,* 292, 303.

20. *Ibid.,* 296–297.

21. *Baird* v. *Bellotti,* 428 F. Supp. 854, 856 (D. Mass. 1977).

22. See the strong criticism of this view in the earlier dissenting opinion of Anthony Julian in the first district court decision in the case, *Baird* v. *Bellotti,* 393 F. Supp. 847, 859 (D. Mass., 1975).

Inquiry 11.   On the Financing of the Liberty: The Courts

1. Charles P. Hall, Jr., *et al.,* "Medical and Cash Welfare Recipients: An Empirical Study," *Inquiry* 14 (1977): 48–49.

2. Karen Davis, "Medicare Payments and Utilization of Medical Services by the Poor," *Inquiry* 13 (1976): 127, 135.

3. *Griffin* v. *Illinois,* 351 U.S. 12 (1956): An indigent defendant, appealing his conviction, must be furnished a transcript of his trial; *Boddie* v. *Connecticut,* 401 U.S. 371 (1971): Access to a divorce court cannot be barred to an indigent by requiring payment of $60 of court and sheriff fees. See the analyses of these cases in Gerald Gunther, *Con-*

stitutional Law: Cases and Materials (Mineola, N.Y.: Foundation Press, 1975), 816–824.

4. *Roe* v. *Norton,* 380 F. Supp. 726 (D. Conn. 1974) at 730.

5. *Doe* v. *Wollgemuth,* 376 F. Supp. 173 (W. D. Penn. 1973) at 189.

6. South Dakota: *Doe* v. *Westby,* 383 F. Supp. 1143 (D.S.D. 1974); Utah: *Doe* v. *Rose,* 499 F.2d 1112 (10th Cir. 1974); Missouri: see n. 10 *infra;* New York: *Klein* v. *Nassau County Medical Center,* 409 F. Supp. 731 (E.D.N.Y. 1976); Minnesota: *Nyberg* v. *City of Virginia,* 495 F.2d 1342 (8th Cir. 1974).

7. *Hathaway* v. *Worcester City Hospital,* 475 F.2d 701 (1st Cir. 1973) at 705.

8. *Ibid.,* 706.

9. *Roe* v. *Norton,* 408 F. Supp. 660 (D. Conn. 1975) at 663, n. 5.

10. See *Doe* v. *Poelker,* 515 F.2d 541 (8th Cir. 1975) at 542.

11. *Ibid.* at 547–548.

12. See *Beal* v. *Doe,* 432 U.S. 438 (1977) at 462 (dissent).

13. *Who's Who in America* (1969).

14. *Doe* v. *Poelker,* 515 F.2d 541 at 548.

15. *Ibid.* at 547.

16. $3,500 for the appellate part of the proceeding, plus an amount for the district court proceedings, see 515 F.2d at 548.

17. *Beal* v. *Doe,* 432 U.S. 438 (1977).

18. *Maher* v. *Roe,* 432 U.S. 464 (1977) at 471.

19. *Ibid.* at 479.

20. *Missouri, Kansas and Texas Ry. Co.* v. *May,* 194 U.S. 267 (1904) at 270.

21. *Maher* v. *Roe,* 428 U.S. 464 (1977) at 478.

22. *Ibid.* at 475.

23. *Poelker* v. *Doe,* 432 U.S. 519 (1977).

24. *Ibid.* at 521.

25. See *New York Times,* June 21, 1977, 20; June 27, 1977, 32.

26. *Beal* v. *Doe,* 432 U.S. 438 (1977) at 455–462 (dissenting opinion).

27. *Maher* v. *Roe,* 428 U.S. 464 (1977) at 482–490 (dissenting opinion).

28. *Beal* v. *Doe,* 428 U.S. 438 (1977) at 462–463 (dissenting opinion).

Inquiry 12.   On the Financing of the Liberty: The Legislature

1. 42 *U.S. Code,* 300 a-6.

2. See Daniel Patrick Moynihan, *The Politics of a Guranteed Income:*

The Nixon Administration and the Family Assistance Plan (New York: Random House, 1973), 493.

3. *Congressional Record* 117 (June 21, 1971): 21089.

4. 42 *U.S. Code,* 1396d(a).

5. HEW, "Effects of General Provision 413 of the Labor–HEW Appropriation Act," September 24, 1974, *Congressional Record* 120 (November 20, 1974): 36695. The admission of Louis Hellman that the 90 percent rate had been used was made to Jim Castelli and reported by him in a *NC News Service Release,* December 13, 1974. The Medicaid rates were set by 42 *U.S. Code,* sec. 1396d(a).

6. *Congressional Record,* 123 (June 17, 1977): H.6084 (Congressman Hyde).

7. See *Congressional Record* 122: H.10312.

8. *Ibid.,* H.10317.

9. John Buggs to Senator Packwood, July 22, 1976, *Congressional Record* 122: S.16115 .

10. *Ibid.,* 122: S.14568. For more on the definition of abortion, see Inquiry 16.

11. *Ibid.,* 122: S.14562.

12. *Ibid.,* 122: S.16120.

13. *Ibid.,* 122: S.16114–16115.

14. See *McRae* v. *Mathews,* 421 F. Supp. 533, 535, (E.D.N.Y. 1976).

15. See Inquiry 11.

16. *New York Times,* October 23, 1976, 1.

17. *Reeside* v. *Walker,* 11 How. 271, 290 (1850).

18. *Cincinnati Soap Company* v. *United States,* 301 U.S. 308, 321 (1937).

19. *Glidden Company* v. *Zdanak,* 370 U.S. 530, 570 (1962).

20. *Stitzel-Weller Distillery* v. *Wickard,* 118 F.2d 19 (D.C. App. 1941).

21. *Lovett* v. *United States,* 104 Ct. Claims 557 (1945).

22. *United States* v. *Lovett,* 328 U.S. 303, 318 (1946).

23. *Lovett* v. *United States* at 581.

24. *Ibid.* at 584.

25. *Doe* v. *Mathews,* 420 F. Supp. 865 (D.N.J. 1976).

26. *McRae* v. *Mathews,* 421 F. Supp. 533, 540–541 (E.D.N.Y. 1976). In this litigation Americans United for Life has appeared as an *amicus curiae* supporting the validity of the Hyde Amendment. In December 1978 the author became a director of this organization. Hence he writes as one who is now associated with a position before the court.

27. *Ibid.* at 543.

28. *Klein* v. *Nassau County Medical Center,* 409 F. Supp. 731 (E.D.N.Y. 1976).

29. Under House Rule XXI, the Hyde Amendment, being an amendment to a general appropriation bill, was in order only if it "retrench[ed] expenditures. . .by the reduction of amounts of money covered by the bill," Rule XXI, *Constitution, Jefferson's Manual, and Rules of the House of Representatives,* ed. Lewis Deschler, Parliamentarian (Washington: U.S. Government Printing Office, 1967), sec. 835. Substantially the present form of the retrenchment rule known as the "Holman Rule" had been adopted in 1876 and employed till 1885. It was revived in 1912 and has continued in effect until the present, (*ibid.,* sec. 835). There is a substantial body of precedents indicating the House's understanding of the rule. These precedents indicate that a limitation on the use of appropriated funds constitutes a decision not to appropriate for that purpose. See, e.g., Ruling of the Chair, January 27, 1931, Cannon's *Precedents of the House of Representatives* (Washington: Government Printing Office, 1935), 7, sec. 1645 (limitation offered by Fiorello La Guardia).

30. William H. Taft IV and Robert H. Bork, *Memorandum for the Secretary of Health, Education and Welfare in Opposition to the Application for a Stay Pending Appeal,* November 1976, filed in the Supreme Court in *Buckley* v. *McRae,* 91 S. Ct. 347 (1976). Senator Buckley was in a very different position from the government, and his request for a stay was summarily denied on November 8, 1976, 91 S. Ct. 347.

31. *U.S. Law Week* 45 (February 11, 1977): 3591.

32. *Congressional Record* 123 (June 17, 1977): H.6098.

33. See Inquiry 11.

34. *Congressional Record* 123: S.11046.

35. Order entered in open court by Judge Dooling, August 4, 1977, in *McRae* v. *Califano.*

36. *Congressional Record* 123 (September 27, 1977): H.10170.

37. *Ibid.,* H.12652 (Congressman Michel, December 6, 1977); H.12774 (Congressman Hyde, December 7, 1977).

38. *Ibid.,* S.18583 (Senator Bayh, November 3, 1977).

39. *Ibid.,* H.12160 (November 3, 1977).

40. *Ibid.,* H.12169 (Congressman Mahon, November 3, 1977).

41. *Ibid.,* H.12771.

42. *Ibid.,* H.12831.

43. Department of Health, Education, and Welfare, "Federal Financial Participation in State Claims for Abortions," *Federal Register* 43,

no. 24, (February 3, 1978): 4842. The regulations were accompanied by an opinion of the Attorney General stating that the proposed regulations were "authorized" by the act of Congress.

44. See, e.g., Ad Hoc Committee in Defense of Life, *Lifeletter,* February 14, 1978, 1, sharply attacking the regulations. *Lifeletter* is published by the Ad Hoc Committee in Defense of Life, P.O. Box 574, Murray Hill Station, New York, N.Y. 10016.

45. Herbert E. Harris, "Limiting Legislation in Appropriations Bills," January 16, 1978 (a "Dear Colleague" letter to other Congressmen).

46. See "General Provisions" from the Departments of State, Justice, Commerce, the Judiciary and Related Agencies Appropriation Act, 1973, 86 Stat. 1109, 1134 (1972).

47. Samuel Flagg Bemis, *John Quincy Adams and the Union* (New York: Knopf, 1956), 336.

48. *Ibid.,* 348.

49. Many state legislatures were not in session or had rules inhibiting the late introduction of legislation when the Supreme Court spoke on abortion funding in June. Three states—Idaho, Illinois, and Utah—acted at once to bar state payments for nontherapeutic abortions. In Illinois, the legislature overrode Governor James Thompson's veto. In Massachusetts the legislature failed, by a margin of three votes in the Senate, to override Governor Michael Dukakis's veto; the following year the legislature overrode the veto and forbade funding. By July 1978 only thirteen of the fifty states were still funding elective abortion.

Inquiry 13. On the Logic of the Liberty

1. Joseph F. Fletcher, "Fetal Research: An Ethical Appraisal," in National Commission for the Protection of Human Subjects of Biomedical and Behavioral Research, *Research on the Fetus: Appendix* (Washington: U.S. Department of Health, Education, and Welfare, 1976, hereafter *Research on the Fetus),* 3-3.

2. *Ibid.,* 3-11.

3. David G. Nathan, "Fetal Research: An Investigator's View," *Villanova Law Review* 22 (1977): 384 at 390.

4. *The Use of Fetuses and Fetal Material for Research: Report of the Advisory Group, Chaired by Sir John Peel, London, 1972,* reprinted in *Research on the Fetus,* 19-63.

5. *Ibid.,* 19-11.

6. National Research Act, Public Law No. 93-348, 88 *Stat.* 342–354 (1974).

7. HEW, "Protection of Human Subjects," *Federal Register,* v. 39, no. 165, August 23, 1974 (also in 45 *Code of Federal Regulations,* part 46), secs. 46.306 and 46.307.

8. The single critic of *The Abortion Cases* was David W. Louisell, Boalt Professor of Law at Boalt Hall, University of California, Berkeley.

9. Charles U. Lowe, "On Legislating Fetal Research," in Aubrey Milunsky and George J. Annas, eds., *Genetics and the Law* (New York and London: Plenum Press, 1976), 354–355. The author also writes from observation of Dr. Lowe as he chaired preliminary sessions on the rules to govern experimentation on the fetus. A failure to appreciate the character and key role of the staff and an overvaluation of the influence of the commission's "consultants" (mere witnesses) leads to an evaluation of the commission's work and HEW almost diametrically opposed to mine. See Jane M. Friedman, "The Federal Fetal Experimentation Regulations: An Establishment Clause Analysis," *Minnesota Law Review* 61 (1977): 961–1005.

10. "Permissible Medical Experiments," in Judgment of Military Tribunal Number 1, August 20, 1947, *The Medical Case: United States v. Karl Brandt, et al., Trials of War Criminals Before Nuremberg Military Tribunals* (Washington: Government Printing Office), v. 2, 181, reprinted as *The Nuremberg Code of Ethics in Medical Research* in *Research on the Fetus,* 17-1. For the defense argument, see *The Medical Case,* v. 2, 90–93.

11. World Medical Association, *The Hippocratic Oath Formulated at Geneva,* in Jay Katz, *Experimentation with Human Beings* (New York: Russell Sage Foundation, 1972), 312.

12. World Medical Association, Declaration of Helsinki, reprinted in *Research on the Fetus,* 18-1; also reprinted in *British Medical Journal* 2 (1964): 177.

13. Declaration of Helsinki; sec. III, 3a.

14. Dennis J. Horan, "Fetal Experimentation and Federal Regulation," *Villanova Law Review* 22 (1977): 325 at 334.

15. Warren Burger, "Reflections on Law and Experimental Medicine," *U.C.L.A. Law Review* 15 (1968): 436 at 438 (emphasis in original). Burger was then Chief Judge of the Court of Appeals for the District of Columbia.

16. Richard A. McCormick, "Proxy Consent in the Experimentation Situation," *Perspectives in Biology and Medicine* 18 (1974): 2–20.

17. See Inquiry 16.

18. Robert J. Levine, "The Impact on Fetal Research of the Report of the National Commission for the Protection of Human Subjects of Biomedical and Behavioral Research," *Villanova Law Review* 22 (1977): 367 at 379. Part of Levine's case seemed to be built on the

premise that nontherapeutic experiments were prohibited as to any patient, so that, if the term were kept, no such experiments could be performed (see pp. 378–379). He ignored the fact that what was crucial was consent.

19. Declaration of Helsinki, "Introduction."

20. Fletcher, "Fetal Research," 3-4.

21. National Commission for the Protection of Human Subjects of Biomedical and Behavioral Research, "Deliberations and Conclusions," C.4, *Report and Recommendations: Research on the Fetus* (DHEW Pub. No. [OS] 76-127, 1975); also printed in *Federal Register* 40 (1975): 33530, and reprinted in *Villanova Law Review* 22 (1977): 297.

22. Fletcher, "Fetal Research," 3-3 and 3-11.

23. Maurice J. Mahoney and others, "The Nature and Extent of Research Involving Living Human Fetuses," *Research on the Fetus*, 1-11.

24. HEW, "Protection of Human Subjects," *Federal Register* 39: 30649, "Fetuses, Abortuses, and Pregnant Women."

25. R. I. Leininger and others from the Battelle-Columbus Laboratories, "An Assessment of the Role of Research Involving Living Human Fetuses in Advances in Medical Science and Technology," *Research on the Fetus*, 15-3.

26. R. I. Leininger, "Response to the Cooke Critique," *Research on the Fetus*, 15-162.

27. Robert E. Cooke, "Critique of Batelle Report," *Research on the Fetus*, 15-159.

28. David Nathan, "Fetal Research: An Investigator's View," *Villanova Law Review* 22 (1977): 384, 388–389.

29. Cooke, "Critique of Batelle Report," 15-155.

30. Commission for the Protection of Human Subjects, "Deliberations and Conclusions," C.4.

31. *Idem*, "Recommendations 5 and 6."

32. *Idem*, "Recommendation 6."

33. *Idem*, "Deliberations and Conclusions," C.4.

34. Marc Lappé, "Balancing Obligations to the Living Fetus with the Needs for Experimentation," *Research on the Fetus*, 4-5. For two commissioners' dissent if proved that fetus can feel pain see "Statement of Commissioner Karen Lebacqz, with the Concurrence of Albert R. Jonsen on the First Item," in Commission for the Protection of Human Subjects, "Deliberations and Conclusions," C.4.

For further discussion of fetal pain capacity, see Inquiry 16.

35. Dissenting Statement of Commissioner David W. Louisell," in Commission for the Protection of Human Subjects, "Deliberations and Conclusions," C.4.

36. HEW, *Federal Register* 40 (1975): 33528, and *Code of Federal Regulations* sec. 46.201–211 (1976).

37. *Code of Federal Regulations,* sec. 46.209(b)(1).

Inquiry 14.   On the Frontier of the Liberty

1. *Brief for the Commonwealth,* 1, 1, citing *Transcript* 14, pp. 15–17, *Commonwealth* v. *Edelin* (Mass.), 359 N.E.2d 4 (1976).

2. *Commonwealth* v. *Edelin* at 6–7.

3. American College of Obstetricians and Gynecologists, *Standards for Obstetrical and Gynecological Services* (1973–1974), 72.

4. *Commonwealth* v. *Edelin* at 8. This is the testimony most favorable to the Commonwealth, that of Dr. George Curtis, the Medical Examiner. Dr. Curtis thought, the body having been soaked in formaldehyde for four months before his measurement, the live weight would have been more. A residential pathologist weighed the body after death at 600 grams (1 lb., 5 oz.).

5. *Ibid.* at 7.

6. *Ibid.* at 9.

7. *Ibid.* at 7; *Brief for the Commonwealth,* 7, citing *Transcript* 20, p. 11.

8. *Brief for the Commonwealth,* 8.

9. *Commonwealth* v. *Edelin* at 8.

10. *Brief for the Commonwealth* 19, citing *Transcript* 24, p. 125. On the time the mother had been under anesthesia, see *ibid.,* 19, citing Exhibit 1 and *Transcript* 19, p. 79.

11. Defendant's Brief, 62, citing *Transcript* 19, p. 87 and *Transcript* 20, p. 111.

12. *Ibid.,* 63.

13. *Brief for the Commonwealth,* 19.

14. American Academy of Pediatrics, *Hospital Care of Newborn Infants,* rev. ed. (Evanston, Ill., 1974), 70–71.

15. *Ibid.,* 82.

16. *Defendant's Brief,* 62.

17. Charge to the jury, *Commonwealth* v. *Edelin, 1975 Reporter on Human Reproduction and the Law,* I-C-129.

18. *Brief for the Commonwealth,* 18.

19. *Ibid.,* 19–20.

20. *Defendant's Brief,* 23–25.

21. *Ibid.,* 50, citing *Transcript* 19, p. 87.

22. *Ibid.,* 50, citing *Transcript* 9, pp. 30–31.

23. *Ibid.,* 49–61.

24. Defendant's *Requests for Instructions to the Jury,* numbers 6, 16, 18, *Summary of Record and Assignment of Errors,* 81–87.

25. Defendant's *Supplemental Requests for Instructions to the Jury,* number 1, *Summary,* 95.

26. Charge, *Reporter on Human Reproduction and the Law,* 1-C-103-133.

27. English common law: *Sims' Case,* 75 *English Reports* 1075 (K.B. 1601); *Rex* v. *Senior,* 168 *English Reports* 1298 (1832). American law: *Abrams* v. *Foshee,* 3 Iowa 274 (1856); *Clark* v. *State,* 117 Ala. 1, 23 So. 671 (1898); *Morgan* v. *State,* 148 Tenn. 417, 256 S.W. 433 (1923); *State* v. *Cooper,* 22 N.J.L. 52 (1849) (dictum). *Contra: Cordes* v. *State,* 54 Texas Criminal Appeals, 112 S.W. 943, 947 (1908).

28. *Dietrich* v. *Inhabitants of Northampton,* 138 Mass. 14 (1884).

29. Willard Phillips and Samuel B. Walcott, *Report of the Criminal Law Commissioners on the Penal Code of Massachusetts,* ch. 7, sec. 33 (1844).

30. Alexander M. Capron, "The Law Relating to Experimentation with the Fetus," *Research on the Fetus,* 13-21.

31. E.g., *Defendant's Motion for Dismissal of the Indictment* and accompanying affidavit of his counsel, October 9, 1974, *Summary,* 33–41; *Defendant's Brief,* 32–39.

32. E.g., *New York Times,* February 14, 1975, 36.

33. *Defendant's Brief,* 34.

34. E.g., *Brief of Planned Parenthood Federation of America, Inc.,* 8–10.

35. *Defendant's Brief,* 35.

36. *Commonwealth* v. *Edelin* at 12. Although this statement appears as part of the main opinion of the court, it is evident that Justices Reardon and Quirico (p. 20) and Chief Justice Hennessy (p. 24) disagreed.

37. *Ibid.,* 15–16.

38. *Ibid.,* n. 41.

39. *Ibid.,* n. 22.

40. *Ibid.,* 13.

41. *Ibid.,* 7. On the term, see Inquiry 16.

42. *Ibid.,* n. 40.

43. *Defendant's Brief,* 144.

44. *Commonwealth* v. *Edelin* at 20, 24.

45. *Ibid.,* 20–23.

46. *Ibid.,* 20, 24.

47. *Ibid.,* 21.

48. *Ibid.,* 14.

49. *Ibid.,* 11.

50. *Ibid.,* 28.

Inquiry 15.   On the Liberty Taken Further

1. The facts are taken from *Appellant's Jurisdictional Statement, Anders* v. *Floyd,* 77-1255, *U.S. Law Week* 46 (U.S., 1978): 3587, supplemented by the records of the hospital. The author was consulted by the appellant and writes from the perspective of one who has taken the appellant's position in the case.

2. Sultan M. M. Karim, ed., *Prostaglandins and Reproduction* (Baltimore: University Park Press, 1975), 1–18.

3. On the nonharmful use of prostaglandins to induce labor, see Michel Thiery and Jean-Jacques Amy, "Induction of Labor with Prostaglandins," in Karim, *Prostaglandins and Reproduction,* 164–167; on intraamniotic injection of PGF [2a], Sultan M. M. Karim and Jean-Jacques Amy, "Interruption of Pregnancy with Prostaglandins," in *ibid.,* 107; on the effect of PGF [2a] on the placenta, *ibid.,* 87; on the 40 percent incomplete abortion rate, *ibid.,* 94; on the effect of the twenty-milogram dosage, A. I. Csapo *et al.,* "Termination of Pregnancy with Double Prostaglandin Input," *American Journal of Obstetrics and Gynecology* 124 (1976): 1.

4. *South Carolina Code Annotated,* 44-41-20 (1976 ed.) = 32-68-1 of the 1962 Code as amended in 1974.

5. *Roe* v. *Wade,* 410 U.S. 113, 160.

6. *South Carolina Code Annotated,* 16-3-10.

7. Edward Coke, *Institutes of the Laws of England* (London, 1809), part 3, ch. 7, 50.

8. William Blackstone, *Commentaries on the Laws of England* (London, 1778), book 4, ch. 14, 198.

9. *Prosser on Torts,* 4th ed. (1971), 335–338.

10. 1 *Moody's Crown Cases Reserved,* 346; 168 *English Reports,* 1298 (1832).

11. *Queen* v. *West,* 2 Carrington and Kirwin 784 (Nisi prius, 1848).

12. *State* v. *Cooper,* 22 N.J.L. 52 (2 Zabriskie 52) (1849); *Abrams* v. *Foshee,* 3 Iowa 274 (1856); *Clark* v. *State,* 117 Ala. 1, 23 So. 671 (1898); *Morgan* v. *State,* 148 Tenn. 417, 256 S.W. 433 (1923); *Contra, Cordes* v. *State,* 54 Tex. Crim. App. 294, 112 S.W. 943 (1908).

13. See Inquiry 14.

14. *Appellant's Jurisdictional Statement.*

15. *Younger* v. *Harris,* 401 U.S. 37 (1965).

16. *Ibid.* at 44.

17. *Ibid.* at 53.

18. *Hicks* v. *Miranda,* 422 U.S. 332, 349 (1975).

19. *Hicks* v. *Miranda* held that the denial of a temporary restraining order by the federal district judge did not constitute "substantial proceedings on the merits."

20. *Watson* v. *Buck,* 313 U.S. 387, 402 (1941), quoted in *Younger* v. *Harris* at 53.

21. *Wooley* v. *Maynard,* 97 S. Ct. 1428 (1977).

22. *Allee* v. *Medrano,* 414 U.S. 802, 835 (1974) (Burger, C.J., concurring).

23. *Juidice* v. *Vail,* 430 U.S. 327 (1977).

24. *Douglas* v. *City of Jeannette,* 319 U.S. 157, 164 (1943).

25. *Younger* v. *Harris* at 46.

26. *Floyd* v. *Anders,* 440 F. Supp. 535, 539 (D. So. Car. 1977).

27. *Ibid.,* 539.

Inquiry 16.   On the Language of the Liberty

1. See *Burns* v. *Alcala,* 420 U. S. 575 at 584 (1975).

2. E.g., *California Penal Code,* sec. 270 (West Supp. 1968).

3. The cases are collected in *Parks* v. *Harden,* 504 F.2d 861 (5th Cir., 1974), at 863.

4. *Burns* v. *Alcala,* 420 U.S. 575 (1975).

5. Editorial: "A New Ethic for Medicine and Society," *California Medicine,* September 1970, 68.

6. Howard P. Gitlow, "Abortion Services: Time for a Discussion of Marketing Policies—Suggestions for Producers, Suppliers, and Consumers," *Journal of Marketing,* April 1978, 71.

7. American Academy of Pediatrics, *Hospital Care of Newborn Infants* (Evanston, 1974), 17.

8. E.g., *Munro Keir's Operative Obstetrics,* 9th ed., rev. by P. R. Myers-

cough (London: Cassell and Collier-Macmillan Publishers Ltd., 1977), 603: "If the sac has been ruptured, the fingers may have to be employed to scoop out the ovum."

9. American Academy of Pediatrics, *Hospital Care of Newborn Infants,* 17.

10. American College of Obstetricians and Gynecologists, *Standards for Obstetrical and Gynecological Services* (1973–1974), 73.

11. E.g., Thomas D. Kerenyi, "Midtrimester Abortion," in Howard J. Osofsky and Joy D. Osofsky, eds., *The Abortion Experience* (New York: Harper & Row, 1973), 393.

12. E.g., *Connecticut General Statutes,* 53-29 (1949).

13. E.g., *Sinkler* v. *Kneale,* 401 Pa. 267, 164 A.2d 93 (1960), where Justice Curtis Bok quoted with approval the Supreme Court of New Jersey: "Medical authorities have long recognized that a child is in existence from the moment of conception and not merely a part of its mother's body."

14. See A. James Casner, *American Law of Property* (Boston: Little, Brown, 1952), 5, 358 (sec. 22.42, discussing gifts by will or trust to "children"): "Up to this point the discussion concerning immediate gifts has not taken into account the possible claims of children in gestation when the instrument takes effect. Such children are treated as children in being and thus are not prevented from taking a share in an immediate gift."

15. American College of Obstetricians and Gynecologists, *Standards,* 73.

16. National Commission for the Protection of Human Subjects, "Recommendations," number 6.

17. American College of Obstetricians, *Standards,* 74.

18. National Commission, "Definitions."

19. *Webster's Third International Dictionary* at "abortus," HEW's proposed regulations of 1974, *Federal Register* 39: 30649, radically expanded the meaning of the term to include *live* children, delivered by abortion and not expected to survive for long. This idiosyncratic usage gave way to "the nonviable fetus ex utero."

20. Definitions 1 and 2 are from *Webster's Third International Dictionary* at "abortion." Definition 3 is from the American College of Obstetricians and Gynecologists, *Standards,* 73; for the same definition in a standard text, see, e.g., Edward C. Hughes, ed., *Obstetric–Gynecologic Terminology* (Philadelphia: F. A. Davis, 1972).

21. See Inquiry 8.

22. *Roe* v. *Wade,* 410 U. S. 113 at 163–164.

23. *Webster's Third International Dictionary* (1969) at "abortion."

24. HEW, "Education Programs and Activities Receiving or Benefitting

from Federal Financial Assistance," sec. 86. 47c, *Federal Register,* June 30, 1974, 27237.

25. Caspar Weinberger, Secretary of HEW, to Senator James Buckley, undated, but written about October 31, 1974. Senator Buckley has kindly made available to me a copy of this letter.

26. See Inquiry 10.

27. George Orwell, *Nineteen Eighty-Four* (New York: Harcourt, Brace, 1949), 17–18.

28. See Inquiry 15.

29. Charles Dickens, *Pickwick Papers,* ch. 51.

30. Lewis Carroll, *Through the Looking Glass,* ch. 6.

Inquiry 17. On the Masks of the Liberty: The Object

1. *Fowler* v. *Saunders, Virginia Reports Annotated* II (Wythe) 284 at 287 (Chancery, 1798). On the use of masks by the slave system, see John T. Noonan, Jr., *Persons and Masks of the Law* (New York: Farrar, Straus & Giroux, 1976), 29–64.

2. Jefferson's legislation: Acts of October 1785, ch. 77, *The Statutes at Large, being a Collection of all the laws of Virginia,* ed. William Waller Hening (1824); Lincoln's lawsuit: Anton Hermann Chroust, "Abraham Lincoln Argues a Pro-Slavery Case," *American Journal of Legal History* 5 (1961):299.

3. Editorial: "A New Ethic for Law and Society," *California Medicine,* September 1970, 68.

4. Selig Neubardt and Harold Schulman, *Techniques of Abortion* (Boston: Little, Brown, 1972), 46.

5. See Inquiry 16, *supra,* at n. 11–14.

6. Victor A. McKusick, *Human Genetics,* 2d ed. (Englewood Cliffs, N.J.: Prentice-Hall, 1969), 8–19.

7. David Epel, "The Program of Fertilization," *Scientific American* 237 (1977): 129.

8. P. S. Timiras, *Developmental Physiology and Aging* (New York and London: Macmillan, 1972), v.

9. Paul Henry Mussen, John Janeway Congar, and Jerome Kagan, *Child Development and Personality,* 2d ed. (New York: Harper & Row, 1963), 29, 57.

10. Alan F. Guttmacher, *Having a Baby: A Guide for Expectant Parents* (New York: New American Library, 1947), 15.

11. C. H. Waddington, *Towards a Theoretical Biology* (Edinburgh: University of Edinburgh Press, 1969) 2, 120. Waddington's view of evolution is improperly evoked, in an attempt to deprive the term "humanity" of its stable components, by Edward Manier, William Liu, and David Solomon, *Abortion: New Directions for Policy Studies* (Notre Dame, Ind.: University of Notre Dame Press, 1977), 170.

12. Samuel Taylor Coleridge, *Biographia Literaria,* ed. George Watson (London: Dent, 1906), 139. Sissela Bok evokes I. A. Richards, who objects to such concepts as "Beauty" in esthetics and "Life" in physiology, because such ultimates, prematurely introduced, "bring an investigation to a dead end too suddenly." Similarly, she argues, to speak of the "humanity" of the fetus is to introduce a "premature ultimate" into the discussion. Sissela Bok, "Fetal Research and the Value of Life," *Research on the Fetus,* 2–5. But when human life is palpable, the true "dead end" is to deny its existence.

13. See Jérome Lejeune, testimony, May 7, 1974, Abortion—Part V, *Hearings Before the Subcommittee on Constitutional Amendments of the Committee on the Judiciary,* 94th Cong., 1st Sess.

14. N. J. Berrill, *The Person in the Womb* (New York: Dodd, Mead, 1968) 42–44; Allan C. Barnes, *Intrauterine Development* (Philadelphia: Lea & Febiger, 1968), 455.

15. Anthony Smith, *The Human Pedigree* (Philadelphia: J. B. Lippincott, 1975), 199.

16. Lejeune, testimony, n. 13, *supra.*

17. W. J. Hamilton and H. W. Mossman, *Human Embryology* (Baltimore: Williams & Wilkins, 1970), 188.

18. Trypena Humphrey, "The Development of Human Fetal Activity and Its Relation to Postnatal Behaviour," *Advances in Child Development and Behaviour,* Hayne W. Reese and Lewis P. Lipsitt, eds. (New York, 1975) 12 and 19.

19. G. S. Dawes, "Breathing Before Birth in Animals and Man," *The New England Journal of Medicine* 290 (1974): 557–559.

20. A. William Liley, "The Foetus as Personality," *Australia and New Zealand Journal of Psychiatry* 6 (1972): 99.

21. Smith, *The Human Pedigree,* 199.

22. I. Timor-Tritsch *et al.,* "Classification of Human Fetal Movement," *American Journal of Obstetrics and Gynecology* 126 (1976): 70.

23. Mussen, Congar, and Kagan, *Child Development and Personality,* 65.

24. A. William Liley, "Experiments with Uterine and Fetal Instrumenta-

tion," in Michael M. Kaback and Carlo Valenti, eds., *Intrauterine Fetal Visualization* (Oxford: Excerpta Medica; New York: American Elsevier, 1976), 75.

25. *California Penal Code,* 597v (kittens); *Penal Code,* 597w (cats); *Agricultural Code,* 19501 (cattle).

26. Liley to the author, November 13, 1977, amplifying the statement, "The fetus is responsive to touch, pain, and cold," made in Liley, "Experiments with Uterine and Fetal Instrumentation," 75. Dr. Liley's conclusion was independently confirmed by Mortimer G. Rosen, professor of reproductive biology at Case Western Reserve University, who, on the basis of electroencephalography (EEG) measuring fetal brain waves, has written, "After twenty weeks of gestation, the fetal nervous system has matured considerably. Specialized nerve endings in the skin make the fetus more sensitive to touch, temperature change and pain." Rosen, "The Secret Brain: Learning Before Birth," *Harper's,* April 1978, 46. As Rosen has already determined that the fetal brain is functioning in a rudimentary way at eight weeks, the capability of experiencing pain, which becomes greater at twenty weeks, is probably present earlier.

27. Ronald Melzack, *The Puzzle of Pain* (New York: Basic Books, 1973), 46–47, 158–163. For further discussion, see John S. Liebeskind and Linda A. Paul, "Psychological and Physiological Mechanisms of Pain," *Review of Psychology,* 1977, 43–48.

28. On the differentiation of transmitters, Timiras, *Developmental Physiology and Aging,* 137; and on the development of the cerebral cortex, Geoffrey S. Dawes, *Fetal and Neonatal Physiology* (Chicago: Year Book Medical Publishers, 1968), 126.

29. The author is indebted to Timiras, Professor of Zoology at the University of California, Berkeley, and to her teaching assistants and graduate students, for a discussion with them on the problem of pain in the unborn, in which ways of reaching a firm conclusion as to pain in the unborn were explored.

30. See Inquiry 15.

31. Sissela Bok, "Fetal Research and the Value of Life," *Research on the Fetus,* 2-6 ("humanity" confusing); Munier, Liu, and Solomon, *Abortion,* 170 ("humanity" too abstract).

32. Shakespeare, *King Lear,* Act III, scene 4, lines 263–264.

33. David G. Nathan, "Fetal Research: An Investigator's View," *Villanova Law Review* 22 (1977): 384 at 390.

34. John Updike, *Couples* (New York: Knopf, 1968), 360.

35. *Ibid.,* 378–379.

Inquiry 18. On the Masks of the Liberty: The Operation

1. Judgment of Military Tribunal No. 1, *The Medical Case, Trial of War Criminals before the Nuremberg Military Tribunal* (Washington: Government Printing Office) 2: 264.

2. "Usefulness of the Experiments" (summary from the defense arguments), *The Medical Case* 2: 61–92.

3. Karl Brandt, "Final Statement," *ibid.,* 2: 138.

4. Gerhard Rose, "Final Statement," *ibid.,* 2: 161.

5. *Ibid.,* 2: 160.

6. Wilhelm Beiglbock, "Final Statement," *ibid.,* 2: 74.

7. Joseph Fletcher, "Fetal Research: An Ethical Appraisal," *Research on the Fetus,* 3-7.

8. All quotations and references to the Chicago clinics in this paragraph are from the series of articles in the *Chicago Sun-Times* by Pamela Zekman and Pamela Warrick (beginning Sunday, 12 November 1978 and continuing through Wednesday, 22 November 1978).

9. Selig Neubardt and Harold Schulman, *Techniques of Abortion* (Boston: Little, Brown, 1972), 46.

10. *Williams' Obstetrics,* ed. Louis M. Hellman and Jack A. Pritchard, 14th ed. (New York: Appleton-Century-Crofts, 1971), 1089.

11. Sheldon J. Segal and Egon Diczfalusy, "New Methods for Fertility Regulation: Status Report," in Roy O. Greep, Marjorie A. Koblinsky, and Frederick S. Jaffe, eds., *Reproduction and Human Welfare* (Cambridge: MIT Press, 1976), 278.

12. Nader Bozorgi, "Statistical Analysis of First-Trimester Pregnancy Terminations in an Ambulatory Surgical Center," *American Journal of Obstetrics and Gynecology* 127 (1977): 763 at 764.

13. Neubardt and Schulman, *Techniques of Abortion,* 46–47.

14. A. Alberto Hodari *et al.,* "Dilation and Curettage for Second-Trimester Abortions," *American Journal of Obstetrics and Gynecology* 127 (1977): 850.

15. Neubardt and Schulman, *Techniques of Abortion,* 68.

16. Magda Denes, *In Neccesity and Sorrow: Life and Death in an Abortion Hospital* (New York: Basic Books, 1976), 60–61.

17. See Inquiry 16, *supra.*

18. Robert G. Douglas and William B. Stromme, *Operative Obstetrics,* 2d ed. (New York: Appleton-Century-Crofts, 1965), 158–159.

19. Hysterotomy is "in effect a miniature Caesarean section." *Munro Keir's Operative Obstetrics,* 9th ed. P. R. Myerscough (London,

1977), 602. Cf. *Williams' Obstetrics*, 1163: "Invasion of the uterus (hysterotomy) is the essence of the [Caesarean] operation."

20. M. J. Sobran, "Letter to a Friend," *Human Life Review*, Winter 1978, 13.

21. A. I. Csapo *et al.*, "Termination of Pregnancy with Double Prostaglandin Input," *American Journal of Obstetrics and Gynecology* 124 (1976): 1.

22. *Ibid.*, 8.

23. *Ibid.*, 3.

24. Richard Selzer, *Mortal Lessons* (New York: Simon & Schuster, 1976), 157–160.

25. Denes, *In Necessity and Sorrow*, 60.

26. Bernard N. Nathanson, quoted in Charles Remsberg and Bonnie Remsberg, "Second Thoughts on Abortion from the Doctor Who Led the Crusade for It," *Good Housekeeping*, March 1976, 130.

27. Bernard N. Nathanson, "Deeper into Abortion," *New England Journal of Medicine* 291 (November 28, 1974): 1189.

28. C. Everett Koop, "The Slide to Auschwitz," *Human Life Review*, Spring 1977, 101.

29. *Ibid.*, 103.

30. *Ibid.*, 109.

Inquiry 19.   Why the Liberty May Be Limited

1. *Roe* v. *Wade*, 410 U.S. 113 at 160.

2. Judith Blake, "The Supreme Court's Abortion Decisions and Public Opinion in the United States," *Population and Development Review* 3 (1977): 54.

3. *Ibid.*

4. *Ibid.*, 52, Table 3.

5. *Ibid.*

6. *Ibid.*, 49, Table 1.

7. See Inquiry 3.

8. See, e.g., Katrina Maxtone-Graham, *Pregnant by Mistake: The Stories of Seventeen Women* (New York: Liveright, 1973), 220, 284. Cf. Linda Bird Francke, *The Ambivalence of Abortion* (New York: Random House, 1978).

9. E.g., "While our psychosocial studies do not allow for any conclusions regarding the relative risk of adverse psychologic sequelae to saline-induced abortion, it can certainly be said that it is a less than

optimal procedure. Indeed, if one might deviate for a moment from the scientific and resort to the vernacular, and if one would view saline abortion in terms of the patient's experience, then this method could be adequately described in one word—'lousy'." (Irvin M. Cushner [Associate Professor of Obstetrics and Gynecology, Johns Hopkins Hospital], "Induced Abortion by Saline Injection," in Sarah Lewitt, ed., *Abortion Techniques and Services* [Amsterdam: Excerpta medica, 1972], 26.)

See also Denes, *In Necessity and Sorrow,* 59–60.

10. Eugene O'Neill, *Abortion,* in O'Neill, *Lost Plays* (New York: Citadel Press, 1958).

11. Ernest Hemingway, "Hills Like White Elephants, in Hemingway, *Men Without Women* (New York: Scribner's, 1927), 72–73.

12. Joan Didion, *Play It as It Lays* (New York: Farrar, Straus, & Giroux, 1970), 96–97, 115, 125, 126.

13. John Updike, *Couples,* 380.

Inquiry 20. How the Liberty May Be Limited

1. Brandeis, J., dissenting in *Burnet* v. *Coronado Oil and Gas Co.,* 285 U.S. 393 (1932) at 407 and 409, lists more than a dozen cases of straight overruling of earlier interpretations of the Constitution. Forty-six years later, Brandeis's list could be at least tripled.

2. *Maher* v. *Roe,* 45 *U.S. Law Week* 4787 (1977).

3. *Chisholm* v. *Georgia,* 2 Dall. 419 (1793).

4. *Dred Scott* v. *Sanford,* 19 How. 393 (1857).

5. *Pollock* v. *Farmers Loan and Trust Company,* 157 U.S. 429 (1895).

6. *Oregon* v. *Mitchell,* 400 U.S. 112 (1970).

7. Alexander Hamilton, *The Federalist,* ed. Jacob E. Cook (Cleveland: World, 1961), no. 85, p. 543.

8. American Bar Association, *Report of the Special Constitutional Study Committee* (1973), 30–31. The unanimous committee was chaired by C. Clyde Atkins and included Judge Sarah T. Hughes, Judge William S. Thompson, and Albert M. Sacks, Dean of Harvard Law School.

9. As to the non-necessity of presidential approval: *Hollingsworth* v. *Virginia,* 3 Dall. 378 (U.S., 1798) (Eleventh Amendment is valid, though not approved by the president), and W. F. Dodd, "Amending the Federal Constitution," *Yale Law Journal* 30 (1921): 321, 329. As to the sufficiency of action by the state legislature without approval by the governor, see *Coleman* v. *Miller,* 307 U.S. 433 (1939).

10. "State Applications Asking Congress to Call a Federal Constitutional Convention," printed for the Committee of the Judiciary, House of Representatives, July 1, 1961, 17.

11. *Congressional Record,* November 2, 1977, S.18494; Ad Hoc Committee in Defense of Life, *Lifeletter,* April 28, 1978; Laura B. Weiss, "Constitutional Convention Sought on Abortion Ban," *Congressional Quarterly* 36 (July 1, 1978): 1677.

12. *The Convention Call,* February 28, 1978. *The Convention Call* is published by Americans for a Constitutional Convention, Suite 1306, 303 Fifth Avenue, New York, N.Y. 10016.

13. E.g., Lisa Cronin Wohl, "Are We 25 Votes away from Losing the Bill of Rights. . .and the Rest of the Constitution?" *Ms,* February 1978, 47; see also *Wall Street Journal,* January 25, 1978, 1.

14. James Madison, *The Federalist,* Number 43, Cooke, ed., 296.

15. *Ibid.*

16. ABA Special Committee, *Report,* 16–17.

17. Robert Byrn, testimony, March 10, 1975, *Senate Hearings, Abortion—Part IV,* 209.

18. James L. Buckley, "A Human Life Amendment," *Human Life Review* 1 (1975): 5. The amendment was sponsored by Senators Bartlett, Bennett, Curtis, Eastland, Hatfield, Helms, Hughes, and Young. *Ibid.* at 14.

19. E.g., H. J. Res. 520, 94th Cong., 1st Sess. (1975).

20. See *Civil Rights Cases,* 109 U.S. 3, 20 (1883); *Jones* v. *Mayer Co.,* 392 U.S. 409, 438 (1968).

21. See Inquiry 12.

22. The words "including the unborn" replaced the words "from the beginning of new life." Dean Emeritus Joseph O'Meara, Jr., had observed to me that the latter phrase gave latitude to a court to say that "new life" began only at, say, viability. The present phrase eliminates the possibility of such misunderstanding. See my testimony, February 5, 1976, "Proposed Constitutional Amendments on Abortion," *Hearings Before the Subcommittee on Civil and Constitutional Rights of the Committee on the Judiciary,* House of Representatives, 94th Cong., 2d. Session (1976), 67.

23. Robert M. Byrn, testimony, *Senate Hearings, Abortion—Part IV,* 107.

24. Abraham Lincoln, Speech at Ottawa, Illinois, August 21, 1858, *The Collected Works of Abraham Lincoln,* ed. Roy P. Basler (New Brunswick: Rutgers University, 1953), 3, 29.

25. Byrn, Testimony, *Senate Hearings, Abortion—Part IV,* 209.

26. As this book went to press, events occurred of significance to the effort to limit the liberty:

1. By a 6 to 3 vote the Supreme Court of the United States invalidated as "vague" a Pennsylvania law requiring abortionists to attempt to bring about a live birth when there was "sufficient reason to believe that the fetus may be viable" (*Colautti* v. *Franklin,* 47 *U.S. Law Week* 4094 [January 9, 1979]). The decision, delivered by Justice Blackmun, drives home how the Court has put the abortion liberty above the life of the unborn even at a late stage of pregnancy. In a dissent joined by Chief Justice Burger and Justice Rehnquist, Justice White observed that "only those with unalterable determination" to invalidate the law could have concluded that it was too vague to be understood (*ibid.,* at 4101). It is this "unalterable determination" of Justice Blackmun and his colleagues which makes a constitutional amendment necessary.

2. Governor Edmund Brown, Jr. of California proposed that the states petition Congress to call a constitutional convention on an amendment requiring a balanced federal budget (*New York Times,* January 10, 1979, p. A-1). The use of such a method of amending the Constitution became widely known and discussed, and the effect on Congress of such petitions by the states became appreciated.

3. The media became more concerned with fairness to the anti-abortion cause. Three instances will show the new trend. Nicholas Von Hoffman took to task the critics of opposition to abortion as playing "single-issue politics." Such politics, he observed, had helped end the war in Vietnam. They manifested "an engaged and enthusiastic civic spirit" (Von Hoffman, "And Just What Is So Terrible About Single-Issue Politics?," *Berkeley Gazette,* February 7, 1979, p. 12). For the first time in the history of the annual march in Washington on the anniversary of *The Abortion Cases,* the press did not understate the number of marchers (60,000 on January 22, 1979). The *Washington Post* even accorded the march page-one treatment. The night before, NBC Television's "Weekend" gave a one hour account of the anti-abortion movement. The account was untainted by religious bias. It focused on the movement's "astonishing and accelerating growth." If such astonishing and accelerating growth continues to be fairly reported, the curtailment of the abortion liberty is certain.

Inquiry 21.   Why the Liberty Must Be Limited and Surpassed

1. For the documentation of the conclusions under "First," see Inquiries 2, 4, and 17; "Second," Inquiries 7, 5, 16, and 19; "Third," Inquiry 10; "Fourth," Inquiries 7 and 16; "Fifth," Inquiry 11; "Sixth," Inquiries 7, 9, and 10; "Seventh," Inquiries 9, 11, and 12; "Eighth," Inquiry 12; "Ninth," Inquiry 12; "Tenth," Inquiry 16; "Eleventh," Inquiries 9, 14, 15, and 18; "Twelfth," Inquiry 7.

Index

Index of Cases

These cases are named or discussed on the pages given.